Talking of Silence: The Sexual Harassment of Schoolgirls

Dedication

This book is dedicated to all girls like Collette, Carmel, Zaheda, Zohra, Jenny, Annmarie, Maria, and Alex who have suffered sexual abuse.

Talking of Silence: The Sexual Harassment of Schoolgirls

Carrie M.H. Herbert

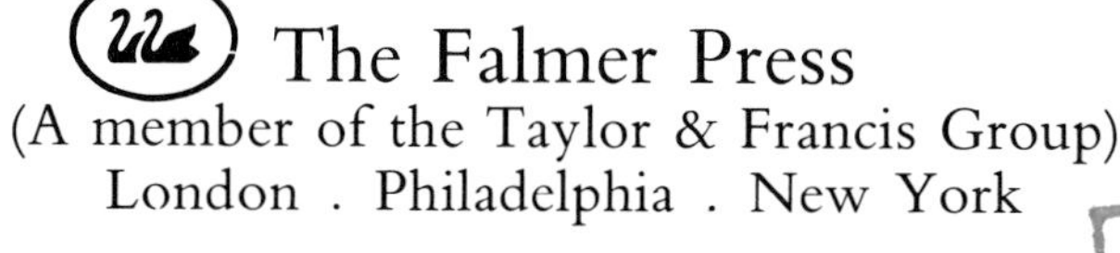

The Falmer Press
(A member of the Taylor & Francis Group)
London . Philadelphia . New York

UK The Falmer Press, Falmer House, Barcombe, Lewes, East Sussex, BN8 5DL

USA The Falmer Press, Taylor & Francis Inc., 1900 Frost Road, Suite 101, Bristol, PA 19007

First published 1989

British Library Cataloguing in Publication Data
Herbert, Carrie M.H.
Talking of silence: the sexual harassment of schoolgirls.
1. Great Britain. Girls. Sexual abuse by adults
I. Title
362.7'044
ISBN 1-85000-585-0
ISBN 1-85000-586-9 pbk

Library of Congress Cataloging-in-Publication Data
Herbert, Carrie M.H.
Talking of silence: the sexual harassment of schoolgirls/Carrie M.H. Herbert.
p. cm.
Bibliography: p.
ISBN 1-85000-585-0.
ISBN 1-85000-586-9 (pbk.)
1. Child molesting — Great Britain — Case studies. 2. Sexual harassment — Great Britain — Case studies. 3. Sex crimes — Great Britain — Case Studies. I. Title.
HQ72.G7H47 1989
362.7'6-dc20 89-32554 CIP

Jacket design by Caroline Archer

Typeset in 10½/13 point Bembo by
Alresford Typesetting & Design, 12 Campbell Court, Bramley, Basingstoke, Hants.

Printed in Great Britain by Taylor & Francis (Printers) Ltd, Basingstoke

Contents

Acknowledgments

Books of this nature are never achieved single-handed, for it is in the very act of discussion and sharing experiences that ideas are generated. There have been many people, women in particular, who have contributed to this process, in an academic, personal and practical capacity.

My thanks go to all the following groups and individuals:

To Dr Martin, the staff and students at the Inner London school, and in particular to all the girls who so willingly participated in the research, and contributed to the development of the revised methodology.

To Garth Boomer, Keith Bovair, Mary Jane Drummond, Jacqui Halson, Judith Hart, John Herbert, Ruth Loshak, Colleen McLaughlin, Charlotte Pembrey, Marlene Schiwy, Heather Wood and Claire Woods, all of whom have helped and assisted me in a variety of ways.

To Dr Felicity Hunt for the enormous part she played in helping me develop my ideas and writing style.

To my family, the Herberts, the Reads, the Lowers and the Heavens for their continual support. Lastly I thank my parents Pamela and Jim Herbert who have constantly given me encouragement.

Introduction

On December 19th 1986, thirteen girls and an educational researcher gathered in the library of an Inner London comprehensive school to say farewell, to mark the end of a nine-month friendship and to celebrate the completion of the data-collecting stage of a research project. The project had been concerned originally with the sexual harassment of girl pupils by male teachers in school. However as the project developed it became clear that the data which were being offered were not the kind I had anticipated and although related in that the information given was about unsolicited, unwanted sexual abuse, the disclosures were of a different calibre. So it became necessary to change the focus of the study away from school-based incidents and to document and analyze the cases the girls described. All the attacks occurred outside the school building and the perpetrators were a variety of men, none however being teachers. Thus the study became a study of the incidents of sexual violence disclosed by these thirteen girls. All the names in this book have been changed to protect the people concerned. In some cases it has been necessary to alter locations of incidents, family sizes and the relationship between those described in order to aid anonymity. The following extracts indicate the type of sexual violence with which the research project was confronted.

> Zohra: Sexually violated by an unknown man, at the age of 4, in a block of flats near her home.
>
> Carmel: Sexually assaulted at the age of 6 by a cousin in his house.
>
> Chanel: Approached by a man in a playground when she was 6 years old. He took her hand and tried to persuade her into going with him but she ran away escaping physical harm.
>
> Zaheda: Forced into playing with her older brother's genitals as a 6-year-old.

Alex: Sexually attacked at the age of 10 by a man 'known' to her family.

Collette: Sexually molested at 13 by a schoolboy outside her home.

Fitti: Sexually propositioned at 14 by a man in an underpass near the school.

Linda: Chased by men in a car one evening at the age of 14. She escaped physical harm.

Maria: Sexually harassed by a boy on a school trip when 14.

Annmarie: Subjected to an attempted rape when she was 15, as she was on her way home from school.

Jenny: Sexually assaulted by two men in an underpass one afternoon, at the age of 15, 300 yards from school.

This distressing catalogue of incidents emerged as the research project developed through an intricate interweaving of issues to do with methodology, close inter-personal relationships and raised consciousness. This book is the story of this research project, how it changed and the way in which a group of Inner London schoolgirls came to disclose their experiences of sexual violence as children.

Chapter 1

Case Studies

The first time sexual harassment came to my attention was while I was working in a primary school in South Australia in the early 1980s. However, although I recognized it as unwanted, unsolicited and embarrassing behaviour which had no specific name, it wasn't until a few years later that the impact of this particular problem and the frequency with which it occurred became of great significance to me. The following cases came to my attention in a variety of ways through professional channels and through personal communications with colleagues and friends.

Miss Spiros

The first case of sexual harassment was that of Miss Spiros, a 34-year-old experienced teacher who was a Cypriot by birth and Australian by adoption. She had taught for many years as a primary teacher in Adelaide and for the last five she had had grade seven children.

Primary schools in Australia have five grades, from year three to year seven. The last year for children in primary education is grade seven where most of the students are either eleven or twelve years old. As in British junior schools, children in Australia stay with their class teacher throughout most of the day, but in contrast to the English system Australian children spend one year longer in this one-teacher environment. Towards the end of their last term in primary education some children are approaching 13 years and as a result it is often thought that they are becoming increasingly 'difficult to handle'. Some students also feel that they have outgrown their class teacher and the 'family-like' community perpetuated in primary education and become disruptive, boisterous, and ready to challenge the status quo.

Miss Spiros encouraged a warm and friendly atmosphere in her room which some children liked but which others rebelled against, feeling her approach was 'childish' and smothering.

The incident of sexual harassment I am about to describe was initiated by two boys who fell into this latter category. Ben and Simon had begun to 'throw their weight about' in a variety of ways. During their last year they had been reprimanded for swearing at teachers, for being disruptive in class, for behaving badly on school trips and for being responsible for obscene graffiti in the school cloakrooms. Towards the end of the third term they went one step further and sexually harassed their teacher.

On the first occasion Miss Spiros arrived in her room in the morning and was confronted with a worn and dirty teenage brassiere which was lying on her desk. The whole class was present. Attached to the article of clothing was a note written in a child's hand which said that it had been left in the car of another male teacher the previous evening. Innuendoes in the note were made as to what Miss Spiros and this teacher were supposed to have done. Two weeks later a new but unpackaged condom was found on her desk with another note making further suggestions as to how she and this same male colleague should use it. The consequences of their behaviour were significant for they directly affected Miss Spiros, the other children in the class and indirectly affected the teachers on the staff.

On the first occasion Miss Spiros ignored the incident but pointedly placed the article in the waste-paper-bin. Nothing was said. On the second occasion Miss Spiros handled it very differently. Initially she lost her temper, but when confronted with silence and indifference by the class she broke down and ran from the room crying. She was shocked and outraged that this behaviour had occurred and immediately asked for support from both her colleagues and the headteacher.

Miss Spiros's appeal to the staff for support was met with claims that the boys were 'just being boys', that it was nothing to worry about and anyway the school year was nearly over and these two boys would be going to high school in a few weeks. The staff were largely unsupportive and saw Simon's and Ben's behaviour as a 'natural' expression of adolescent youth and blamed Miss Spiros for inciting their 'high spirits' by keeping the class on 'too tight a rein'. In this way it was concluded that she had 'asked' for it. When Miss Spiros wanted disciplinary action to be taken it was interesting that the headteacher asked the deputy to 'see' the boys.

This incident raised four important issues. Firstly, it was apparent that 12-year-old Ben and Simon had already 'learned' that one way of asserting their power was to sexually harass a woman teacher by placing artifacts on her table which undermined her confidence. They had the knowledge that this both embarrassed her and asserted their power. It is interesting to ask where they had 'learned' this tactic; from school, from home, from the media, from literature? The second issue is the way in which the incident was handled by the staff in particular and the school in general. Implicit in the headteacher's delegation of responsibility over the boys' reprimand could be the interpretation that the matter was not of a serious enough nature and could be handled by someone with less authority than him. Thirdly, there is the issue of what the girl students in the class learned about their place in society. Little is known about how they felt for no questions were asked, but it can be surmised that they could have been embarrassed and humiliated. However the major point they probably learned was that incidents of this kind were not taken particularly seriously, nor would they be dealt with in a rigorous way. They may also have realized that if they set themselves outside the boys' goodwill they too may receive similar treatment. The fourth issue is that of silence. It has been documented by other researchers (Farley, 1978; South Australian Education Department, 1984) that incidents of sexual harassment, if ignored, do not 'go away'. By ignoring the first display of sexual harassment, it could be argued that Miss Spiros implicitly gave the boys the feeling that what they had done was not worth remarking on, thus promoting a more vicious repeat attack.

There were two results of this case. One was in the short term. The two boys were summoned to the deputy headteacher's office, where I was asked to be present. Mrs Wilkins talked briefly about manners and more formally about the boys' weak academic performance in class and their poor behaviour in the school generally. She stressed that if they wasted time in this way they would never 'succeed'. 'Success' in her terms was academic. The sexually harassing behaviour was ignored and the boys were not confronted on the unacceptable use of this intimidating strategy.

The long-term effect had more significance. Seven weeks later, at the end of term and the school year, Miss Spiros was 'counselled' by the headteacher to take a lower grade as he felt her teaching style was more suitable for younger children, despite the fact that she had successfully taught grade seven children for many years. The implication was that the problems which had arisen during the year were as a result of her inability to control the boys and that the case of sexual harassment was a manifestation of this lack of discipline. Interestingly this complaint was a direct contradiction to the previous accusation; that it was because she had kept the children on a tight rein that they had behaved in this manner.

During the summer holidays Miss Spiros applied to the South Australian Education Department for a transfer. She was moved to another school. Her confidence in teaching, in her colleagues' professional and personal support, and in the school's disciplinary procedures had been undermined. Here was a case of the victim being further victimized for making public an incident of sexual harassment, those responsible for the unwanted sexual attention exonerated, and those with the authority to challenge such interpretations of male behaviour remaining ignorant of the miscarriage of justice. Miss

Spiros's departure from the school enabled the staff to believe that indeed it was Miss Spiros's fault and that she could not 'cope'.

Liz

Although in the previous incident sexual harassment was a problem for the girls in the class only by default, there are cases where they have been the direct target and where the harasser has been their teacher. A friend told me about her experience as a 13-year-old. Liz was asked by her geography teacher to be the 'cupboard monitor'. After a lesson it was her duty to return the used text-books to their place on the shelves. On one occasion, at the end of the school day, Liz was asked by this man to get a set of books he needed from one of the top shelves. He followed her into the cupboard and suggested that she stand on a stool to reach, then he ran his hand up her leg and tried to touch her genital area. Jumping down Liz said she had to go and ran out of the classroom home. She told her mother of the incident and pleaded with her to go to the school and report the teacher. Her mother refused to believe this incident had happened and told Liz that she had 'imagined it'. Liz's attempt at reporting sexual harassment had been silenced by disbelief.

This example shows how easy it is for girls to be disbelieved, for parents to disregard the subject and ignore the claim, and for the harassed girl to begin to 'see' how some societal attitudes are predetermined by the male perspective. On the other hand it also shows how the male teacher has been allowed to believe he has 'got away with it'. According to many definitions of sexual harassment, repetition of unwanted sexual behaviour is one of the criteria for recognizing 'it'. Thus it could be assumed that perpetrators are recidivists, men who constantly use sexually harassing behaviour on a variety of women and girls. Farley found evidence of the recidivism of sexual harassers. In her research (1978, p. 23) she quotes a policeman who said of a man they were trying to arrest for propositioning, 'if he tried it (propositioning girls at job interviews) with one he might be trying it with others, might have already tried it'. Indeed they found he had used the same approach with a number of applicants who had applied for jobs in his fast-food restaurant but the young women had remained silent about the advance.

If complaints are not followed through, as Liz's was not, no one is aware of the unwanted sexual attention received. It could be that the geography teacher was at one level unaware that he had sexually harassed this girl or that his actions were unwanted. When one looks at the recidivism of sexual harassers as cited by other researchers, it is unlikely that this was his first indiscretion, and because of the silence which surrounded this case, it is unlikely that it would be his last for he had never been openly confronted. Although he was probably aware that this was not appropriate behaviour he could continue to try the same approach with other students. The silence of sexual harassment must be broken, and men confronted with the unwanted behaviour if they are to stop.

Alison

Another case which came to my notice was also described to me by a friend. Alison was a boarder in a convent school in the early 1960s. One day, whilst playing netball, and thus dressed in a short PE skirt, she was told by one of the nuns that a friend of the family was in the 'school parlour', a room set aside for important guests, and wished to see her. This 'family friend' was a Roman Catholic priest and had known Alison for many years and at one time had been her parish priest. When she entered the room he was sitting behind a desk. He told her to come around and stand next to him and not to be scared. She obeyed. Whilst he talked to her about various family details he slipped his hand under her skirt and into her pants. She moved but he told her to stand still. She did and this time he tried to touch her genitals. She ran out of the parlour and back to the netball courts. Alison told no one of her experience for twenty years.

This incident raises a number of issues not dealt with in the first two examples. Firstly, Alison was in a Roman Catholic boarding school. Such places are historically renowned for their protection of girls' emotional, spiritual, educational, sexual and physical development. Most boarding schools, whether church-founded or not, are considered places where wealthy parents can send their daughters to avoid incidents of sexual interference. Great care is taken to protect boarders from men and boys and thus any sexual encounters. Yet here in a convent Alison was sexually attacked. This example shows that experiences of this kind are not confined to the state sector or to girls who have relative freedom, but affect girls from all strata of society.

Secondly there is the issue of confidence and trust. As a Roman Catholic Alison had been trained to believe that priests were servants of God. In this capacity the priest was endowed with special and particular attributes. It is to a priest that one is taught to confide one's human frailties and whom one asks for forgiveness and guidance. Here was a man in this capacity taking advantage of a girl's training and upbringing, certain in the fact that she could never divulge what he had done. If Alison had reported this incident and claimed that a family priest was responsible for such behaviour, it is likely that she would have suffered ostracism, ridicule, persecution and charges of 'wickedness', be accused of being sexually perverted herself and of lying. No one would believe that a priest would be capable of such an indiscretion. Alison knew that she had no alternative but to remain silent.

Louise

I have shown from these last two examples how girls can be victims of sexual harassment from men in positions of *loco parentis*. In this next case it is not a schoolgirl who suffers from unwanted sexual attention, but a female teacher: the perpetrator is a male peer. In 1985 I was engaged in a research project for the Centre for Applied Research in Education (CARE) at the University of East Anglia. I was to evaluate the extent to which the TVEI programme (Technical and Vocational Education Initiative), which was being trialled in a number of Suffolk schools, had achieved equal opportunities. One probationary female teacher, Louise, talked to me about the way in which she was treated by her head of department.

'Sometimes [I get] a greeting like "ah, just the voluptuous young lady I wanted to see". Well that sort of greeting can make the hair on the back of your neck stand up on end. It has happened more than once. But short of saying "I don't like that", and getting aggressive about it, it is easier to let it rest and change things gradually. I can see getting rattled with people is not the best way forward. If you get aggressive with people they switch off or get aggressive back, and it is now that I can see the gradual way is best . . . in stages, not one huge bound. A bull in a china shop would be more damaging. East Anglia is very resistant to change of any sort.' (Herbert, 1985, p. 23).

The way in which Louise chose to handle this senior teacher's unwanted sexual comments was with a 'softly softly' approach. Yet did she have an alternative? How else could she have responded? As a first-year teacher she was dependent on him for a good report, a recommendation for her 'passing' her probationary year and possibly a reference if she wanted to apply for another job. Within that school's environment she also needed to 'get on'. It was certainly not in her best interest to get her head of department 'rattled' or to encourage a response of aggression, so she kept quiet.

Chloe

The last case I wish to cite was told to me by a teacher friend, Ann. 'How's school?' said Ann to 5-year-old Chloe. 'It's alright, except for the boys'. 'What's wrong with the boys?' Chloe describes how at break times the boys, led by two ringleaders, gang together, decide on a victim, who is always one of the girls, chase her and cut her off from her friends, and once isolated try to look at and touch her knickers. During this pursuit they grab, hassle, touch and shout. Their objective is to lift the girl's skirt to look at the girl's underwear and if they successfully corner her, to tell her to take down her pants. Chloe has been one of these victims on a number of occasions. She is frightened by this behaviour, dreads free times when children are allowed to play in the extensive grounds and is now reluctant to go to school. The school is a well known and respected traditional prep school which ten years ago opened its doors to girl students. However it is still predominantly male in that there are two boys to every one girl. One reason that there are less girls is that at the senior level the school reverts to an all boys' public school, where the boys can complete their education but the girls have to transfer elsewhere.

Ann was talking with Chloe at her parents' home and at that stage had told no one else. Chloe, at 5, has already begun to experience unwanted sexual attention by males. In this 'exclusive' environment the boys pursue, corner and frighten the girls, once more showing how sexual harassment is not class-based, and neither has it to do with age. Although it could be assumed that the boys are unaware of the sexual connotations of their behaviour, it is clear that they have already, at the age of 5, begun to assert their masculine power and authority in a way which undermines, intimidates, embarrasses and humiliates girls. Similarly Chloe has already learned that she has less power than boys. Although she has chosen to tell Ann what has happened at school it is interesting to ask why she had not told her teacher or parents.

Carrie

The next example is my own experience of sexual harassment which occurred in 1984 whilst I was working as a lecturer in South Australia. In the mid-1980s in South Australia the problem of sexual harassment was taken up by the State Government for it was recognized that it was a serious problem for state employees and students in schools. Moves were made to make the behaviour unlawful, and steps were taken to protect women and girls and to re-educate the male harassers.

In Adelaide, the new Bill was to be introduced into South Australian law in November 1984. Because of this Bill, there was an urgent need for all personnel working with the government to understand the implications of the new clause in the Equal Opportunity Act, which would make sexual harassment unlawful. I was employed to run day conferences for all employees on this subject. The participants ranged from domestic and gardening staff working in the Education Department residential centres, to the Superintendents (a British equivalent would be an HMI) of education.

The day conferences were intended to allow personnel to identify sexual harassment. Certain types of behaviour were defined and named as sexual harassment. This was followed by a consolidation period where a film was shown (two films which dealt with sexual harassment at work which I used were '9 to 5' and 'Give us a Smile'), a discussion organized and pamphlets on sexual harassment from various unions were distributed to the different union members. Once it was felt that the conferees understood the range and breadth that sexually harassing behaviour could take, there followed a session on personal experiences and anecdotes.

One of the strategies for getting people to talk about personal experiences was to put them in small groups. However if this was left to the conferees they usually joined groups with people whom they knew and worked with. In most cases this was a mixed group and consisted, for example, of a manager and a project team, or the staff from one department. In most cases the manager was a man, the team members were of both sexes, but the secretary of the team was always a woman. When groups like this met little discussion of sexual harassment was forthcoming, in fact such groups often declared that their members had experienced no sexual harassment at all. When the conference members were divided up by me into single-sex groups (triggering much criticism from both the women and men), this helped some women to discuss incidents of sexual harassment amongst themselves.

In these groups women had the opportunity to share experiences, clarify definitions, name particular behaviour as sexual harassment, exchange feelings and strategies for coping, as well as give each other support and validation in an environment that was supportive of such disclosures. Another way women disclosed incidents of sexual harassment was on a one-to-one basis with me, often at the end of the day when everyone was leaving, and it can be assumed that they knew that I would be sympathetic towards their story. One woman I remember came to ask me if the incident she had in mind was sexual harassment. She was the secretary at a residential centre, and on more than one occasion, the same senior department manager had asked her to photocopy for him a range of sexually explicit and derogatory cartoons about women to pass round to his colleagues during the evening 'social'. I assured her that this was sexual harassment.

There was much hostility from both men and women in these conferences. One reason was that they were compulsory, every employee in the Education Department having to attend a one-day course. The sessions were also very difficult for me. After the first four or so I realized that I could no longer continue to do them on my own for in the sessions I was challenged, laughed at, trivialized, dismissed, humiliated by sexual innuendoes or told that this issue was a leftist feminist bandwagon, and was of little interest to most ordinary people. In addition, given the opportunity, some members of the conference would insist on giving explicit details of a particular woman's behaviour, a description of her clothes, and how she acted provocatively, all these interwoven with sexual asides and double entendres. From then on I organized a colleague to work with me, for at least in this way we could 'field' some of the more abrasive comments in turn. Most of those who were antagonistic were men, but some were women. Many of the men attending the conference were senior to me in the Education Department. For the women I believe I challenged perceptions of their concept of femininity, for unlike many of them I never wore make-up and I was a woman who had some, albeit limited, authority over their bosses which they resented. The forces exerted by both sexes were in an effort to silence me, to show me my place, and to deny the phenomenon under discussion. I finished these day sessions depressed, angry, disappointed, humiliated and embarrassed.

The account of this personal experience serves two purposes. Firstly it shows how if a government decides to take an issue seriously it can be assumed that it feels that there are changes which need to be made and attitudes which can be altered. By amending the Sex Discrimination Act, the South Australian Government attempted to change the environment in which women and girls have to work. Their method of achieving this was to make attendance at a day's conference on sexual harassment compulsory. A substantial financial commitment was necessary to fulfil this aim. The long-term effects are unknown, but recognition of the statewide challenge to sexual harassment must be acknowledged.

The second point is to show how theory can develop from an autobiographical experience, or in other words, how the personal becomes the political. After I had left Australia and that particular job, I reflected on the feelings and circumstances around which the conferences were held. Naming and labelling, I believed, were 'change agents' in that they gave people the necessary tools with which to re-identify past experiences. I had been intimately involved with organizing and implementing sexual harassment conferences, giving the legal definition, explaining the effects it had on women, showing how it could be differentiated from other male behaviour, and pointing out how harassers would be treated. The fact that some women had changed and made the connection was borne out in the example of the woman and the cartoons. She had made the link between experience and a newly named phenomenon.

Yet change is not necessarily a corollary of labelling. I had been unaware that during each of these conferences I was being subjected to unwanted sexual attention, that this constituted sexual harassment and the behaviour displayed was to do with power and silence. I accepted the sessions as being difficult and regarded the antagonism as being to do with my lack of skill, their resentment at having to attend, and the content of the conferences. It is clear on reflection that I suffered from a range of appraising gestures and looks and sexually orientated innuendoes and jokes. I was thus a victim of the very behaviour I was addressing; the consequences being consistent with symptoms associated with sexually harassing behaviour, although I did not make the connection until many months later.

Conclusion

These examples show some of the different ways in which women and girls are sexually harassed and their different ages and social classes, and also the diversity of position and status of the sexual harasser. Boys, teachers and priests are cited as perpetrators. Girls, both privately and state educated, and women teachers and lecturers, as well as office workers, can be the victims of sexual harassment. The behaviour in these examples ranges from verbal sexual harassment to intimidating and embarrassing behaviour and includes sexual molestation. But further issues can be extrapolated. It can be argued that in cases where the behaviour had become public, as in the case of Miss Spiros, the machinery for dealing with the incident was very poor and in fact could be interpreted as being supportive of the perpetrator. It is clear, too, that in some of the examples there was the woman's or girl's reluctance to report the incident because of her belief that as a result of publicizing the incident more serious repercussion would ensue. So the event remained a private experience. For some, sexual harassment begins early. At 5, Chloe is already beginning to learn that there is a difference between girls' and boys' positions in Western society. There is also the issue of being able to recognize sexually harassing behaviour whilst being sexually harassed, rather than the ability to recognize it from other people's experiences or written examples. Until these two factors have effectively converged, behaviour which constitutes sexual harassment can remain unlabelled.

Lastly there is the issue of perception. In Liz's case her attempt to report the case had resulted in disbelief and claims of 'imagination'. Whilst girls are treated in this manner it is likely that they will learn that to have faith in their own perceptions is dangerous. Because of this influence they will be encouraged, albeit tacitly, to perceive sexual harassment as 'normal' and 'typical' male behaviour and as such unremarkable.

All these cases of sexual harassment convinced me that this was a significant problem for females, but it was the way in which it affected girls in schools that interested me most. I decided that I must conduct some research on the subject of sexual harassment in classrooms to ascertain how frequently it happened, how it manifested itself, how girls perceived and described it and what effects it had on them. However, before this could be successfully organized or achieved I needed to uncover how others had defined this behaviour and what were the inherent problems with conducting research into this phenomenon. Thus the next chapter describes sexual harassment and some of the problems with definition and labelling and the confusion which arises because of the similarity sexual harassment has with 'normal' male behaviour.

Chapter 2

Sexual Harassment

The experiences I have already described allow a preliminary definition of sexual harassment which is that it is unsolicited and unreciprocated sexual male behaviour towards women and girls, which may be obscured by what is considered 'normal' behaviour. It is a social construction founded on inherited male power and gender conditioning and serves to undermine the autonomy of women and girls. It may include an explicit or implicit threat for non-compliance. I now wish to turn to an analysis of the process of defining sexual harassment in the late twentieth century in 'Western' society.

The most usually cited examples of sexual harassment are those which depict a male boss and a female secretary. In a classic scenario the boss, because of his masculinity and status, is able to use sexualized language and familiar gestures as a way of extracting both sexual and non-sexual favours from the woman employee. Women who are employed because they will add an 'attractive dimension' to the office are examples of women who are being viewed by their boss as sex objects first, and workers second. In order to remain in employment many women accept a variety of unwanted sexual advances, silently, regarding it as 'normal' male behaviour.

In discussing sexual harassment I will focus on the reasons why women began to see this social interaction as detrimental, and how sexual harassment was and is perpetuated. As the chapter develops it will become clear that the status of sexual harassment is changing. 'Sexual harassment' may be a new term, but the practices which constitute the behaviour are classic and commonplace. Initially regarded as a 'normal' male practice, it is now considered unlawful in some parts of the world such as Canada and South Australia, and at least undesirable in some places amongst some groups in society.

Challenges to men's unwanted sexual attentions had been made before the twentieth century but either had not been taken seriously or else had been ignored. Some women have always considered this 'normal' behaviour 'aberrant', but their protests were suppressed. Over the centuries essays, plays and books have been written which have challenged and condemned men's 'romantic' and 'knightly' behaviours. Some women writers found chivalry and gallantry to be in men's best interest and belittling and controlling of their own sex. Further, some recognized that by encouraging women to be passive and pretty, and to accept and be flattered by such behaviour, they could be easily denied educational opportunity, and thus by default become dependent.

Some women were aware that their resources were used by men, that women had to trade their bodies in return for financial support and that in defying the traditional role of womanhood they were considered 'abnormal' and 'aberrant'. These women were the precursors to those who named the unwanted behaviour 'sexual harassment'. Aphra Behn (1640–1689) was one of the first feminists to speak on behalf of women and present her different experiences in a male-dominated world. According to Spender (1982, p. 26), Behn vociferously defended the right of women to an education, and the right to marry whom they pleased. Mary Astell in 1694 wrote 'A Serious Proposal to the Ladies for the Advancement of their True and Greatest Interest', and stated that '[w]omen are from their very Infancy debarr'd those advantages [of education] with the want of which they are afterwards reproached, and nursed up in those vices with which will hereafter be upbraided them. So partial are Men as to expect Bricks when they afford no straw' (cited in Partnow, 1985, p. 201). Mary Wollstonecraft (1759–1797) (1982, p. 97) was critical 'of idle superficial men, whose only occupation [was] gallantry', and suggested that co-education was the answer to debauched and selfish boys and weak, vain, indolent and frivolous girls. 'I presuppose, that such a degree of equality should be established between the sexes as would shut out gallantry and coquetry, yet allow friendship and love to temper the heart for the discharge of higher duties' (1982, p. 288).

By the middle of this century there was a growing interest in the understanding of power relationships between men and women. Simone de Beauvoir's (1949) analysis of women's oppression attributed its cause to society not biology and this formed the basis for most debates up to, and including, the 1960s. In the late 1960s and early 1970s, much attention was given to the same problem, the cause of women's oppression, and to understanding the construction of male power and dominance. Feminist writings were divided into two main strands. Both concentrated on finding the source of women's oppression in society, but one was academic (Millett, 1970; Firestone, 1970; Mitchell, 1971; Rowbotham, 1971, 1973; Rich, 1972), the other grew out of the Women's Movement and was more experiential in nature, focusing on the manifestation of male power through the use of direct and indirect violence (Griffin, 1971; Brownmiller, 1975). This strand reinterpreted the personal experiences of women who had been victims of male abuse, challenging the previously accepted view that men's aggressive behaviour was 'typical' and 'normal', resulting in behaviour being viewed from a different perspective. It is this strand with which I am concerned.

Attention up until the late 1970s had been focused on extreme forms of violence against women, initiated in particular by Susan Griffin (1971) in her paper 'Rape, the All-American Crime' and consolidated by Susan Brownmiller's book, *Against Our Will* (1975). Amir's (1967) study of known male rapists in Philadelphia in the late 1960s helped to give a different perspective to rapists and their victims, questioning the stereotype of the uncontrollable sex-maniac, indiscriminately attacking women. He showed that in 48.9 per cent of cases the woman 'knew' her assailant (by 'knew' Amir meant acquaintances, neighbours, friends, family friends and relatives) and that rape was most likely to occur in the assailant's home, or the woman's home. In fact 55.7 per cent of rapes took place in the home, 14.9 per cent in a car and only 29.4 per cent elsewhere. Further, he showed that in 70 per cent of cases the rapes listed in the police files were planned and only 15.9 per cent were 'explosive' acts or totally unplanned. Amir found the 'uncontrollable urge' myth to be inaccurate.

This evidence, which successfully challenged the belief that rape was a result of uncontrollable male lust, also indicated that individual women were less 'responsible' for the attack than was usually assumed to be the case. The new information provided women with a lever with which to argue for change. Women's shelters (in 1972 Canada and the UK opened the first Women's Shelters; the Netherlands, Australia and the United States opened shelters in 1974 (Seager and Olson 1986)), rape crisis centres (the London Rape Crisis Centre opened in 1976), and demonstrations for women to 'Reclaim the Night' (the first 'Reclaim the Night' demonstration was held on November 12th 1977 in cities such as Leeds, London, Manchester, Newcastle and York, and similar marches were held throughout the USA; at the end of the decade this developed into a large and more explicitly political campaign, 'Women Against Violence Against Women' (Coote and Campbell, 1987, p. 42)) resulted, drawing attention to the fact that women were subjected to and controlled by male violence. By the end of the 1970s, though, women had become interested in other less dramatic forms of female abuse, and everyday intimidation and exploitation of women came under scrutiny. Sexual harassment was one of these issues.

There are a variety of definitions available to us to describe sexual harassment, all of which have been evolved in the last decade or so. Farley (1979, p. 33) defined sexual harassment as behaviour in the workplace which men use to gain power and includes 'staring at, commenting upon or touching a woman's body, requests for acquiesence in sexual behaviour, repeated non-reciprocal propositions for dates, demands for sexual intercourse, rape'.

During her three years' research on women in employment, Farley (1978, pp. 11–12) spoke to many female employees about their work experiences. '[W]hen we had finished there was an unmistakable pattern to our employment. Something absent in all the literature, something I had never seen although I had observed it many times, was newly exposed. Each one of us had already quit or been fired from a job at least once because we had been made too uncomfortable by the behaviour of men. . . . Sexual harassment seemed to come about as close to symbolizing the problem as the language would permit'. (Although Farley is attributed with the coinage of the phrase, there is evidence of it being used prior to 1978. Sexual harassment appears twice in the index of Susan Brownmiller's book *Against Our Will* (1975). Although not in the text itself, sexual harassment is used to label general male aggressive behaviour towards women. There are two entries given (pp. 247–8 and p. 390). The first is an incident involving a 14-year-old youth who asked a young married woman for a date. She chased him off, but 'in a gesture of adolescent bravado . . . [he] wolf whistled at her' (p. 246). The second example is more generalized and describes sexual harassment as behaviour which ranges from abusive four-letter words and animal noises grunted at women on the street, to the media exploitation of 'faceless naked female bodies' (p. 390). These two examples locate sexual harassment as a problem experienced by many women in ways and places which are both public and private. However, Brownmiller's early recognition of the phenomenon was not taken up by the media or others until a few years later.) Farley coined the term 'sexual harassment' because there was no appropriate phrase in current usage, revealing an absence of meaning, insight and naming for women in the standard language.

Farley (1978, p. 17) argued that men view women workers as sexual objects, rather than as employees employed for a specific task, and that any act of male aggression which contributes to the ultimate goal of keeping women 'in line' constitutes harassment. Whether the behaviour is demanding of sexual favours or generalized annoying behaviour which assumes familiarity, both are assertions of male power. She identified the protagonists of sexual harassment as men in the workplace, usually in positions of power and authority, whilst the victims are women who occupy relatively inferior positions. In her study (1978, p. 261) she recognized that the reward for men using this behaviour is the maintenance of both personal and group power.

MacKinnon's (1979) work took a different perspective from that of Farley. She argued that in American law sexual harassment constitutes sexual discrimination. She argued that sexual harassment in the workplace was behaviour men adopt and the process by which they seek to gain sex or sexual favours. The initial behaviour does not have to contain a sexual act, and unlike Farley who saw men's reward as power, MacKinnon argued that the reward is one of sexual gain. She broadly defined sexual harassment as the unwanted imposition of sexual requirements levied on another person in a relationship of unequal power (1979, p. 1). Her definition extends along a continuum of severity and unwantedness. It includes verbal sexual suggestions or jokes, constant leering or ogling, brushing against a person's body 'accidentally', giving a 'friendly' pat, squeezing or pinching or putting an arm against a person, a quick kiss, the indecent proposition backed by the threat of being sacked and forced sexual relations.

Studies in Britain on behaviour which resembles sexual harassment covered a broader perspective than the American research. In 1978 an article by Hanmer (1978, p. 190), 'Male Violence and the Social Control of Women', although not using the term sexual harassment, clearly discussed behaviour which belongs to this category. '[I]n a woman's life fear of violence from men is subtle and pervasive' and is located in 'certain neighbourhoods or streets and parks and open spaces' as well as in the home (1978, pp. 191–2). Hanmer's continuum of behaviour ranges from the covert use of force which 'may appear friendly or joking', to violence, which includes rape and murder and included 'modes of behaviour that coerce compliance.' The research was conducted in private houses and aimed to record the extent to which women were harassed in this setting. In the study the label sexual harassment was not used. Was this because sexual harassment was seen as a problem confined to the workplace?

In another article published the same year, Dinny (1978, pp. 142–144) described her experiences with a general practitioner. Here is another example of an incident which is not named sexual harassment but which describes feelings which are consistent with the feelings of other women who have been sexually harassed. In this example unwanted attention is enacted in a location previously ignored as a possible site, that of a doctor's surgery. The doctor, according to Dinny, was patronizing, petulant, wielded his power and 'made a big joke' about the fact that on her last visit she had been told she had a 'touch of thrush'. Unlike the doctor, Dinny did not find this amusing. She felt humiliated, anxious, angry and powerless.

By the early 1980s, sexual harassment had become an employment concern for the Trades Union Congress and an issue for human rights campaigners. When the TUC realized the detrimental effect that this behaviour had on women members a number of pamphlets were written by various unions to bring the problem into the open. The TUC defined sexual harassment as 'repeated and unwanted verbal or sexual advances, sexually derogatory statements or sexually discriminating remarks' (TUC, 1983, p. 3). Sedley and Benn (1982, pp. 7–8) in the pamphlet published by the National Council for Civil Liberties (NCCL), defined sexual harassment as ranging from patronizing language to behaviours such as 'he put his hand up my skirt', 'a pin-up of a woman with her legs wide open', 'blowing down the neck of her jumper', and 'a remark such as "your nipple's sticking out" ' (pp. 3–12). The NCCL defines harassment as any unwanted male behaviour.

However as time continued the definition of sexual harassment became less exact: in 1987 Wise and Stanley did not make any distinction between sexual or non-sexual behaviours because for them every aggressive male action constituted sexual harassment. However I feel this all-encompassing definition is dangerous and I argue that sexual harassment must be explicitly sexual in form and can be distinguished from any other behaviour of an aggressive and harassing nature by this very characteristic. Intrusive male behaviour in which gender plays a part, but which is devoid of a sexual component, is not sexual harassment but 'sexist harassment'. This new term includes unwanted comments, gestures, remarks, innuendoes and actions, from a stereotyped assumption about the role of women but with no actual sexual content. Thus expressions such as 'damn women drivers', 'let me help you, women are no good at this', or asking a woman to perform certain tasks because of the expectations that she is more suited for it, are not examples of sexual harassment, but 'sexist harassment'. The distinction between these two forms of harassment is rarely made in spite of its importance (the distinction between sexist and sexual harassment emerged following a conversation with Jacqui Halson, currently lecturer at the University of Kent, Canterbury), and will aid differentiation whilst refining definition.

Dziech and Weiner's research (1984, p. 24) also made a distinction between sexual harassment and other forms of sexualized behaviour, and this was a necessary and important distinction. Their research focused on those they described as 'lecherous professors', and was conducted in universities in America. Although the majority of their study was concerned with the sexual harassment of female students by male lecturers, they discussed sexual behaviour in the form of unwanted sexual overtures and flirtations made by women students directed at male lecturers and professors. Dziech and Weiner argued that although this behaviour may meet the criteria of sexual harassment in that it is unwanted, unreciprocated, unsolicited, sexual in nature, and could be disruptive and anger a male professor, it does not constitute sexual harassment because there are fundamental differences in its nature. They argued that female students do not have the socially constructed power of birthright, for whatever power they have is held individually and is not collectively organized. 'There is too much difference in role and status of male faculty and female students to make flirtation or even seduction by students harassment. "Harassment" suggests misuse of power, and students simply do not have enough power to harass.' Dziech and Weiner state that as a consequence however annoying or uncomfortable this 'crush' may be for the professor, the behaviour cannot destroy his self-esteem or endanger his intellectual self-confidence. Instead of calling this behaviour sexual harassment they call it 'sexual hassle', because it does not incur retaliation, punitive treatment, bad grades or withheld recommendations. Ultimately, the professor has the power to control the situation whatever the consequences because of the inherited power bequeathed the male gender. Dziech and Weiner imply that sexual harassment can only be regarded as having occurred if the protagonist is male and the victim female, for they see power as being at the centre of such practices. Women, they argue, are relatively powerless and the strategies they use to undermine men constitute 'sexual hassle'. Because sexual harassment is a strategy used exclusively by those with access to the privilege of power, men, they indicate, are free from sexual harassment.

Now that a picture of the frequency with which sexual harassment was occurring and the diversity of the ways in which it was manifested was becoming clearer, it was important to study other researches which had specifically looked at this problem in schools.

Sexual Harassment in Schools

Sexual harassment was located in schools by a number of researchers, teachers and writers. However most of the research seems to have been collected by default rather than by design. Mahony's work is a case in point. Initially studying students on teaching practice, she found that by sitting in classrooms and observing she saw that sexual harassment was clearly a significant problem for many girls. Her research was based on letters from, and interviews with, girls and women teachers who had experience of this behaviour either as an observer or as a victim. Many forms of harassment were related. One example of verbal sexual harassment was told to her by some students: 'We were walking along, talking when a couple of boys aged about fourteen began edging towards us. One passed unnecessarily close and growled to his mate, "cor I'd like to squeeze her tits" '. Other examples of sexual harassment included 'grabbing breasts', as well as non-sexual behaviour such as 'ridiculing'. Both of these, she argues, have the effect of controlling girls whilst furthering male power.

She also documents incidents of 'servicing', which she argues is a form of sexual harassment (1985, pp. 50–53). 'Servicing' comprises male-imposed tasks which not only control the girls but extract a service, resulting in humiliation and oppression. The 'services' the girls provide include homework, shopping, mothering, 'lending' money, providing food and school equipment. For these 'services' the girls have a 'good name, image and reputation'. This definition which includes the power reward for the male, is similar to that described by Farley. The boys, like men, are 'active in structuring relationships of dominance and subordination', effective in that they maintain both personal and group male power.

Sexual harassment can be manifested in schools in a visual way. Carol Jones (1985) found examples of 'magazine cutouts and pictures of women (often put up to brighten the building)' in the school corridors which had been crudely defaced by male students. This visual sexual harassment affects teachers and students alike, to say nothing of women visitors who come to the school. She also found that girls complained that boys 'teased them with pornography'. Copies of *Playboy* were being used as a way of embarrassing and intimidating some girls. Having one's learning-space invaded by distorted or defaced images of the female body, by hearing abusive language in which 'cunt', 'slag', 'pro' and 'bitch' are used with such alacrity to describe females, can only provide an unhappy and stressful work environment.

In schools it is not just girls who are subjected to sexual harassment, neither is it only men in traditional positions of power who can sexually harass. In 1980 Whitbread's empirical study identified unacceptable male behaviour between schoolboys and female teachers. She found that women teachers, especially those in the lower echelons of the school, were subjected to 'unidentifiable boys' milling around in a group, grabbing and making obscene comments and appraising remarks. Jones (1985, p. 28) found examples of female staff members being harassed by boys too. She cites an incident of a woman teacher who 'discovered a boy masturbating in a classroom to a photograph of a naked woman. He ejaculated to the cheers of other boys.'

Researchers found numerous examples of sexual harassment or evidence of unwanted sexual behaviour in schools and they also found that sexual harassment was accepted as part of the hidden curriculum for female students and one of the hazards of teaching for women staff. Sexual harassment was either ignored as a problem detrimental to women or it was regarded as 'normal' or 'typical' behaviour.

Other research studies themselves displayed this very problem with recognition for when looking at educational issues in classrooms they failed to recognize sexual harassment when it presented itself. Some male behaviour, depending on the setting, the people involved or the way in which it is interpreted, can be seen to be at one and the same time both sexual harassment and 'normal' male behaviour. The difficulty in pinning down particular actions and labelling them as sexual harassment has resulted in women and girls becoming confused with what is genuine and wanted sexual attention and what is unwanted sexual attention. More often than not behaviour which falls into this grey area is either described as 'normal' or 'typical', or it is ignored and not spoken about.

One such example of this can be found in the research conducted by Measor and Woods (1984, p. 120). They looked at the transition of students from middle to upper schools and part of their data and their analysis shows how male sexual behaviour can become confused with sexually harassing behaviour. The incident they describe involves one male teacher and the way in which he speaks to and acts with particular girls. 'Mr Hill [a teacher], always addressed one sixth form girl, named Erica, as "Hey Erotica" ', and '[h]e would walk with his arm around the shoulders of a younger girl who was upset.' Measor and Woods fail to recognize that this behaviour may well have been sexual harassment and describe it as him showing friendliness, justified because according to the researchers the girls liked him and he was 'forgiven for it.'

What Measor and Woods fail to discuss is any alternative interpretation, or indeed the possibility that the girls may have been unable to regard Mr Hill's behaviour in any other way. Girls' perceptions of male behaviour are likely to be informed by the predominant interpretations prevalent in our society. These, on the whole, are male-centred. For the most part it seems that girls are silent. For the girls in Mr Hill's school, it is likely that they find his actions and comments 'normal' behaviour, and to have complained about them as unwanted or unwelcomed would have suggested that their 'learned' interpretation of this behaviour is somehow different from that of Measor and Woods. Thus a male teacher joking, flirting and consoling his female students whilst using a sexually inappropriate diminutive is considered quite acceptable.

There is however a different perspective on this behaviour. Erica and the younger girl are in positions of subordination, based primarily on age and gender inferiority, and secondarily on their educational, emotional and financial vulnerability. Measor and Woods ignore this perspective. Implicit in the text where Mr Hill is described as 'young . . . good looking [with a] good sense of humour', is the assumption that this is 'normal', healthy behaviour for a young male teacher and can be condoned. The incidents then are described (and dismissed) as a reflection of 'normal' heterosexual interactions.

Even by the mid-1980s many education researchers were not using the term 'sexual harassment' even though they were describing behaviour which clearly fitted the various criteria. The criteria for sexual harassment had not, it seems, been adequately clarified or recognized. Davies (1984), Measor and Woods (1984) and Stanworth (1984) are three such examples of studies where the term sexual harassment is not used, even though examples are given of demoralizing statements from men teachers (Davies, p. 37; Stanworth, p. 45), aggressive male behaviour in the form of annoying touches (Measor and Woods, p. 104), and sexually oriented remarks (Measor and Woods, p. 86). Instead what emerges from the literature is a confused and inconsistent range of behaviours some of which are labelled sexual harassment and covering a broad range of actions, whilst others which clearly describe sexual harassment are ignored or described as normal or acceptable male behaviour.

Whilst definitions of sexual harassment remain inconsistent or contradictory, gaps occur through which sexual harassers or sexually harassing behaviour may pass unnoticed or uncontested. For example, the TUC's phrase 'unwanted verbal' advances makes the definition too broad, for surely many people receive unwanted verbal advances which would not be considered sexual harassment? Farley and MacKinnon's discrepancy over whether the harassment is a sexual act or one to gain sexual favours, further confuses. 'Repeated' means more than once, but clearly rape, or attempted rape, of a secretary by her boss on just one occasion constitutes sexual harassment. Unclear definitions enable the practice to continue, for specific cases go unrecognized or unremarked.

The Problems with Sexual Harassment

Sexual Harassment — 'Aberrant' or 'Typical' Behaviour?

Sexual harassment can in some cases be described as 'normal' or 'typical' behaviour, or described as something else. One of the problems, as I have already shown, is that girls do not readily name the behaviour as unwanted for they have become inured to it. However there are further reasons for sexual harassment passing as unremarkable, and these are to do with the line between what constitutes 'normal' male behaviour and that which is described as 'aberrant'.

The definition of 'normal' and 'typical' dress, speech, attitudes, actions, and roles for women and men, is largely influenced by what society has determined as femininity and masculinity. This division between women and men is artificially created and exaggerated, according, among others, to Rubin (1975, p. 179). Social conditioning has manufactured the differences, accelerating and promoting traits and denoting specific ones as female or male, rather than accepting those traits as human. Yet what is deemed feminine behaviour and masculine behaviour are social constructions. De Beauvoir (1949, p. 249) was one of the first to declare of females: 'One is not born, one rather becomes a woman', indicating the power of the conditioning process. According to Greer (1970, p. 29), the 'normal sex roles that we learn to play from infancy are no more natural than the actions of a transvestite', and 'in order to approximate those shapes and attitudes which are considered normal and desirable both sexes deform themselves.'

Traditional behaviours, Rubin (1975, p. 165) argues, become embedded in society and regarded as that which is 'normal' and 'typical' for that group of people. Gender identity is not based on an expression of natural differences but on the suppression of natural similarities. (In differentiating between gender and sex I take Warren's (1980, p. 181) definition. Gender is used 'to refer to the socially imposed dichotomy of masculine and feminine roles and character traits. Sex is physiological, while gender, in the latter usage, is cultural.') Conforming to one's gender role has the effect of 'repressing some of the personality characteristics of virtually everyone, men and women', and is a 'socially imposed division of the sexes' (Rubin, pp. 179–180). Physical differences between women and men are exaggerated by specific gendered expectations and training, rather than individual physical potential. The evidence here shows that this is equally true of behavioural traits.

There have been many studies (Rosenkrantz *et al.*, 1968; Bem, 1974; Spence *et al.*, 1975; Williams and Bennett, 1975), that have asked people to describe 'typical' women and men in order to understand what society perceives as 'normal' for a particular gender. Perceptions of 'typical' feminine and 'typical' masculine traits often fall into stereotyped categories. They provide a very familiar picture, since the 'commonsense' judgements have been made by people within the culture in which the investigation was carried out. Not surprisingly the findings reflect the society's gender divisions. According to Williams and Bennett (1975), submissive, emotional, attractive, flirtatious, gentle, highly-strung, charming and fickle describe some of the characteristics of the female gender whilst male characteristics apparently include being sexually interested, initiating, aggressive, dominant, cruel, forceful and unemotional (cited in Archer and Lloyd, 1982, pp. 38–39). As most women and men wish to conform to their gender-assigned category, they exhibit behaviour which is in keeping with that social definition. Gender characteristics and behaviours are learned from role models and from constant reinforcement. By displaying the appropriate characteristics, people gain a sense of belonging to their gender group. However, the more these characteristics are displayed, the more the behaviour is regarded as being inherently feminine or masculine. Consequently the images of women and men and the ways in which they operate become embedded in the society and come to form a stereotype.

It is also in the best interest of individual women and men to acquire and reveal their assigned gender characteristics, for to reject one's gender results in being, according to French (1986, pp. 80–81), labelled 'monsters and unnatural fiends . . . beasts', if female, or 'fools, freaks, fags or saints', if male. However, this has consequences for the way in which women and men behave and lead their lives. According to Cole (1985, p. 27), a 'normal' man's behaviour is the same as that of an abusive father, for he is 'hard-hearted, no nurturing sense, inarticulate, unable to express feelings, controlling, intimidating, [and] able to back up his demands with the threat of physical force.' What has become confused is behaviour which is considered appropriate for the 'standard' male, and behaviour which is abusive and controlling.

The behaviour of men towards others, especially those weaker or more vulnerable than themselves, reveals that when detailing 'aberrant' and 'typical' behaviours, the descriptors are interchangeable, because 'normal' and 'aberrant' male behaviour can be one and the same. The difficulty in pinning down particular behaviour, and describing it as 'aberrant' and thus sexually harassing, is one reason why sexual harassment has been able to persist. For in one setting with certain people, particular behaviour can constitute sexual harassment, but in the same setting with different characters the same behaviour can be wanted sexual attention.

Many people assume that sexual harassment is a man 'naturally' showing his recognition of a woman's attractive face, figure or way of moving and that his appreciation can be shown in a variety of ways such as a wolf-whistle, a slap on the bottom, repeated requests for dates, sexual innuendoes, pats, winks, kisses and touches. This raises the question of why, if women do not like this behaviour, they fail to make this clear. Why do women remain silent about unwanted sexual attention? It is clear that women do not remain silent about other forms of violence, such as an attack by a man or boy purely on a physical level, for example if a woman's handbag is stolen, her car is broken into, she is mugged, or she is verbally abused by her angry boss for incompetence. These incidents do not silence her, in fact she would probably tell a number of friends and work colleagues about all of them. Is it because she does not consider that sort of attack her fault and therefore she cannot be called 'provocative'? Is it because people are more likely to believe that she is 'telling the truth'? Is it because sexually harassing behaviour can mean unwanted sexual intimacies, which can be embarrassing to talk about? Is it that the victim believes, even though she doesn't like the behaviour, that it is a 'natural' way for a man to behave? So as long as sexual harassment is considered sexually motivated, women and girls find it hard to understand it in the same way as they would a mugging. For a mugging is regarded as something which is outside their control but sexual harassment immediately implies, quite erroneously, women's complicity.

In other situations, however, sexual harassment can be regarded as men showing friendliness or concern. This raises further problems. To get men to understand that some women do not like to be touched, petted, patted, cuddled, winked at, whistled at, patronized, helped, or protected goes against the way in which many men have been taught to respond and behave. Nevertheless it must be accepted that such behaviour is learned social behaviour: men do not 'naturally' wink at, whistle at or pet women.

Confusion between what is aberrant and what is normal is so distorted that when a female student complained that a male teacher passed her a love note during her O-level English exam the headmaster replied, '[a] young woman of your age should be flattered' (*Guardian*, 16 February 1988, p. 16). According to our society's standards women should be pleased that men take notice of them and make comments to show their appreciation or interest. This type of social construction is readily understood by most people, and women who complain of sexual harassment can be told that they are killjoys or 'prudish'.

It must also be recognized that there are women and girls who engage in sex-stereotyped behaviour which leads some men to believe that sexualized comments and touches are appropriate. Coquetry, coyness, incompetence, frailty and inefficiency are ways in which some women gain sexual attention. These, as much as men's stereotyped behaviour, are learned social interactions. However the problem arises because these are the very behaviours which are said to promote the use of sexual harassment by men. Indeed there are some women who would feel ignored and sexually 'unappreciated' if such comments and gestures were not forthcoming.

The Lack of Language

The inability to recognize sexual harassment as a phenomenon per se has meant that it has had no place in the language. As language is one of the ways people describe and shape their understandings of the world, the absence of a label makes talking about something unnamed, difficult. Spender (1980, p. 172) argues that language is so powerful 'in structuring thought and reality that it can "blind" its users to the evidence of the physical world; objects and events remain but shadowy entities when they are not named'.

Having the ability to name new phenomena has in the past been in the hands of men who have had control of this important medium. There are many women who have written about the monopoly which men had and have over language. Millett (1970, p. 25), argues that 'every avenue of power within the society' lies within the male preserve. Those who have power are in positions to generate more power, both for themselves and for people they denote as belonging to their powerful group. Belonging or not belonging to the powerful group, according to Millett (1970, p. 24), is the result of birthright, not ability. Having inherited power to construct reality, men are able to construct and represent the world in the way that makes sense to them. De Beauvoir stated that men 'describe [the world] from their own point of view, which they confuse with the absolute truth' (cited in MacKinnon, 1983, p. 249). Spender (1980, pp. 163–165) makes a similar point. Her analysis of the perpetuation of male control shows that language plays a central part, and that naming the world is 'essential for the construction of reality'. Her thesis is that the process of naming phenomena and encoding meanings is conducted by those who have that power and authority to name. The names selected to represent the material world are not chosen arbitrarily, but are the outcome of 'partial human vision'. All naming, Spender (1980, pp. 163–165) argues, is of necessity biased, because emphasis, selection and omission in naming forms the core of the process. 'When one group holds a monopoly on naming and is able to enforce its own particular bias on everyone, . . . bias is embedded in the name it supplies . . . '. From this it can be seen that those who have the power to name the world are in a position to influence reality. Cameron's (1985, p. 29) argument is that 'sex differences in language are related to the power of men and the powerlessness of women, and . . . that even our speech behaviour reflects and perpetuates patriarchal norms'. Language, she continues, is an essential component for understanding the world. If the language we use does not represent the 'real world', but a version of it which is already filtered, definitions become problematic, 'effectively creating our perceptions of reality and they . . . produce a repressive and one-sided picture' (Cameron, 1985, p. 94).

One of the ways in which discussions about sexual harassment were curtailed was because of namelessness. Dworkin (1976, p. 32) argued that because men were the engineers of this culture and had named all the words, women had had their values, perceptions and understandings defined for them. 'We use a language which is sexist . . . developed by men in their own interests; formed specifically to exclude us; used specifically to oppress us . . . '. Having a deficient language, or one that omitted various concepts, gave people the power to trivialize and ignore particular experiences which could not be adequately described in the existing language. Behaviour which was not experienced by the naming party would remain nameless or be made 'normal', and by default be regarded as unproblematic by most women and men alike.

Up until recently many women and girls who were 'sexually harassed' were at a loss as to what to call this unwanted behaviour. Because of a language deficiency there was an inability to express feelings adequately, or to describe a man's unwanted approaches. Not being able to communicate the existence of such a problem prevents women from sharing the experience with others, forcing them into an isolated, vulnerable and thus silent position. Spender argues that it is through their control over meaning that men are able to impose on everyone their own view of the world; 'women without the ability to symbolize their experience in the male language, either internalize male reality (alienation) or find themselves unable to speak at all (silence)' (cited in Cameron, 1985, p. 108).

However, with the 1960s came a new strategy, devised by women, which had the power to create an environment in which phenomena could be discussed and named. This strategy in turn challenged the accepted naming procedures, because specific women-based problems were at last diagnosed and given credence.

Much of the information for the debate on the oppression of women, for example, was promoted by this strategy. It consisted of groups of women discussing relevant issues, sharing information and personal experiences, which were found to be conducive to self-education and advancement and for making political connections. These were 'consciousness-raising' groups. From these groups came the phrase 'The personal is the political', a major slogan used by feminists, which argued that personal and intimate experiences were not isolated or individual, but were social, systemic and had political implications. Throughout the 1960s and 1970s, and on both sides of the Atlantic, groups of women spent evenings in each other's homes, or in local halls, discussing issues which were directly related to their wellbeing. Out of these discussions grew the awareness that women shared many common problems which, when analyzed, were seen to have political consequences in that all were detrimental to women's advancement and autonomy.

An example of one of the well known 'findings' from this type of information generation, though not related to sexual harassment, is that of the American Betty Friedan. Friedan (1963) interviewed college-educated women graduates about their lifestyles. All were living in comfortable detached houses in wealthy suburbs, married to successful high-earning men, all had children and all thought they should be fulfilled in their lives. 'But on an April morning in 1959, I heard a mother of four, having coffee with four other mothers . . . say in a tone of quiet desperation, "the problem". And the others knew, without words, that she was not talking about a problem with her husband, or her children, or her home. Suddenly they realized they all shared the problem, the problem', Friedan (1963, p. 17) called it, 'that has no name'.

Sexual harassment then came into conscious thought in the late 1970s via this method. Women in a research project organized by Farley were in a supportive and sharing environment in which concepts and issues which affected mainly women were beginning to be defined and labelled. However it cannot be assumed that, because sexual harassment had reached the notice of some groups of people, it became a common or household word. Indeed, although it had been labelled and defined, there were many people who still did not recognize it, although there were some people who knew what it was but who were not able to match theory and practice.

Chapter 3

Why Sexual Harassment is Silenced

Although sexual harassment has been labelled as a widespread problem and there is a better understanding of how, why, where and to whom it happens, those who challenge and confront sexual harassers or institutions which allow harassment to continue are often limited to those involved with feminist theory, legal implications, or officials in the trade unions. Despite the publicity surrounding this issue there are still few women and girls who are able to submit a complaint to an employer or challenge the harasser themselves. Women remain silent about their experiences of sexual harassment, changing jobs or avoiding the person who is the protagonist.

One reason why women may be reluctant to complain of sexual harassment may be that there is a discrepancy between what is understood in theory, read about in papers or policy statements, and how it is depicted on television, and what is experienced on a personal level. This was exactly the case with me in South Australia. Although theoretically competent to talk about and identify sexual harassment for others I was unable to recognize that I was a victim of this phenomenon.

If one of the problems is the ability to identify the behaviour when it affects oneself, perhaps the issue is to do with raised consciousness. To be able to describe sexual harassment and recognize it in the abstract does not necessarily mean that people can automatically transfer that information into an understanding of the situation when it applies to them personally. It is possible that one's perceptions of 'normal' male behaviour, translated into justifications of 'he was just being friendly' or 'he didn't mean it', persist, and victims turn inwards to seek for reasons as to why they are feeling embarrassed, humiliated or angry.

So how does one know when one is a victim of sexual harassment? From a theoretical point of view, some feminists argue that sexual harassment occurs when a person feels she has been sexually harassed. For others, sexual harassment has occurred when behaviour which a woman or girl experiences meets the 'objective' criteria of unwanted, unsolicited verbal or physical sexual abuse. Yet these definitions are not foolproof, for the situation may occur when the 'objective' criteria have been met, yet the person claims she does not feel she has been sexually harassed. Who should decide when sexual harassment has taken place, the woman herself, or an outside observer who is an 'expert' in the field? In this case it could be argued that a woman who receives unwanted sexual advances, which are persistent, abusive and have negative consequences, but who does not consider this 'harassment' has not been harassed. But this raises interesting questions for it is undoubtedly true that perspectives and personal awareness change. What one considers to be 'normal' male sexual joking may a few years later with a raised consciousness be perceived differently. Was the treatment received five years ago not sexual harassment?

Conversely a person may say she has been sexually harassed but the 'objective' conditions have not been met. Once more is it the 'expert' who should decide or should the woman be allowed to make the judgement herself? There is also the question of whose perception is accurate? One woman's perception of what may be a sexually harassing experience for her, may be different from another woman's perception of the same behaviour. In one setting with certain people, particular behaviour can constitute sexual harassment, but in the same setting with different characters the same behaviour can be wanted sexual attention.

The difference in point of view does not necessarily mean the difference between a male perspective or a female perspective. As I have shown in the previous section, women and girls experience such a wide range of situations in which sexually harassing behaviour takes place, that no single statement can adequately encompass all their experiences or all the different interpretations of these experiences. Education, social conditioning, maturity, sexual experience, and political awareness all play a part in a woman's or girl's perception of what constitutes sexual harassment.

But there is a further complication. If it is accepted that a woman can claim to have been sexually harassed this can take many forms. Is it possible that a particular look, a postcard or a pin-up, the raise of an eyebrow or a quietly muttered sexual innuendo constitutes sexual harassment? Many groups of people in society would find these actions difficult to accept as examples. But in some instances each of these actions could be sexual harassment if women are enabled to decide what constitutes sexual harassment, for each could embarrass, trivialize and humiliate.

However there may be other reasons why women and girls do not disclose that they have been subjected to unwanted sexual attention. It is clear that there are a number of social pressures and expectations placed on girls and women which militate against them telling. One of these is the issue of 'intention'.

Whether a man 'intentionally' sets out to sexually harass a woman or accidentally harasses her can confuse and thus make her keep silent. If she thinks the man 'didn't mean to', but was 'just being friendly', (even though she may be embarrassed, feel humiliated and trivialized) she is likely to ignore his attentions and 'put up with it'.

If we take the scenario of a young woman in a short skirt and high heeled shoes walking down the street and a building labourer whistling and shouting 'cor what nice legs you've got', the question is 'did the man intentionally harass her or not?' Here however there are two sets of 'intentions'. On one hand it can be argued that the woman was deliberately asking for attention and that her 'intentions', by dressing the way she did, were to provoke comment. On the other hand it can be argued that the man's 'intentions' were merely to indicate that her dressing, walking and presence had not gone 'unappreciated'. In both of these interpretations the onus for the harassment has fallen on the shoulders of the woman and the man is exonerated. If a woman were to complain she would be seen as being prudish, provocative or lacking a sense of humour.

But if a man who has no intention of embarrassing or humiliating a woman still does this from a position of being unaware, he is no less culpable of sexual harassment per se, than if he deliberately harassed her knowing what she might feel. Irrespective of the man's perceptions, the definitions of sexual harassment must, to some extent, rest with the person being harassed, certainly not with the assailant. If a man sexually harasses a woman 'by mistake', this is still harassment even though the usual interpretation excuses the man, and blames the woman for over-sensitivity or exaggeration. The question of intention must be side stepped so that the harassment can be more easily identified. Intentions are irrelevant for the harassed woman. Whilst intentions are allowed to colour the issue the woman learns that sexually harassing men mean no harm and that their behaviour must be accepted, not challenged. It is a central facet of my argument that irrespective of the man's intentions, unwanted sexual attention is sexual harassment.

Another central issue is the claim that particular male behaviour is in fact flattery and thus 'normal'. Let us examine the cases of sexual harassment I cited earlier in the context of an assumption that sexual harassment is sexually oriented and a 'natural' display of men's sexual desires. In some of the examples it could be argued that sexual attraction may have been the motive behind the action. Perhaps Louise's head of department was sexually attracted to her; perhaps the priest was infatuated with Alison, as was the geography teacher with Liz and both felt sexual desire. Although the actions are inappropriate in the case of the two schoolgirls, spectators of Louise's harassment may interpret the senior teacher's actions as a man 'naturally' paying a compliment to a young member of staff.

However it is important to look at some of the other examples cited earlier. The intentions of Ben and Simon, and the intentions of the 5-year-old boys at the prep school and the men at the conferences were not to 'flatter' or to make women feel 'better', nor was the behaviour designed to show appreciation. In fact the intentions of all these males were to denigrate, embarrass, humiliate or to frighten in order that they should gain power. In these instances 'flattery' played no part in the intentions of the men or boys.

At its basic common denominator, then, sexual harassment is about power, and about the wielding of that power in an effective manner in order to extract favours or have particular services performed. I have argued that the notion of power however is usually subsumed beneath the rhetoric of 'sexuality'. Thus women who get wolf-whistles, or who are followed, or get appraising looks are being as effectively harassed as women who are physically touched. Chloe was being effectively sexually harassed even though it would be difficult to argue that her assailants were sexually motivated because of their relative naivety or young age. Sexuality in this case must be eschewed for the more obvious motivation of power. This position both results in a consolidation of male power on an individual level, and furthers men's power on a much wider scale. On the other hand women are diminished both individually and collectively.

One of the outcomes of silence is that men and boys are not repeatedly challenged in any way about the inappropriateness of their behaviour. Thus we have a situation in which men do things for which they are then subsequently never challenged. For the head of department, the priest, the geography teacher, the boys in the junior school, the men at the sexual harassment conferences, their behaviour which was perceived in one way by women and girls, existed in these men's minds on a completely different plane. The silence of the girls and women actually protects male behaviour and allows it to continue unchallenged. For men their perception of what they have done remains on a level of at best acceptable and condoned behaviour and at least unremarkable.

I have already described why it was impossible for Alison to report her sexual harassment because of the further victimization that might occur. This situation is a common feeling amongst women and girls who have been sexually attacked. Sexual harassment is usually not a 'public' affair. The harasser and the harassed are often alone, or the harassment is slight, subtle and directed inconspicuously. For complaints to be levied at older, more mature, 'father-like' figures, at bosses, at heads of department or priests are often dangerous steps to take. With no witnesses, physical signs or other proof, harassed women and girls remain silent. Unfortunately it is the case that if women did talk about the behaviour to each other then it might become apparent that the harasser was victimizing many others. But silence brought about by fear of repercussions and claims of lies isolates girls and makes the unwanted attention 'invisible' to others.

Some girls do try to break the silence, like Liz, yet are just not believed. Once a girl has tried to 'tell' and has been rejected by someone such as a mother, it is likely that she will soon learn that such behaviour although unwanted, dirty, degrading and violating is in fact unmentionable and thus legitimate, the implicit message being that one 'puts up with it'. Secondly there are those who remain silent because they know they will not be believed because of how society sees male behaviour. If sexual harassment is more usually categorized as 'normal' male behaviour, and it is believed that men cannot help but do this because it is 'natural', and that women and girls who receive this attention should feel flattered, women and in particular girls are hardly likely to challenge societal attitudes in any overt way. Their best chances are to remain silent, try and avoid further occasions when this behaviour might occur and to structure their lives around prevention rather than cure.

Many girls and women remain silent about their experience of sexual harassment because they believe that in some way they have 'asked' for it. For whilst a male interpretation is used the man is exonerated and excuses or rationalizations are used for his behaviour: he was drunk; she provoked him; she was wearing the wrong clothes; she was in the wrong place at the wrong time; he thought she liked his attentions; she didn't say 'no'; her protests really meant that she was 'playing hard to get'; she is very pretty and she really wants to be noticed; and 'I was only being friendly'.

All these justifications for men's behaviour are assimilated by girls and women throughout their lives until they believe them themselves. Whilst they believe that men are allowed to behave in this manner women will continue to feel guilty and will blame themselves for any incident of sexual harassment.

The Consequences of Sexually Harassing Behaviour

The consequences of sexual harassment are numerous and varied. Both Farley (1978, p. 11) and MacKinnon (1979) show how sexual harassment acts as a control for many different kinds of women irrespective of class or colour or financial position. Farley argues that it keeps women subordinate in their employment, constantly reminding them of their sexual and economic vulnerability whilst undermining their autonomy and personhood as workers (1978, p. 3 and p. 34). The effects include demotion, dismissal, quitting, nervous and physical disorders, negative job evaluations, financial and professional loss, as well as the personal toll all these have on a person's self-esteem, confidence and ability to find a new job (Farley, 1978, pp. 41–48).

Research in America and England has described some of the negative controls sexual harassment for women entails. As a victim of sexual harassment a woman's life is curtailed in a variety of ways including her sexuality, her autonomy, her professional advancement, her financial independence, her rights to a fair and equal dealing in law, medical attention and educational opportunities and her rights to peace of mind and happiness.

Miss Spiros who was a victim of sexual harassment certainly suffered lack of professional advancement and the right to peace and happiness. The extent to which she was financially or educationally disadvantaged by moving school is unknown. The complaint she made to the headteacher was not seen as a serious complaint, the boys were largely exonerated, whilst Miss Spiros was not only told that she was to blame for their behaviour, but was later penalized and asked to teach another grade, so like many other sexually harassed women quit the job. Incidents of men's aggression force women either to succumb to the attention or to escape by quitting. Either way women forfeit their independence and their equality, and either way this helps men maintain their control of female labour and the female body (Farley, p. 261).

From the research it is clear that women's main way of handling this unwanted attention is to hand in notice. According to Read (1982, p. 23) the Alfred Marks survey notes that most women who have experienced sexual harassment find it easier to change their jobs than report the action. However this method of dealing with the problem has other consequences. To admit that one has been sexually harassed is to court disaster socially and professionally. Complaining of being harassed does not augur well for promotion prospects. Leaving employment for no apparent reason makes finding another job more difficult. To change employment frequently does little to enhance one's long-term employment prospects.

With Miss Spiros's case there is a further consideration seldom recognized which is that women can be sexually harassed by younger men and boys. Here it could be expected that women should have the status or authority to prevent behaviour of this kind and that sexual harassment in this situation would not be regarded as harassment. The two boys who harassed her were clearly her juniors in terms of age, size, experience, maturity, knowledge and education, yet they still had the ability to undermine, embarrass and humiliate.

Some victims of sexual harassment, on the other hand, choose not to leave the job, hoping that they can ignore the treatment or avoid it. Louise accepted the situation in this manner, preferring to ignore and avoid rather than confront.

The consequences for girls in schools has been noted in research projects by Mahony (1984) and Jones (1984). Sexually harassing behaviour has the effect of controlling girls whilst furthering both collective and individual male power yet is largely 'unseen' as a problem. The result for the girls is detrimental in that they become more subordinated, less autonomous and less capable of resisting. This behaviour controls the girls through intimidation, embarrassment or humiliation.

The girls who have been sexually harassed by adult men and by men who have been in positions of trust also suffer consequences. Fear of school, mistrust of adults, mistrust of male teachers and men in positions of power, remaining silent about the experience because of the feared consequences revelation might entail, results in girls becoming preoccupied with other concerns, avoiding certain teachers, places or lessons.

However unsatisfactory it is for Miss Spiros and other teachers to leave their jobs, for girls this is often not a viable proposition. If girls are disbelieved, like Liz, not only can they not escape the school environment but they are likely to have to be confronted by the harasser on a weekly, if not more frequent, basis. Alison could not ask for a transfer either. What would the grounds be? She felt that she could not discuss the incident with anyone so she was in a position where nothing could be done. Chloe too is in no position to ask to be sent to another school, and anyway if she did there is no guarantee that the same behaviour, with different protagonists, would not be repeated.

How does this affect girls' learning? Although most of the research conducted into the effects of sexual harassment has been conducted with adult women it is realistic to suppose that the effects on girls would be similar. In many cases depression, fear and feelings of guilt combine to act on the person making them miserable, lacking confidence and therefore unable to perform at their best. For some women, job satisfaction is diminished, promotion is unobtainable unless they are sexually acquiescent, and the daily avoidance of a particular man or men is stressful. Women's energies which could be more productively used elsewhere are spent on avoidance strategies or tense interactions. For women in jobs where overtime is expected, being left alone with a man who may be her boss and sexual harasser, makes her position untenable. Some women feel debarred from jobs where night shifts involve late travel and they are put at risk. Some locations or districts carry the same embargo for women, as do some jobs which are dominated by men.

In this chapter I have tried to give an overview of the problems associated with sexual harassment by drawing on examples in the literature and from my own and others' personal experiences. The research has shown that sexual harassment has a detrimental effect on the way in which women perform the job for which they are paid. The actuality of sexual harassment, or even just the fear of it, affects women in a number of ways which have numerous consequences.

The Research I Wanted to Conduct

It was with a sense of intrigue that I began to gather together ideas about establishing a research project into the sexual harassment of schoolgirls. From my readings I realized that sexual harassment was a complex and difficult topic to describe. From my personal experience I knew how it could be misinterpreted and ignored. From the numerous incidents that had been described to me I realized how sexual harassment could be silenced and remain unchallenged and how victims lost confidence and self-worth and chose to leave the situation in which it occurred.

It was with these problems in mind that I decided to design a research project to find out to what extent girls felt that sexual harassment was a problem for them, the ways in which it was happening, how they described it and the ways in which they coped with it. I have already shown that there has been some research on the way in which adolescent boys sexually harass girls, but I was more interested in the role of the male teacher in the area of sexual harassment. To what extent was his 'normal behaviour' unwanted sexual attention? How did the girls perceive this behaviour? How did they describe it?

I chose such a particular and specialized project for a number of reasons. Firstly, as I have already shown, teaching and education is the area of work with which I am most familiar and was of greatest interest to me, and therefore it was the most appropriate situation in which to work. Secondly there were already books written on other aspects of sexual harassment such as women in the workplace and girls being sexually harassed by their male peers, yet there was no in-depth study on the sexual harassment of girls by their male teachers. Thirdly, many of the educational research books which purport to study girls and boys in equal proportions are clearly male-dominated. Furthermore, there are more educational research projects carried out on the male culture and the male ethos than on women's culture. Thus I decided that the research project which dealt with the sexual harassment of girls would exclusively focus on girls' problems and perceptions, not on the boy's or male teacher's interpretations or perceptions. Fourthly, I had come to suspect from my work as a teacher that one of the reasons that girls become 'disenchanted' with schooling may have to do with this phenomenon. I believed that maybe unwanted sexual attention, or confusing sexual attention which on one hand the girls would have been taught to call 'flattery' but which embarrassed and angered them, might be one of the reasons for girls' lack of achievement. It has been documented that between the ages of thirteen and sixteen some girls in schools lose confidence, become more passive, publicly contribute less in class and generally lose their eagerness to participate in the way in which they did as pre-teenagers (Spender and Sarah, 1980; Spender, 1982).

One example of this is in the approach that girls have to maths and the sciences in general. For example although girls may be achieving at an above average level in maths at their primary schools, they drop to a level at the secondary stage whereby A-level maths is neither contemplated nor expected by many girl pupils or their teachers. This can be seen in the difference between boy and girl students' examination entries. The figures of A-level mathematics entries in Summer 1980 were 73 per cent males and 27 per cent females (Whyld, 1983, p. 19). The lack of higher and particular education manifests itself later in life for women and men, for women consistently occupy jobs at the lower end of any employment structure, education and the health service being two such examples.

There are of course many pressures contributing to the change in achievement and attitude on the part of the female students. Some of the 'normally' accepted reasons within a male defined paradigm is that the shift from childhood to adolescence is in itself traumatic, socially, emotionally and physically. It is thought that perhaps because biologically girls' bodies are maturing, this results in an exaggerated concern with sexuality and personal identification. It is also argued that on the whole girls are more emotional than their male counterparts as they try to cope with their changing position in society. And finally some argue that it is in fact 'natural femaleness' which accounts for the developing passive behaviour.

All these justifications for diminished success are valid if one accepts a male-as-norm paradigm. However I believed that this way of looking at the world does not give a fair and just interpretation from a feminist perspective. I believed that more credence had to be given to the social pressures and sexist influences on girls which made them see themselves in a less than positive light. And it was from a feminist perspective that I wanted to conduct this research.

I believed that sexual harassment might have some bearing on the change in the female students' attitudes to their academic abilities and their personal self-esteem. I hypothesized that this particular phenomenon was present in the everyday interactions between male teachers and female students and was regarded by the perpetrator, the girls and society in general as 'normal' or at least unremarkable male behaviour. I believed it was present in speech, choice of words and intonation, in glance and gesture, in innuendo, facial expression, deliberate touches and other physical contact. Some of this behaviour was sexual violence, other behaviour was less clearly identifiable as such. I believed that it affected many female students, irrespective of their racial and class backgrounds. Because it was so deeply embedded in the daily exchanges between pupil and teacher some of it had become invisible and 'normalized'. When it was confronted a range of 'justifications' were made, or it was assumed that the girl had lied or imagined the incident. Its pervasiveness was so institutionalized that people found it difficult and embarrassing to confront. However it was my belief that it had the effect of slowly but systematically reducing the girls' confidence in themselves, making them accept their 'place' in society, which in turn had an effect on their learning and on their ability to foresee an alternative role other than the stereotyped feminine role.

This was the phenomenon I wanted to research. By closely working with a small number of the girls I wanted to find out how they constructed this behaviour for themselves. I wanted to find out the language they used to describe it, the methods they used to cope with it and the strategies they employed to avoid or thwart it. In short I wanted to reconstruct with the girls what it was like to be a 15-year-old in a comprehensive school, as a recipient of unwanted sexual attention.

However although there were pockets of interest it was not an issue with which many people concerned themselves in a large way with the exception of some states in Australia, America and Canada. Sexual harassment is still a difficult, intangible and elusive area with which to deal because of the subjective nature of the behaviour and because it is still a relatively new and unpublicized problem.

If all the publicity to do with sexual harassment had made an impact on the girls and women in this country sexual harassment would not still be a problem. But theories of sexual harassment do not necessarily mean that people can convert theory into practice, or that someone else's experience of sexual harassment will be equated with one's own.

So I anticipated that there would be many problems in setting up a research project with girls in order to answer some of those questions on sexual harassment. There would be problems in identifying the phenomenon; with changing the 'normal' perspective from 'flattery' to 'aberrant'; in getting the girls to understand that it was in no way their fault; in getting the girls to have enough confidence to talk to me about their experiences, given what I knew about how silent victims can be; and in having enough time for the project to allow the girls to change and develop their ideas as they became more aware of how unwanted sexual attention could affect them.

Chapter 4

Methodology

Sexual harassment, I anticipated, was going to be a difficult topic to study. The fact that sexual harassment had been mislabelled in the past and was still being mislabelled by many women and girls, that some girls believed that sexual harassment was 'normal' male behaviour or that they thought that they had provoked it, that the usual interpretation of a man's behaviour was that he was only being friendly and kind and that to describe any incidents of intimacy could well prove to be embarrassing for the girls, would all hinder the collecting of information on this subject. For it was not the men's perceptions, or my perceptions, but the girls' perceptions, understandings and ways of dealing with the problem that I wanted to document. Thus it was necessary to construct a specific methodology in order to cope with the problems of silence, suppression, misinterpretation, guilt, embarrassment, intimacy, privacy, trust, and the language of naming concepts and behaviour.

Given the nature of sexual harassment, an unusual and hybrid design would be necessary, and particular but complementary strategies, not normally used in other projects of an educational nature, would be required if it was the girls' perceptions of sexual harassment that were to be revealed rather than the researcher's interpretation of these incidents.

The research design was influenced by several factors, the most crucial being how to collect data from schoolgirls on a phenomenon which they might not be able to 'see', might dismiss as 'normal' behaviour or label 'flattery'. On the one hand a finely tuned methodology would be needed which was sensitive, supportive, slow, careful, and unfolding, yet which would also include an element of challenge and confrontation of 'normal' interpretations. On the other hand it was important that it be respectable, rigorous, valid, and acceptable to the academic community.

There were four possible sources of research methodology from which I could draw in designing this project, all coming under the broad category of ethnographic research: traditional ethnography (Lacey, 1970; Ball, 1981); action research (Kemmis, 1982; Davis, 1983); democratic research

(MacDonald, 1974; Walker, 1974); and research conducted by feminists (Mies, 1983; Oakley, 1981). Traditional ethnography, as described by such researchers as Lacey (1970), Woods (1979, 1986), Ball (1981), Hammersley and Atkinson (1983), Burgess (1983), Hammersley (1983), and Shipman (1985), did not give the scope for the political issues, the personal input or the interventionist factor that I needed to incorporate, although strategies were used which would satisfy the rigour and validation required. Action research gave the 'interactive' and spiralling effect, and feminist inspired research and democratic research provided the political aspect for which I was looking.

To these ends I planned two offensives. The first was to use the time-honoured techniques of participant observation and diary writing found in classic ethnographic research and the second was to advance into the area of feminist inspired research methods and experiment with the more unorthodox use of group meetings, devolved power and reciprocity. The decision to combine these four particular research methods was taken in order to construct a methodology which would be able to cope with the inherent problems of collecting data on sexual harassment and it was from these methods that the principles and procedures which underpin this project were taken.

Four techniques will be discussed; participant observation, diary writing, group meetings, and interviewing. Some were traditional, others less orthodox. The range gave me the security of the tried and trusted strategies whilst allowing me the flexibility and excitement of experimenting with new ones. This chapter describes the broad field of ethnographic research, the strategies of participant observation and diary keeping and action research. The next chapter describes the research methods used by feminists, followed by a discussion of the group meeting and interviewing techniques used.

Ethnographic Techniques

Ethnography is a broad category of social research and under this label comes a wide variety of methods, adapted and reshaped according to the needs and preferences of the various researchers. There are, however, definable characteristics for the traditional model. Edwards and Furlong (1978, pp. 57–58) describe ethnographers as researchers who quite deliberately adopt a 'catch what they can' approach, and who make no attempt 'to control or ignore irrelevant features'. Their account was 'intended to be derived from what happens' and no attempt is made to impose on it from outside. Unlike the systematic observer with a checklist of researcher-chosen categories, ethnographers categorize and analyze the data retrospectively at the end of the fieldwork. They usually explore a single situation, rejecting completely the systematic observers' insistence on 'knowing precisely what to look for' (Ober *et al.*, 1971, p. 6, quoted in Furlong and Edwards, 1977). The advantage of this approach is that it retains considerable flexibility, allowing the researcher to move from one hypothesis to another throughout the period of the research. This freedom is essential to an enquiry which aspires to be genuinely exploratory, and which makes few claims for highly generalizable findings.

The two most useful strategies that I felt ethnography offered my research were first, those of participant or non-participant observer, the chief methods according to Woods (1986, p. 33) of collecting data in this genre, and second, diary keeping.

The difference between participant and non-participant observer lies in the way in which the researcher operates in the research setting. Most ethnographers agree that their presence in any situation, especially that of a classroom, has an effect but that the researcher's own political views are suppressed. The main practices involved in observation are, according to Woods (1986), 'diligently keeping "field notes" and a generally reflexive attitude . . . the extent of the commitment, the observer's reaction and changes, all become part of the account'. Classically, then, observers enter a research milieu, have an effect on that setting however insignificant, take notes and leave after a reasonably long period of time to analyze and write up. I felt that part of this process was consistent with what I intended to do.

Although some ethnographers avoid the issue of telling those being observed what it is about them that is of interest, or what the research is, this would not have been helpful for me. The role these ethnographers adopt is the non-participant role. King (1978) was a non-participant observer, trying to affect the scene as little as possible. Participant observers, on the other hand, are more open about their presence and consequently have more licence to ask questions, move about and generally interact with the proceedings. I wanted to watch and take notes and I did not want to try to 'disappear', for this I felt would be impossible and unethical. I felt that to document incidents of sexual harassment covertly was unfair and would undermine the teachers' authority. As it was my intention to find out the girls' perceptions, research which was not explicit about the area of interest would be impossible anyway. Describing sexual harassment would be difficult enough, without misleading the girls as to the nature of my questions. As I intended that the teachers and the girls should know what it was I was researching, and I knew my presence would have some effect on the classroom dynamics, I anticipated a lengthy presence hoping that given time the effect of my intrusion would diminish. But I felt there were more ways in which the research would be compromised if I engaged in the method King advocated.

As sexual harassment is a political issue I felt it was important that the school community in general was aware of the existence of this phenomenon. To have used covert methods would have denied its presence, colluded in the silencing of this issue and perpetuated the suppression of information. Being overt would encourage the girls to be open too. An important aspect of being a researcher is building up trust and, according to Woods (1986, p. 29), to show 'that you are a person of some worth and integrity'. I expected the girls to be honest with me about their experiences as I too would be honest about what I was collecting. Woods (1986, p. 29) also argues that '[i]f people are not happy that the information would be put to good use, confidences observed, and their own interest and identities safeguarded, they will block access to it'. As collecting data, feeding it back, reflecting on it and developing theories about it were all part of the process envisaged, a covert approach would have been counter-productive. In a research project designed to continue for nine months, working in one school with a few pupils, effectively concealing one's real intentions would, I believe, have been difficult, if not impossible. The question of collecting data from unsuspecting respondents is an ethical issue. As a researcher one is often in a position of relative power because of access to information, and more knowledge of the matter under consideration. To take advantage of these is, in my opinion, to abuse the participant's willingness to cooperate. To enter a classroom under a pretext is to disregard a teacher's professional status and personal rights. Thus the research project on sexual harassment would be conducted overtly.

It was my intention therefore to use participant observation and to be overt about the research question to both teachers and students. However this raised the issue of validation. If I told the girls what it was I was looking for, would they fabricate, exaggerate or lie about particular incidents? To circumvent this possibility I decided to use the method of 'triangulation' to validate the data.

'Triangulation', as described by Elliott and Adelman (1976, p. 74, quoted in D. Hopkins, 1984, p. 201) 'involves gathering accounts of a teaching situation from three quite different points of view; namely, those of the teacher, his (sic) pupils, and a participant observer. Who in the "triangle" gathers the accounts, how they are elicited, and who compares them, depends largely on the context. The process of gathering accounts from three distinct standpoints has an epistemological justification. Each point of the triangle stands in a unique epistemological position with respect to access to relevant data about a teaching situation. The teacher is in the best position to gain access via introspection to his own intentions and aims in the situation. The students are in the best position to explain how the teacher's actions influence the way they respond in the situation. The participant-observer is in the best position to collect data about the observable features of the interaction between teachers and pupils. By comparing his own account with accounts from the other two standpoints, a person at one point of the triangle has an opportunity to test and perhaps revise it on the basis of more sufficient data'.

The way in which I intended to use triangulation, however, was not exactly in line with that described by Elliott and Adelman (1976), for I did not wish to know the men teachers' interpretations of specific incidents: rather, I wanted to have confirmation that particular incidents had occurred. Thus, if I saw behaviour which I called sexual harassment, and the girl agreed that the same act had happened, and the male teacher also confirmed that he had done this, whether or not these two considered the behaviour sexually harassing, this was proof enough that the incident per se had occurred.

Within the broad category of ethnographic research, but used also by other researchers besides ethnographers, was the provision for diary keeping. I decided to use this technique to collect data to augment the participant observation fieldnotes for two reasons, and from two perspectives. Firstly, I planned to have the girls write a diary. This, I hoped, might help some girls overcome the embarrassment of articulating experiences of sexual harassment. This method is one cited by Kemmis and McTaggart (1982, p. 40) as a strategy in their action research projects. 'Students may be encouraged to maintain diaries on the same topic [as the teacher] to provide alternative perspectives'. I also wanted the notebook to be used for recording incidents of sexual harassment which they saw in the classrooms when I was not present. In this way they might observe another girl subjected to sexual harassment and write down the facts of the incident. It would also be a tangible record of each girl's developing awareness.

Secondly, the use of diary writing would be employed by me. This process is one often used by ethnographers. However, it must be distinguished from 'field notes' which are observations taken by participant observers which I would be doing also. For Allport (cited in Burgess, 1984, p. 128), the intimate journal is the best form of personal documentation, recording thoughts, events and feelings which are considered important. Burgess (1983, p. 222) used the technique of diaries, encouraging the teachers he studied to keep a record of classroom events. My diary would contain my impressions, feelings, questions and concerns, which would not have a place in the observational notes.

These, then, were the principal techniques derived from the traditional ethnographic methodologies. However, there were particular problems with aspects of this approach. Firstly the role of the ethnographer is to enter a research setting, collect data and return to his or her university, or study and write up the findings from the field notes without consultation from the respondents. This approach is often derived from a position of 'the expert'. Although I was obviously an 'expert' in understanding the theory of how sexually harassing behaviour operated, I was not an 'expert' in how different girls experienced the behaviour. For, as I argue in the previous chapter, sexual harassment is a personal and highly specific experience. What one person regards as sexually harassing behaviour may be described totally differently by another girl. Although it would be important to get the girls to understand the power relationship underpinning unwanted sexual approaches, it was not my intention to describe their feelings for them. Feedback and discussion on this phenomenon would increase the girls' awareness and provide them with an alternative perspective as to what they felt was happening. But providing new and relevant information to the respondent was not a part of traditional ethnography.

Further, as the information I wanted was the girls' personal perceptions of sexual harassment, it was essential that I spend time with them to discuss what they experienced and felt. Also because of the nature of the research question it was necessary that I ask both personal and sometimes intimate questions, and also challenge some of their preconceived ideas. Answers to these questions and personal challenges would not be acceptable if a relationship of trust had not been established. Traditional ethnographic research often did not provide the opportunity for these strategies to be used.

Lastly, as Edwards and Furlong (1978) said, ethnographers caught what they could. I was not interested in 'catching what I could', I was interested in documenting examples of sexual harassment of girls by their male teachers, for this area had been largely neglected in the research literature. Also ethnographers, according to Edwards and Furlong, do not impose on the research setting. King (1978, p. 5), for example, tried to 'reduce the effect' he may have had on the events he was trying to document in his research at a primary school and he felt he succeeded 'in effectively disappearing'. This was not what was required in this research, for to leave the research subjects to describe for me what they saw would probably result in the conclusion that sexual harassment was not happening, for it would be regarded as 'normal' male behaviour. Intervention was needed, and this was not usually a technique found in traditional research.

However, ethnography provides the researcher with freedom to explore flexibly different themes or influences that evolve, and to move from one hypothesis to another. This was an important aspect of my proposed research for I did not know the effect intervention and challenge to the girls' perceptions might have on them and the project. Lastly, the realization that findings in a particular setting are non-generalizable was crucial. I was proposing not only working with a small group of girls in one school, but also with individuals and it was unlikely that any universal findings would be forthcoming.

In order to incorporate techniques which would enable an on-going and developmental framework I turned to action research, a method renowned for its problem identification, reflection and ability to change depending on the data uncovered.

Action Research

There are many different interpretations of action research, mainly because it is such a personalized method. Rapoport's (1970) definition is that it aims to 'contribute both to the practical concerns of people in an immediate problematic situation and to the goals of social science by joint collaboration within a mutually accepted ethical framework' (cited in D. Hopkins, 1984).

According to Cohen and Manion (1981, p. 49), the conventional definition of action research is 'small-scale intervention in the functioning of the real world and the close examination of the effects of such intervention' or more basically an on-the-spot procedure designed to deal with a problem that has been located in a specific situation. Kelly's (1983, p. 3) use of action research within the Girls into Science and Technology project (GIST) suggests that action research is particularly suitable for projects which are explicitly value-laden but that it is essentially a teacher-based activity. Ebbutt (1983) argues that educational action research is 'the systematic study of attempts to improve educational practice by groups of participants by means of their own practical actions and by means of their own reflections upon the effects of those actions.' Elliott (1983) argues that it should be 'practitioner based and characterized by an absence of a division of labour between practitioners and researchers', but that the teacher's perspective is central and the problem should be defined from his or her perspective.

Action research classically involves two (or more) professionals who bring separate but complementary skills to the investigation, e.g. a teacher and a researcher. Although not necessarily confined to the classroom, this is where action research has been seen to operate well. Together the professionals seek to understand, monitor, analyze and refocus a particular problem or set of problems collaboratively. The problem of the 'expert' (researcher) investigating the non-expert (e.g. a teacher) is diffused in an attempt to understand and change particular aspects of, for example, classroom activity.

There are four fundamental features to an action research model in the classroom according to Kemmis and McTaggart (1982, p. 7):

- to develop a 'plan' of action to improve what is already happening,
- to 'act' to implement the plan,
- to 'observe' the effects of action in the context in which it occurs, and
- to 'reflect' on those effects as a basis for further planning, subsequent action and so on through a succession of cycles.

It is suggested that these four activities be carried out collaboratively by the teacher and researcher, involving the others, i.e. the students, in the action research process. One of the crucial components of action research is the provision for alteration. The combined aim is to improve some aspect of teaching through systematic modification. Within this model is the scope for negotiation, input of new ideas from the teacher, researcher and student, change of direction, as well as continued reflection from all three parties.

Action research is a method that helps professionals, and teachers in particular, improve their practice. With the help of an outside researcher, and the cooperation and insights of others concerned, it is possible, for example, for teachers to monitor and assess the learning progress, or to find out the problems and/or effects of a particular programme in their own classroom with a view to alteration, modification and change, within a non-threatening environment.

Many principles of action research lend themselves admirably to the project on sexual harassment. Firstly, action research incorporates an element of negotiation between the participants. Each is encouraged to contribute to the design, the implementation and the analysis of the project. This would play an essential part in my research for it was expected that the students, or 'participants' as they were called (rather than 'respondents'), would partake in the decision-making process of how time should be allocated to different activities, how best to observe in classrooms, how interviews should be conducted, and what the area to be discussed would cover. Secondly, strategies are incorporated into the action research model to ensure that all involved are aware of the change, or characteristic 'spiral effect' of action research, as the research develops. It was anticipated that the interviews I conducted with the participants would be transcribed and a copy of the transcript returned to the author to read. This would involve the girls in reflecting on what they had said as well as providing them with a written record of the interview. The transcripts could also form the basis for subsequent interviews and discussion if necessary. In this way it was anticipated that change or at least an alteration of perception and understanding would occur and be documented. Thirdly, another characteristic of action research, that of collaborative decision-making, was to be adopted. I had decided that in order to meet this principle it would be necessary to organize regular group meetings. In this way it was anticipated that opportunities would be created for sharing ideas and initiatives for the research. Fourthly, action research attempts to educate the participants involved by encouraging reflection, analysis and decision-making. In this way it is thought that change is most likely to be effective. It was anticipated that during the research project the girls with whom I would be working would become more knowledgeable, more informed and thus more articulate and better able to discuss the area of sexual harassment with confidence.

However there were several problems with the classic interpretation of the action research model. Firstly, the principles of action research are based on the problem being 'actor'-identified. Establishing a typical action research project on sexual harassment would have entailed the male teachers identifying the problem with an explicit intention of changing their behaviour, once information had been collected and viable alternatives explored. But in this project the male teachers were not invited to be part of the research process and were classically not 'participants', but 'subjects'. The focus of the study was girls and to these ends all effort was to put into understanding their perceptions of sexual harassment, not the perceptions of men or boys.

Secondly, this research question was identified by the researcher, not by the girls, and although one of the anticipated long-term effects was that it may have become 'their' problem, this was not an issue for them prior to the research starting and was one imposed from the outside. Furthermore, action research encouraged 'actors' to identify a problem and seek ways of gathering information with a view to altering practice. Not only was this problem chosen by the researcher, but there was a great chance that the girls would not even, at least initially, 'see' sexual harassment as an issue. The researcher would need to be the 'teacher', in order to help the students define and locate incidents for recording.

Thirdly, this research was to involve only the girls and the researcher. Unlike a classic action research project there were not two or more 'professionals' who were to bring 'separate but complementary skills' to the investigation. This project was to involve participants with great differences in experience, age, skills and intentions.

Thus action research as defined by researchers such as Elliott, Kemmis, Kelly and Ebbutt provided certain ways of working which were seen to be applicable to the type of research I was implementing. Collaboration between the students and myself was desired, as was negotiation of ways of operating. The feedback would be consistent with an action research model, reflection encouraged and alterations negotiated. However the model was only partially suitable and it was because of this that I decided to investigate the method called 'democratic research'.

Chapter 5

Democratic Research

MacDonald (MacDonald and Walker, 1974, pp. 17–18) defined democratic evaluation in the SAFARI project as 'an information service to the community about the characteristics of an educational programme. It recognizes value-pluralism and seeks to represent a range of interests in its issue-formulation. The basic value is an informed citizenry, and the evaluator acts as broker in exchanges of information between differing groups. His (sic) techniques of data-gathering and presentation must be accessible to non-specialist audiences. His main activity is the collection of definitions of, and reactions to, the programme. He offers confidentiality to informants and gives them control over the use of the information. The report is non-recommendatory, and the evaluator has no concept of information misuse. The evaluator engages in periodic negotiation of his relationships with sponsors and programme participants. The criterion of success is the range of audiences served. The report aspires to "bestseller" status. The key concepts of democratic evaluation are "confidentiality", "negotiation" and "accessibility". The key justificatory concept is "the right to know".'

Democratic research originated from the tradition of ethnography, but adapted the principles and practices in order to take account of sensitive and political issues. This method grew out of the work begun by Lawrence Stenhouse in the mid-1970s at CARE, the Centre for Applied Research in Education, located at the University of East Anglia. This research group was interested in understanding more intricately the processes of education and in their attempt they became involved in developing a research methodology which would assist them in this task. It was from a project called 'Success and Failure and Recent Innovation' (SAFARI), that particular questions were raised which challenged traditional ethnographic principles. Traditional ethnographic research, as I have shown, expected the 'expert' researcher to enter a setting, collect the data, with or without the respondents' approval or agreement, and with or without informing them what it was they were documenting, without becoming politically engaged in the milieu, and returning to write up the findings in isolation. Norris (1977, p. 5) argued that democratic research asked the question, 'information for whom and for what purpose?' and it was in attempting to answer this that negotiated success, shared data collection, negotiated meanings, feedback of both transcribed interviews and writing up were developed.

According to Norris (1977, p. 6) one of the key justifications for employing these techniques is the 'right to know'. In setting up a democratic research model, not only the researchers and the funding body must understand what is happening, but so must the respondents, who, like those in action research, have been deliberately renamed 'participants'.

According to Norris (1977, p. 6), the key concepts of democratic research are 'confidentiality', 'negotiation' and 'accessibility'. These three are fundamental to democratic research principles for they are all 'political' strategies and they will be discussed separately. Firstly, confidentiality in the past had not been assured for the respondents, and as researchers were often 'working' for the respondent's superior or employing group, it was not in the respondent's best interest to divulge information that might be used against him or her. However, by being ensured of confidentiality, as in the democratic model, subjects could be assured that the data they provided would not be identified as originating from them.

The second key concept, negotiation, according to CARE, happens on a number of levels. The sponsoring body is expected to negotiate with the researchers as to the actual task in hand, but this of necessity is open to further negotiation depending on the way in which the research project moves. Each participant has the opportunity to negotiate the way in which the data he or she provides is used. In an extreme case the participant, to whom the data belongs, could withdraw from the research, thereby withdrawing the data. However in most cases it is anticipated that the researcher and participant work together, or collaboratively (Kushner and Norris, 1980), and in this way misunderstandings can be eliminated quickly. Part of the research task is to help the participants become more aware of what it is that is being researched, more aware of their role in the organization, school or other setting, and more 'politically' aware of the power structures within their own organization, for according to MacDonald (MacDonald and Walker, 1974, p. 9) research is a political activity. Further, by working together on the data collected, the researcher is in a position to 'negotiate meaning' (as Elliott (1980) describes), that is to have clarified any ambiguities or misunderstandings, and in return the participants have the opportunity to change any information that they had previously given, or indeed to have the information deleted from the records if necessary. In this way democratic research actually provides a service, in the form of raising the awareness of everybody in the research. The researcher is helped in understanding more implicitly the research milieu, the participants are able to provide positive input into the research and learn more about the organization, and the sponsoring body is kept in touch as to the changes and progress the research is making.

Accessibility is the third key concept, and this was a new strategy incorporated into the research method. Often in the past researchers had been employed to conduct research in a particular place because a funding body or sponsoring group had wanted this to happen. Under their authority researchers collected information on the subject that was required from the respondents and disappeared to write up the findings which were then presented to the funding body. The researchers at CARE implemented a new principle which meant that in order to enter the research site chosen, those in the site would have to be approached and the research methods laid out before them along with the research question, the ways in which the researcher was intending to operate and any other information the participants wanted to know. This meant that the researchers would have to negotiate access in order to gain information, give the site an exact description of how they intended to operate and how they intended to use the material collected. Not only had access to each site to be negotiated, but those concerned in the project had to be asked, the research design explained and release of data negotiated.

Democratic research has made explicit many assumptions and secrets about research and researchers that have been hidden in the past. Because researchers have to be 'up-front' it is impossible not to reveal their 'political' and personal stance. Usually in ethnographic research the researchers had not been expected to reveal their personal biases, yet clearly one's political stance affects the way in which data is collected through questioning or notetaking, how responses are given, how data are analyzed and the reports written. In the past this skewing of the data has mostly been ignored under a rhetoric of 'objectivity'. 'Objectivity' has traditionally been regarded as an infallible means of validation. The researchers and evaluators involved in the SAFARI project (MacDonald and Walker, 1974; Norris, 1977; Kushner and Norris, 1980) confronted this traditional method claiming that 'objectivity' was impossible because each researcher, however carefully suppressing her or his biases, could not do this effectively or consistently. It was better to admit the bias, allowing the participants to know what the researcher felt about political issues. By being open about one's political stance, by sharing information, by negotiating access, meaning of data and release of data and reports, the concern with objectivity and validity could be eschewed for the concepts of 'accuracy', 'fairness' and 'relevance'. Using a democratic approach ensured that these three concepts would be embedded in the research methodology.

Some aspects of 'democratic' research as presented by the researchers at CARE seemed to be suited to gathering data on the sexual harassment of 15-year-old girls. Firstly, democratic research was genuinely exploratory offering flexibility in a way that did not try to solve or alter any particular teaching or learning programme, unlike the action research model. In addition the researcher could be directed by the insights and ideas of the participants. Secondly, democratic research was not designed to be generalizable, for it was often small-scale and location-specific. This suited the proposed study on sexual harassment, for the research group was to be small. In addition, because of the problems with defining sexual harassment, the study did not aspire to make general comments applicable to other schools or groups of girls. Thirdly, the political element was well suited, for the content, the process and my own interests were all politically oriented. The democratic research process, in itself reflecting political activity, would provide strategies for negotiating the process with the participants, providing them with feedback for further discussion from the taped and transcribed interviews, negotiating meaning, use and release of data, as well as trying to fulfil the ideal of 'the right to know' in providing information to the school community about the characteristics of sexual harassment. My own political bias would be openly declared at the onset of the research to both participants and the teachers who were to be observed. This would be part of the negotiated access to the school.

Although democratic research had appropriate techniques for data gathering and presentation of the research findings, this method in its entirety was not trouble-free. It was anticipated that the report would be accessible to non-specialist audiences such as the general school community, the girls themselves and their parents, reflected in the way in which the report was written. Confidentiality to participants was assured and it was anticipated that control over the use of the information would belong to them. This 'control' over the data was important, although I recognized, as Simons (1977, pp. 28–32) did, the manipulatory strategies open to a researcher when dealing with a participant reluctant to part with data. But there was a further complication with democratic research in this particular aspect, and that was the tension created by the 'right to know' and 'confidentiality'. Where information should be made public, and where an individual had the right to suppress or delete a particularly sensitive issue, was problematic. One of the phrases CARE used to protect people on both sides of this divide was 'nothing is off the record', implying that as a researcher incidents 'seen' or told about, even if they were later retracted, would inevitably affect the researcher. I recognized the power of negotiating, building relationships and the potentially sensitive nature of the data I might collect and it was not my intention to damage or discredit in any way the male teachers, about whom I might collect controversial information. Rather it was to present my findings to the school community in a way that was supportive and potentially educative. I resolved that this aspect should be discussed with the teachers in particular, when negotiating access.

There were further problems with democratic research. Although this method intially accepted that the participants would become more politically aware, and this was crucial for my research, there was no place in the process for 'intervention'. In CARE's view democratic research provided a picture which represented a range of interpretations or 'ways of seeing' (Norris, 1977, p. 6). In my case sexual harassment was often not made problematic because of the factors already explained about perceiving it as 'normal' male behaviour. I knew that because of this problem an interventionist approach would have to be included, for the information I was seeking (based on what I knew about the other female-controlling-practices) was often not visible to the 'unpoliticized' eye. To the girls, sexual harassment might well fall into the 'normal' male behaviour category. Therefore it would be necessary to confront particular perceptions. Also, democratic research sought to represent a range of interests, but I was only concerned with the interests or perceptions of the girls who were the participants, not those of the teachers or anyone else. In seeking to gain a number of different interpretations the democratic researcher is meant to act as broker in exchanges of information between differing groups. This was not my intention either, for I was not anticipating discussing the girls' interpretations of the men's behaviour with the teachers, and for these reasons I had to find some additional strategies for my research.

Research Conducted by Feminists

There is a problem with the term 'Feminist Methodology' for research conducted by feminists often has no one 'right' way of operating, nor one exclusive use of particular techniques. The research that feminists use is often an amalgamation of existing methods adapted to the particular topic in hand and thus I will use 'research conducted by feminists' or similar terms.

The research methods developed by feminist inspired researchers arose out of the realization that in the past most research projects had been conducted from a male-dominated perspective and that men's version of events had been accepted as the 'real' version. One of the fiercest challenges came from anthropologists who felt that women's lives had been excluded or ignored. Edwin Ardener (1975) argued that this was due to the fact 'that in their own societies, and as subjects of research, women [were] often more "inarticulate" than men, and thus pose[d] special technical problems for the inquirer.' Shirley Ardener (1975, p. viii), stressed that Edwin Ardener was not saying that women did not 'utter or give tongue', but that because public discourse tended to be characteristically male-dominated and the appropriate language registers often seemed to have been 'encoded' by men, women may have been at a disadvantage when wishing to express matters of particular concern to them.

The theory of 'mutedness' was not necessarily based on the silence of a particular group. The group may have spoken a great deal, but whether they had the opportunity to say all that they wanted to say, where and when they wished to say it, and whether what they said was considered important or relevant, or even understood, is at issue here. Thus in the past women and girls may have spoken of their sex-specific concerns, but due to the 'gender blindness' of the researcher, the spoken women's issues went 'unheard' and 'unseen'.

This debate was taken up by women ethnographers, who argued that distortions would arise if men alone took part in the research. Leavitt, Sykes and Weatherford (1975, p. 111), for example, asked how was 'it possible for the male ethnographer, socialized from birth to his superior status in his own culture and in no way held accountable for androcentrism, to report objectively on the relationship between women and men, and on the roles and status of women in other cultures?' The difference in perspective of women and men is rarely acknowledged and the male perspective is usually accepted as being the 'normal' interpretation. George Simmel remarking on this said: 'Man's position of power does not only assure his relative superiority over the woman, but it assures that his standards become generalized as generically human standards' (quoted in Hey, 1986, p. 8).

In order to develop a feminist oriented research method (according to Daly (1973, pp. 11–12), 'under patriarchy, Method has wiped out women's questions so totally that even women have not been able to hear and formulate our own questions to meet our own experiences. Women have been unable to experience our own experiences') a researcher aware of feminist politics was needed, argued Mies (1983). She suggested that members of subordinate groups were in a better position to appreciate fully the everyday reality of oppression, a quality that members of the superordinate group lacked. This quality meant that women and other members of oppressed groups were better sensitized towards psychological mechanisms of dominance. As objects of oppression they had been forced, out of self-preservation, to know the motives of their oppressors. Equally they had experience of psychological and bodily oppression and exploitation, and could empathize with others in a similar position. According to Nash (1974, cited in Mies, 1983, pp. 121–122), due to this 'inner view of the oppressed', women social scientists were better equipped than their male counterparts to make a comprehensive study of their own exploited groups.

Working with children entails the same sort of problems for are these not an 'exploited group' too, and perhaps made 'mute' by researchers? This difficulty was described by Okely (1978, p. 111), who argued that age and the concomitant features of limited experience and immature language command could also inhibit data collection. For children, she argued, 'cannot articulate their experiences in the language of adults. Only after childhood can it be thus expressed'. In recounting her personal experiences of boarding school she wrote: 'When young we found the school world the reality, the norm, the only rationality. That was its power. My mother has often said since, "But why didn't you tell me?" We, my sister and I, could not discriminate that which now seems bizarre'. The problem of a child's limited experience and perception is supported by Steedman (1986, p. 28). 'Children do not possess a social analysis of what is happening to them, or around them, so the landscape and the picture it presents have to remain a background, taking on meaning later, from different circumstances . . . Detail . . . provides retrospective labelling.'

In preparing a methodology to investigate sexual harassment of 15-year-olds, I was confronted with not only the silence surrounding the subject and the 'invisibility' of sexual harassment as a problem, but also these two issues: the mutedness of women (would I be able to hear what they were saying?), and secondly, would they be able to differentiate the 'normal' from the 'unwanted' as they were relatively young, inexperienced and unpolitical?

To answer these problems I turned to women who had researched politically sensitive areas to see how they had tackled this problem. Mies's (1983) research methodology grew out of what she ironically called an 'action research' project. A group of women students initiated a programme in Cologne in 1976 which aimed to make practical provision for battered women. They founded an association called Women Help Women and started a campaign to organize a safe house where women who had been physically attacked by husbands or friends could shelter.

No explicit research component was envisaged at the outset, but as the project grew there arose the need to document and analyze the development. The research method evolved by default and, as Mies argues, was not a systematic attempt to apply a certain methodology of social research, but to further the objectives of the action group. Principles emerged which underpinned Mies' research. They included: raising women's consciousness; implementing an egalitarian, non-hierarchical research process; establishing an on-going self-supported group; using other women's research and information to locate the project in a wider context of feminist and female oriented work; encouraging participation at all levels to eradicate partiality; ensuring that the research served the interests of the oppressed, incorporating women-centred research methods for interviewing and recording; choosing research topics which were immediate and useful; developing a political awareness in the participants and for the oppressed, where possible, to carry out the research themselves; and for the researcher, in her case a woman and a feminist, to use her relative power as a scholar and to take up issues which were central to the Women's Movement. Mies (p. 127) argued that in order to do this, dialogue on methodology with other feminists was necessary and 'interviews of individuals . . . must be shifted towards group discussions, if possible at repeated intervals.' Mies (p. 128) states that '[t]his collectivization of women's experiences is not only a means of getting more and more diversified information but it also helps women to overcome their structural isolation in their families and to understand that their individual sufferings have social causes'.

These principles contained strategies that I could utilize in my project. Mies was legitimizing a form of intervention which politicized women. Through the use of group discussions she encouraged women to make links between personal and political oppression. In this process one could expect that not only would women become better educated and more aware, but that new labels and new concepts would emerge. Mies was making research not only into a political enterprise, shifting women's consciousness towards understanding the political consequences of certain male actions, but she was also using particular strategies to intervene in order to achieve naming and re-conception so that these ideals be met. This methodological strategy had taken MacDonald's and Walker's (1977) 'democratic' research further than they had suggested, using individual and regular group meetings to further the participants' understanding.

This particular research methodology used by Mies had similarities with consciousness-raising. Consciousness-raising was a term initially coined by Sarachild (1975, pp. 131–137) in 1967. The original concept was of a self-interest group interested in discussing the problems facing women. It was a method of practice which gave women the opportunity to describe their own experiences in a shared supportive environment, and to make connections between these experiences and the political position of women in relation to men. There was no one method of consciousness-raising, and the method was less important than the results of insights and understanding. The basic principles, according to Sarachild (p. 135), were 'going to the original sources both historic and personal, going to the people, women themselves, and going to experience for theory and strategy.'

This technique had been used successfully by Farley (1978) in her research on working women. When Farley (1978, p. 11) had begun teaching a course on Women and Work, at Cornell University, the lack of relevant materials forced her to turn, like 'many women before me, to consciousness-raising, a remarkable tool for unlocking that vast storehouse of knowledge, women's own experiences.' She continued: 'Our first "C-R" (consciousness-raising) session was devoted to work, and my students and I determined at the outset to discipline ourselves to focus on what had happened to us on our jobs because we were women . . . we each took our turn speaking, I was a peer . . . when we had finished, there was an unmistakable pattern. . . . Each one of us had . . . quit or been fired from a job at least once because we had been made too uncomfortable by the behaviour of men.'

Here was a research technique which had effectively documented incidents of 'normal' male behaviour made problematic, and thus recordable. Farley had set up a non-hierarchical research group and had been prepared to share her own experiences. She had been dependent on, yet confident of, the power of the personal experiences of the students, which when pooled made political statements about the oppression of women, and by using this unorthodox method, she had located a yet unnamed phenomenon.

The transference of this particular technique to a group of 15-year-olds was one which incurred problems. Was it possible or desirable to organize a consciousness-raising group for 15-year-olds involved in an imposed research topic, meeting on a weekly basis in school time with members drawn from across a year's intake so that in all likelihood they would be relative strangers, in an environment hostile to sharing honest and personal disclosures? I doubted the possibility of organizing such a group and began to conceptualize it as a teaching and discussion session instead. The research participants were far younger than those with whom Farley and Mies had worked, both their groups being adult women, with many years of experience to draw on. My participants lacked not only political awareness, through lack of maturity, but simply years of experience. Would 15-year-old girls, as Okely suggested, be able to articulate their experiences or 'discriminate that which now seems bizarre'?

A second problem that I envisaged was the differentiation between the girls and myself. For both Sarachild and Farley the findings, whether strategic or political, had emerged from people in an exploratory mode. Although I was 'exploring' the girls' perceptions of sexual harassment. I was not exploring the area of sexual harassment per se for I knew what I wanted to document. The girls did not, and were in a politically vulnerable position, while I, as the researcher, could be open to charges of manipulation, promoting propaganda and contamination.

However there were strategies that I felt were adaptable which could by-pass these charges. Consciousness-raising, according to Sarachild, gave women the opportunity to describe their own experiences in a shared supportive environment. If a group was set up which met regularly every week and the girls were encouraged to give personal accounts of their experiences, a sense of shared perception might emerge. My role in this group would be one of 'teacher'. In general classroom discussions it is the teacher's role to draw together threads and make generalizations with which students either agree or not. Learning is a personal experience and although links can be made by teachers, ultimately the connection will be made by the learners. If the teacher's remarks are valid for the individual because what has been said is relevant and makes sense, learning may take place. I therefore envisaged that the group discussions would be general in nature and my role that of a 'teacher'. The use of consciousness-raising or group discussion, however, would not necessarily override all the problems of 'mutedness' inherent in this project. I believed that another technique for facilitating accounts of personal experiences was necessary. Privacy, anonymity, time, space, individual attention, questions both asked and answered, support, with access to all these at the girl's discretion, was essential. Interviewing was a classic way of gathering data, and it was also an appropriate way of providing a 'safe' and 'private' place for in-depth discussions.

There has been much written on how to conduct an interview effectively, yet what is often ignored is the admission that the style chosen reflects the political stance of the researcher. Some research methods promote particular techniques which perpetuate hierarchal research relations on the grounds that these ensure validity, such as disinterestedness and objectivity, but paradoxically this approach has resulted in criticisms on the grounds of invalid data. It has been observed that data gathered in this way often reflects 'expected' behaviour rather than 'real' behaviour. In Campbell's (1984, p. 3) view social interaction is a creative process in which people select to present themselves as a particular type of person, and then offer accounts of their actions which support that view. In a formal research interview, for example, she argues the 'one chosen for presentation is probably a function of the relationship between the questioner and ourselves.' So the accounts that the respondents gave were 'likely to be a function of their conceptions of themselves and the persons they wanted to present' to the researcher.

Certainly a closely scripted list of questions will yield different types of data to that of an open-ended conversation-style approach. Classically, researchers of the 1960s counselled 'never provide the interviewee with any formal indication of the interviewer's beliefs and values. If the informant poses a question . . . parry it' (Sjoberg and Nett, 1968, p. 212, cited in Oakley, 1981, p. 35). Reasons for the interviewer remaining neutral were to eradicate 'bias' and 'contamination'. However, this type of research method encouraged two other problems. Firstly, the interviewer and the interviewed remained estranged both from each other and from the research question, and secondly, by remaining aloof the researcher took on a psychoanalytic role, possibly alienating the respondent. Selltiz *et al.* (1965, p. 268, quoted in Oakley, 1981) described such an approach. 'Perhaps the most typical remarks made by the interviewer in a non-directive interview are: "You feel that . . .", or "Tell me more" or "Why?" or "Isn't that interesting?" or simply "Uh huh".'

According to Oakley (1981, p. 38), the quasi-psychoanalytic and mechanical interview 'owe a great deal more to a masculine social and sociological vantage point than to a feminine one', appealing more to the values of objectivity, detachment, and hierarchy. Oakley's (1981, p. 41) challenge to this form of interviewing came after interviewing several hundred women over a period of ten years, and resulted in her using an alternative technique. First, 'the use of prescribed interviewing practice is morally indefensible; second, general and irreconcilable contradictions at the heart of the textbook paradigm are exposed; and third, it becomes clear that, in most cases, the goal of finding out about people through interviewing is best achieved when the relationship of interviewer and interviewee is non-hierarchical and when the interviewer is prepared to invest his or her own personal identity in the relationship.' Formal interviewing on this basis was not appropriate for this research project, but the techniques Oakley advised would be of value.

Oakley had further valuable strategies which could be adopted too. Maintaining trust and openness was dependent on the way in which the researcher treated the participant once the interviewing began. This in turn would be reflected by the interviewee's response to the researcher, manifested both in the degree in which she was trusted, and in the quality or depth of data gathered. Oakley (1981, p. 47) set out to convey to the participants whose co-operation she was seeking, the fact that she 'did not intend to exploit either them or the information they gave'.

Oakley (1981, p. 42) inspired openness and intimate disclosures from her participants too in the way that she chose to answer questions asked of her. When analyzing the tape-recorded interviews she had made in a research project on pregnant women, she listed 878 questions that had been asked. Of these three-quarters were requests for information. She (p. 49) found that an attitude of refusing to answer questions or offer any kind of personal feedback was not helpful in terms of the traditional goal of promoting 'rapport', and '[a] different role, that could be termed "no intimacy without reciprocity" seemed especially important in longitudinal in-depth interviewing.'

I felt that Oakley's interviewing principles had the potential to encourage a generally open and intimate relationship between interviewer and participant. Because the girls with whom I would be working were relatively young, and the nature of the research personal, these techniques would assist the generation of data. It was important then that I establish a non-hierarchical relationship in the initial stages as well as remain consistent in this role throughout the project, for once the research had been set up it was vital that my commitment to these principles remained explicit, else distrust or scepticism would occur. Therefore I decided that I would endeavour to explain the nature, purpose and style of the research to the girls. I would explain that the sessions would be taped using a portable cassette recorder and I would assure them of the confidentiality I intended to observe. I would reassure them that no one would listen to the taped interviews, that when used in a report or book the names and locations would be altered to provide anonymity, that they would receive a copy of every transcript for checking, and that writings using their data would be sent to them for approval. These principles were those to which researchers in the democratic tradition adhered, and which many feminists had adopted for their research too.

I anticipated interviewing the girls on average once a week, for approximately one hour, in order that a deep relationship could be established. Although disclosing incidents of sexual harassment may well be found embarrassing, humiliating, disloyal and thus difficult to talk about, I anticipated that the closer we got the less difficult it would become. In addition to the interviews initially being instigated by me, I hoped the girls would eventually take responsibility for determining the need for interviews as well as the frequency, duration and topic. I also intended to have a open-style, unplanned, conversation-type communication. If they asked me questions about my life I would be willing to answer on the understanding that they too respected my privacy and accorded me confidentiality. The underlying principle to which I subscribed, one of Oakley's (1981, p. 49) already quoted, was 'no intimacy without reciprocity'.

I envisaged, however, that there could be a criticism made that the girls may lie to me especially if they knew the topic to be researched and wanted to 'help' me in providing information. Campbell (1984) took up this point in her study of girls in American street gangs. She argued (1984, p. 2) that if the research was designed so that the researcher remained with a group for a period of time it would be 'quite difficult for either researcher or subject to sustain false impressions: it [would be] hard to maintain a systematic deceit or an alien persona for six months, and members of the gang or the community [were] apt to give the game away'.

The research design would take account of this issue for it was planned that I would work with a small group of girls in a school for nine months and would be seeing them on a regular basis, thus ensuring that a close relationship developed between us. In addition the weekly meeting might help prevent girls making up stories because of the peer pressure from others. However, I was not anticipating that girls would make up stories, for the benefit of me or the research project, or for their own aggrandisement. That girls lie is, as will be argued, more of a myth than a reality. Further, that girls or women should want to make up false allegations of sexual harassment by male teachers was unlikely, given the special stigma accorded women who had been sexually harassed or raped.

What I was prepared to accept was that any incidents that they reported to me I would accept as data. 'Ample research', according to Campbell (1984, p. 3) 'in the study of memory generally and eyewitness testimony in particular indicates that errors frequently occur in the rehearsal of "facts".' This was echoed by Ronald Frazer (quoted in Steedman, 1986, p. 145), in a conversation he had with his analyst. 'What actually happened is less important than what is felt to have happened. Is that right?' His analyst agreed. Okely's (1978, p. 110) research discussed a similar problem with what constituted data. Her study was largely autobiographical for she was the main informant in analyzing her own boarding-school education, supported with accounts from other former residents of similar schools. Okely explained that her study was based on memory, not on a diary, and in the absence of a written record there would inevitably be a loss of memory. She argued that some 'forgotten experiences may nevertheless [have] affect[ed] the narrator unconsciously'. The past would have become distorted but the 'accuracy of childhood events may, however, have been less important than the child's perception of them.'

Chapter 6

The Research Process

January–June 1986

Negotiating Access

It had been anticipated that because of the potentially controversial nature of the project, finding a school to accept the research would prove difficult. During January and February I spoke to a number of colleagues about finding a suitable local school but none was available. However at a conference in March I met Dr Martin, a headteacher from an Inner London Education Authority (ILEA) school. We discussed my proposed topic, research methodology and the problem of finding a suitable site. He said he would welcome such a project in his school, but to be consistent with the ideals of democratic research, he would take the proposal to the teachers at the staff meeting at the end of the Easter term to ask if they were interested.

The teachers were sympathetic towards the project but wanted to find out more and elected two representatives who were to investigate further and were given authority that if they approved the project would be accepted. At a meeting with me, the representatives asked many searching questions about the research and in particular the steps to be taken to assure confidentiality and anonymity for the male teachers and the students. They approved of the project. Dr Martin also took the proposal to the parent and governors' meeting in March 1986, and approval was given by this body too.

It had taken three months to find a school and arrange access but negotiating had been conducted overtly and explicitly. The school community was aware of the nature of the research, the data collection process and my political stance. With the exception of the students, opportunity had been given for people to voice their opinion and reject the project. Within a few weeks some students would be asked if they would like to join the project. In this way the principles of democratic research had been met.

I began work at the school in April 1986. The project was allocated an office, conveniently placed off the library, which was small and had a 'safe' feel to it. The librarian, Liz Armitage, and the other library staff were most supportive of the research throughout the nine-month period and, for example, when the informal 'chats' and interviews began, allowed the girls to wait if necessary until I was able to see them.

In the first few days Dr Martin wrote a memorandum (Appendix 1) and I wrote a description of the research project, including the principles and procedures to be observed (Appendix 2) for publication in the school newsletter. Dr Martin had assigned a senior staff member, Mike Stroud, to act as 'mentor'. His role was to assist me in setting up the research, smoothing over any problems, helping with staff introductions, room locations and questions I had about the school generally. To these ends it was Mike who wrote a letter to each fourth year tutor, and every head of subject, asking them to announce the need for candidates for a research project on 'Women's Issues', and to recommend girls who they thought would be interested.

Forty girls applied so that interviews had to be organized to reduce this number to fifteen. There were four criteria on which the girls were chosen. Firstly, I had decided that girls who were aware of 'women's issues' were preferable as they would more quickly, it was assumed, be able to provide the data for which I was looking. Thus questions about sex discrimination and sexism formed the basis of the interview. Secondly, as it was male teachers who were to be observed, those girls with only women teachers were excluded from consideration. Thirdly, because the school was multi-racial it was necessary to reflect the diversity of nationalities and so a range of girls from different cultural backgrounds was selected. (The birthplaces of the girls' parents were: Iran 2, Turkey 1, Morocco 1, Barbados 1, Jamaica 3, Spain 1, Italy 1, Britain 4. The birthplaces of the girls were: Britain 10, Iran 2, Spain 1, Israel 1, Turkey 1.) The fourth criterion was how well the girls and I related to one another. This was a subjective decision but it was important that there was reciprocity for we would be working together for a relatively long period, discussing incidents of an intimate nature, and I felt that the project would fare better if we 'liked' each other.

Every girl was interviewed separately (when Alex came for her first interview she brought with her Chanel, her best friend. Although not one of the candidates, Chanel became a 'silent' member of the research group by default just because she was always there. She never spoke and if I suggested she leave, Alex would leave too. By the beginning of September, however, she had begun to join in, have private interviews with me, join in the weekly meetings and she came to the Stansted weekend organized in November) between 29 April and 14 May, and each interview began with an informal exchange and an introduction about the research in general terms and ended with a question as to their interest in being involved. Fifteen girls were offered a place, based on the criteria already discussed. The girls involved in the research were: Zohra, Lucy, Annmarie, Collette, Carmel, Alex, Linda, Jenny, Ashley, Fitti, Efrat, Jane, Marit, Christina, Hattie, Chanel, Zaheda and Maria. In Efrat and Jane's cases, their fathers refused permission. Marit, Christina and Hattie left the project before June, and Chanel, Zaheda and Maria joined the project after June.

On their acceptance I sent a letter to their form tutors (Appendix 3), and Dr Martin wrote a letter (Appendix 4) to each girl's parents asking permission for their daughter's involvement.

Implementation

There are two dimensions to the account of the period between 19 May, when I began working with the girls in earnest, and 25 June; the first is an analysis of the relationships that were built up through the informal 'chats', the formal interviews and the group meetings; the second is a discussion of the ethical issues that emerged as the research process was put into practice. These aspects of the initial weeks of the project will be discussed separately. Both accounts draw upon a number of different sources including the girls' recorded comments, my own field notes and the research diary. The girls found it difficult to keep diaries and after four weeks I stopped asking to see them because they had not been written.

Building up Relationship through Formal and Informal Interviews and Group Meetings

Between 19 May and 25 June three group meetings were organized and seventeen formal interviews were conducted. The first three meetings were directed by me. The first was practical (19 May 1986), a session of filling in forms, explaining the project, the commitment the girls would be asked to make, the project's duration, my availability, the techniques of participant observation, interviewing, diary writing and the weekly group meetings. I also explained the concepts of confidentiality and anonymity which were to be observed by me as the researcher, and which they were to observe as group members. It was explained that the interviews would be taped, transcribed and two copies made, one for them and one for me. We would use these transcripts for further discussion and reflection and they were to check that the information was accurate, changing or deleting pieces if they chose, for the data belonged to them. It was also explained that if during an interview they wanted to say something that they did not want recorded the tape recorder could be turned off. (Some of the girls did ask for particular pieces of information to be deleted and this was done. It so happened that none of these deletions were central to the research.) I asked the girls to complete a timetable showing their lessons, including the teacher's name, subject taught and room number. From these I later compiled a list of teachers whose classes I would be observing and wrote them a letter (Appendix 5).

The first meeting was difficult because the girls were reluctant to talk. My diary notes that 'I was rather disappointed with the response, there seems to be dissension, and "this school is not sexist in any way, we are all taught the same", is their attitude' (Diary, p. 37),[1] which was in direct contradiction to what they had said in the selection interviews. I reflected on the meeting and I realized that what the girls were prepared to say in private and what they were prepared to say in public was different. My diary after the first meeting records: 'Having thought about their negativeness, I have decided that this is reasonable. The girls do not know each other particularly well, if at all. They come from different houses, different tutor groups and are all in a variety of classes, depending on their options. It would have been surprising if there had been a high level of trust. I have decided that I must spend some time getting the group to function as a unit' (Diary, 19 May 1986, p. 37).

The division between the public and the private disclosure became an important part of the analysis. As the data emerged there were some incidents which were disclosed publicly, but others which were closely guarded and to which few people were privy. This division will be discussed later.

At the end of the first meeting one of the girls decided that she was not interested in the project and left. Within a few days I had received the replies from the parents to the headteacher's letter. Two fathers had refused permission. This reduced the number in the group to twelve, but I realized that if I wanted to interview the girls regularly, transcribe and return the scripts, as well as visit classrooms, I could not be as effective with fifteen participants; twelve was a more realistic number. I therefore decided not to recruit any more and to restrict my time in London to three or four days a week depending on the project's needs.

As a result of the constraints apparent in the first meeting, the second (2 June 1986) was planned to knit the group together. On their suggestion everyone introduced themselves and a tentative but 'directed' discussion began about who their parents were and what they did for a job. For the third meeting (10 June 1986) I had duplicated a poem for discussion (Sarah Hook: 'Teenage Sexism', from Hemmings, 1982). According to my notes 'this incited quite a lively discussion around the topic of sexism and feminism. Collette is very articulate and strong about her views. We argued for some time about what were the criteria for being a feminist. Carmel put forward the view that feminists are extremists and do more damage to women than if they did nothing. She also believes that feminists "put down" women who want to have a "traditional" female role' (Diary, 10 June 1986, p. 50).

These general meetings were supported by two types of interview, the 'formal' and the 'informal'. The first type could be initiated by either the girls or myself. If a girl asked to talk to me about a particular problem, a time was booked and the session was recorded and transcribed and the hard copy returned to the author. Similarly, if I felt I hadn't seen a particular girl for sometime, I would ask for an interview.

The second type of interview was the 'informal' and unplanned type, for the girls would arrive at my door and ask to have a 'chat'. Sometimes there was already a girl there, and they would either wait, or join in with whatever was the discussion in hand. The topics covered in these 'informal' interviews ranged from homework to boyfriend and girlfriend concerns and to family issues. Because these were informal and not specifically related to the project, but were a crucial process in building relationships, many were not recorded. In retrospect this proved to be a mistake, for as the research developed it became clear that some of these 'informal' chats were signalling the future disclosures which ultimately became the concern of the research, but at the time my focus was school-based sexual harassment, and personal problems at home were not, I thought, relevant.

The Research Process and the Ethical Issues which Emerged

This section is divided into two. Both parts are concerned with ethical problems generally, but the first part discusses participant observation and the second part the interviewing process.

Participant Observation

Participant observation began after half-term on 2 June. The timetables from the girls had been completed and it was possible to arrange days on which to 'follow' particular participants through their day. I decided that for practical reasons it was better to devote one day to one girl, but when other girls from the research were in the same lesson I would observe them all. Each girl contributed to the arrangement by choosing a day to be observed when she had the majority of lessons with men.

It rapidly became clear that participant observation would be extremely difficult to implement effectively for three reasons: the reactions of the girls, the teachers and the boys in the classes. Although each group reacted differently they had in common an element which was to contribute to a fundamental reassessment of the research design. Each group was unsettled by the knowledge that participant observation was taking place and appeared to behave in an atypical fashion.

The girls with whom I was working reacted in a variety of ways to my presence in the classroom. Some were particularly conscious of me and were silent, some made sexual comments to the teacher, and some kept up a running commentary with me about what 'usually' happened.

> 'Carmel constantly looking at me, giggling, making gestures and comments for me to hear' (FN, 3 June 1986, p. 45).

> 'Carmel made comments to the teacher, Mr Weston; "This is my favourite teacher, he loves me to death". I think Mr Weston is embarrassed, I certainly am' (FN, 3 June 1986, p. 45).

> 'Christina was asked to write down her completed work. She refused to cooperate. The teacher did it for her. Both of these actions I feel are unusual behaviour' (FN, 9 June 1986, p. 49).

> 'I went with Collette to Mr Gough's lesson. The teacher called the register, and called her by her full name which she doesn't use. She wrinkled up her nose and looked at me, mouthing some obscenity' (FN, 10 June 1986, p. 50).

My sense that teachers were changing their usual practice, content of the lesson and behaviour too, was confirmed by the girls. In an interview with Fitti I asked her how my presence had affected the class. She said that she had 'carried on as normal', but that the other students and the teachers had behaved differently. Mr Ennis 'showed off', but the students had been 'quieter'. Mr Hethering had surprised them with a maths lesson that was very much out of the ordinary (Int., 19 June 1986, pp. 1–2).

In other classes the teachers themselves came to me to discuss the girls in the project, but it was not always clear what were the intentions behind these actions.

> 'Mr Jacobs had spoken to me in the corridor to ask me when I was going to go to his room. He talked to me about the girls that he taught who were in the project and said that he was presently having "fun" with Carmel. At the last lesson there had been a supply teacher and she had been disruptive. He told me that her contribution in the class was poor, and that her work was below average' (FN, 21 June 1986, p. 38).

> 'Mr Weston came up to me after the lesson to tell me that Carmel was always "difficult", and that he put it down to the fact he refused to direct her work' (FN, 3 June 1986, p. 45).

> 'Mr Newcombe came and talked with me about problems of non-attendance' (FN, 11 June 1986, p. 53).

> 'Mr Ash came and talked to me about Fitti in his lesson and gave me some detailed family information' (FN, 18 June 1986, p. 59).

> 'Mr Hethering began by calling all the students together and said "this morning we are all going to be doing an investigation". The whole class groaned loudly'. (Apparently the usual lesson format was individual maths cards.) (FN, 18 June 1986, p. 55).

> 'The teacher went out of the room to get some pencils. Collette began handing out sweets. (Mr Gough returned and said;) "Not in the classroom". Collette looked at me and said: "we always do this and he usually has some"' (FN, 10 June 1986, p. 50).

The third group who made the participant observation difficult were the boys. Once it became known who I was and what I was doing, they began disruptive action. They hassled me about not including boys, they stared, made comments about girls in my hearing, made overtly sexist comments to test my reaction, called me 'sexist' for only researching girls, disparaged and trivialized the research and generally made collecting data difficult.

In some classes the boys would openly discuss sexual issues, as was the case in one of Collette's lessons.

> 'The boys on the back row began talking about women with three or four breasts. The girls (Collette and others) were aware of this conversation and said, "Oh can't you talk about something else". Then one of the boys apparently passed wind. Another boy said, "Excuse me Sir, David has just excreted some smell from his bottom". The teacher addressed this second boy and told him he was immature for calling it to everyone's attention, and the boy who was the perpetrator was neither admonished nor spoken to, he was ignored. Then the boys started burping very louding and talking through their burps. No one made any comment or took any notice. They continued to burp all lesson' (FN, 10 June 1986, p. 50).

In Fitti's class the boys sexually harassed the girls and made sexist comments. Text-books had been handed out, but one girl did not get a copy.

'Girl: "Can I have a book?"
Mr Ennis: "I'll give her one . . ."
Boy: "Yes do give her one" (sniggers)' (FN, 10 June 1986, p. 58).

'Efrat starts to read. Mr Ennis corrects her pronunciation. Another girl offers to read. Loud objection and laughter from one of the boys' (FN, 10 June 1986, p. 58).

I spent many other days in classrooms observing all the girls in turn. By the end of June it was becoming clear that this strategy was not an effective way of collecting data on sexual harassment. There were examples of sexist behaviour, sexual discrimination, sexual hassle, and sexual harassment by peers, but up until now I had found no examples of sexual harassment from teachers.

Interviewing Strategies

Because of the nature of the research project, it was necessary for me to have a number of roles. Sometimes I was a confidante, sometimes a friend, sometimes a parent figure, sometimes a student like them with little power in the school, sometimes a teacher, for example, when I led the group discussions at the beginning of the project, and sometimes a political figure challenging their beliefs, for I was not a 'neutral' researcher.

At the weekly meetings my function was to give information, chair the procedings and facilitate. This position was only used at the group meetings for I did not wish to be regarded as authoritarian by the girls and to these ends I seldom went to the staffroom or spent time fraternizing with teachers. Thus when I was asked by a senior teacher to check that the girls were attending lessons I was in a dilemma. Carmel and Collette, unknown to me, were continually choosing to see me in the same lessons. Although I realized that the research was partly responsible for the girls missing some of their lessons, when questioned about this they told me they usually 'bunked' that lesson anyway and if they didn't come to the research room they would go home. Because the integrity of the project was dependent on the girls coming to see me when they chose, I felt it would harm the research if I was seen as a teacher or authoritarian person, and I wanted this avenue kept open. I discussed this with the girls stressing the repercussions that repetitions of their truanting might have.

My function in the private interviews often changed too, when I revealed my political views. In one of the initial interviews I was asked whether I was a feminist (FN, 28 April 1986, p. 25). When I answered 'yes', Collette said in a way that sounded conspiratorial, 'right, what do you want to know?' Approximately three weeks later when my role was that of a 'researcher', I asked her to clarify the incident for me. What had she thought at the time? Had my answering her question in this way affected her response? I felt it was important to reflect on past interviews with the girls in order to find out how they thought the project was going, and to make sure that we were understanding each other, or in Elliott's (1980) words 'negotiating meaning'.

> 'Carrie: "Do you remember that first morning you walked in here and you said to me, well do you remember what you said to me?"
> Collette: "Are you a feminist?"
> Carrie: "And what did I say?"
> Collette: ". . . 'Yes'".
> Carrie: "Then what did you say?"
> Collette: "I said 'So am I'. You see at that point I felt comfortable."
> Carrie: "If I said 'no', what would your response have been?"
> Collette: "Then why are you doing this [research]?"
> Carrie: "If I had said, 'Well that's an interesting question but I am here to ask you questions', what would you have said?"
> Collette: "'Oh bloody hell, I ask her a question, what are we here for?' I would have felt 'Oh this is really it, she's looking down on me'. She's saying 'oh yes, this is a very interesting question', but she is evading it. I would have thought that straight away, because here I'm giving you a chance to form a relationship, because I am walking in and asking you a question. I'm not walking in, sitting down, and [just] saying 'yes', I'm giving you a chance"' (Int., 3 June 1986, p. 3).

In order for the researcher to be accepted by the subjects it was important that I be honest. To have avoided, parried, or ignored the question would have undermined the project, and the ambience I wished to create. The research project was to be built on reciprocal relationships and if asked a question I would endeavour to answer it. However in order for a researcher to provide subjects with knowledge which would further the research project and extend the girls' understanding, sometimes it was necessary to change roles again, this time to challenge them. One such occasion was with Carmel at her inaugural interview. She made some racist comments and told me that the men who committed rape were all black, because all black people had an anger towards white men and their way of retribution was to rape white women. At this point I had some choices. Either I ignored this racism, or I used what Oakley (1981 p. 38) called a 'quasi-psychoanalytic' tactic, 'ah, tell me more, that is interesting', or else I confronted it and told Carmel some facts about rape and rapists. It was the third choice I made as the interview transcript demonstrates.

'Carrie: "Can I tell you a few facts about rape. I am not disputing that there are some black men who feel that way, but the majority of rapists are white men, some married, perfectly sane, quite normal, and the majority of people who are raped, something like 80 per cent are known either well or . . ."
Carmel: (interrupting) "family, that kind of thing?"
Carrie: (continuing) ". . . casually by the rapist. So only 20 per cent of rapes happen in the streets, in dark alleys . . ."
Carmel: "Listen, if I am a multi-millionaire do you think I am scared of being raped? Do you think that would be my main worry? Do you think I am going to walk down an alley, do you think I am not going to take a car?"
Carrie: "But you can still be raped if you are a female millionaire . . . you may get raped by your chauffeur."
Carmel: (Begins talking about her childhood and how she used to take a taxi to school; suddenly she says:) "I never had to sit down and think, 'what will happen if I get raped?', because it was totally unlikely. But I will tell you that in that kind of condition (sic), to get sexually abused is very likely."
Carrie: "By whom?"
Carmel: "By cousins and that. I think it happened to me, I am not sure. I think I got sexually abused as such, and I think it's going to affect my life"' (Int., 29 April 1986, p. 18).

This disclosure, I argue, was as a result of the challenge that I made to Carmel's misconceptions about the relationship between the rapist and the woman. The link that rapists 'knew' their 'victim' in many attacks gave her the necessary information to connect and name an incident in her life. Intervention in this situation was a powerful tool to unlocking experience, memories and information.

The methods that I had chosen to use had been expected to generate data on sexual harassment from male teachers directed at girls. However, as has been shown no data of this nature were forthcoming and I could find no justifiable explanation. I was convinced by writers such as Mahony (1985) that this particular female-controlling-practice did occur in schools so I assumed that this school was no exception, yet I was unable to 'see' it, and, further, despite the conversations we had had, both public and private, the girls were not 'seeing' it either. As the term progressed I realized that the school was more comprehending of the importance of gender issues that I had anticipated. However I was also aware that the principles of open and overt data collection to which I had adhered had created false and unrealistic tensions in the classrooms. As the term began to draw to an end I reflected on the progress of the research. Firstly the research was sterile in terms of information on sexually harassing behaviour. Secondly the research was productive in terms of having developed close personal relationships with most of the girls which were already beginning to reveal experiences which I had not anticipated.

June–December 1986

Summer Term

The data that I was collecting was not what I had anticipated, either in form or content. This suggested that some modification might be needed in my approach. However there was an incident which had the power to influence the girls and my ideas of what the research could do. This change in direction happened only gradually, but was followed by another incident in September after which the research project's revised course plunged deeper into this new area, consolidating the tentative beginnings which had been made.

The first incident involved two students, a girl and a boy. (Sources for this were field notes, diary notes and the students' own writings.)

Maria was 14, a Bulgarian who had arrived in England with her parents approximately eighteen months earlier. Her father was a journalist for a Bulgarian news agency, living and working in London on a four-year contract. Her mother was a highly trained engineer, but was currently unable to get a job in England because she had not been granted a work permit. Although when she arrived Maria could not speak English well, she had been put into a class above her chronological age, because she was considered an academically able student, and her parents wanted her to complete O-level and A-level examinations before she returned home. Her written English was very good but she spoke text-book, as opposed to colloquial, English. To help her improve she was involved in the English as a Second Language Programme. However, when I first met her she did not understand many of the slang expressions which the other students used every day. Maria spoke with a marked European accent, wore plain and demure clothes (white blouse, dark skirt, flat shoes), was tall for her age, had long, dark hair usually worn tied back, was always very polite to teachers and adults, was academic by inclination and did not like sports lessons. Her social life was limited; she was not allowed out in the evenings for her parents expected her to study. At the weekend she enjoyed visiting museums and art galleries. On Saturdays she attended Bulgarian School.

Rani Etal was 16, Indian by race, from a family with two older brothers and a younger sister who was 6 years old. His mother took most of the responsibility for the family for Mr Etal was often away on business trips to Singapore and Hong Kong. Rani was very interested in sports, especially tennis, and spent many evenings and much of the weekend practising. He aspired to play tennis professionally. He was a popular boy with both boys and girls, worked hard at his lessons and was regarded generally as a polite and respectful student.

One of the teachers, Jon Robinson, brought Maria to see me because she had been sexually harassed by Rani and he felt that I might be able to help her. The three of us sat down and Maria told us what had happened. This conversation went unrecorded as Maria was not a member of the research group, and the content of the incident, although related, was not central.

After we had heard the details, Jon and I decided that discipline was in the hands of the Head of House. Jon wanted my support in order that the case would be 'taken seriously', so together we went to the staffroom where the Head of House was sitting. Although sympathetic at a verbal level she seemed uninterested in the incident. Whilst talking, we were joined by Chris Morrison, who was not only Head of the Fourth Year, but had also been the teacher in charge of the students when the incident happened. After a discussion it was decided that Mr Morrison would see Dr Martin regarding punishment and Rani to get his version of the incident, whilst I would get the exact details from Maria. I returned to Maria who was waiting in the library and wrote down the details.

> 'It began at Hatton Hall [a country house in Shropshire, used by the school for field trips]. Rani asked me something and I didn't hear. And I said "yes". The next day in the evening about five o'clock he asked me to go out of the house into the garden of Hatton Hall with him. I followed him out. He stopped just behind the fence where there were some people just about to come outside to play football. I went into the garden and Rani said "Lie down on the grass" and he started asking me if he could make love to me.' [Apparently Rani had not used this expression, but had used the local vernacular, "fuck", a word which Maria had not understood at the time.] 'And I said "no", but he started begging and asking me to hurry because there were some people coming and he wanted to go and play football.
>
> 'He was very angry when I said "no" again. He went very red. He then said, "Alright, you will see in school, I'm going to have my revenge. I am going to tell the whole world about you and that you are a slag and that you are saying 'yes' to everyone . . .". When I was coming out of the Hall to get on the bus home, Rani said that

he had some witnesses, and that they would spread the news around the school that I had said "yes" and that I had "done it with him".

'I was away from the school for about a week. Although I was ill with a sore throat and temperature, I was embarrassed to come to school because people would be talking about me and calling me a slag. I didn't tell my parents because they would be very worried about me and I prefer that they do not get mixed up in this. I told my [13-year-old] sister, Sophia, and she told me to tell the teachers. I decided to tell the teachers after Annmarie [one of the girls in the research project] had talked to me for twenty minutes. I didn't go to the teachers before because I thought Rani had witnesses and that Mr Morrison would not believe me, and I didn't think it would stop Rani talking to people. We decided to go to another teacher [a sympathetic person], before Mr Robinson. . . . We didn't say any names because we wanted to find out what would happen. If nothing had happened we wouldn't have said anything to anyone. I was afraid of it getting worse and that teachers would believe Rani and his witnesses' (Diary, 24 June, pp. 64–65).

The following day (25 June), Chris Morrison gave me the written statement made by Rani. He had written:

'I asked Maria in Oswestry [for a sexual relationship]. She said "yes", so at (sic) the same night I asked her again and she said "yes", which was not to my surprise even though she has a speaking and understanding problem in English. What I asked her is known worldwide and you [Maria] cannot deny this by giving a stupid excuse, "I don't understand him", to get away with it.

'So to make her feel it, for her stupidity, I got a few mates waiting without her knowing. I had no intention of any physical contact, that's why I had a few boys waiting. I don't like or fancy her and I never have. Throughout her year as a 4th year we haven't spoken much. This shows you that we are not even good friends at all. I have never ever taken for granted anybody boy or girl. What Maria said to people I didn't like. It's not my fault she said "yes". I cannot believe that her misunderstanding can be an excuse. I've heard from other people [that she had slept around], so it wasn't a surprise. I just taught her a lesson. She never expected this from me so maybe from now on she might say "no" more often. The verbal abuse I've given her was only on the same matter. I repeatedly said to her "why didn't you say no". She knew what I said without any hesitation and answered me knowing 100 per cent the future outcome' (Diary, 25 June 1986, p. 68).

As Maria was not one of the girls in the group, I had not intended to spend very much time in sorting the problem out. I was willing to help the teachers concerned decide on an appropriate way to handle this case and other similar incidents, and I thought it would be cleared up rapidly, but this was not so. I spent many hours with Maria sorting out her feelings, including what she wanted from Rani. She wanted to talk to him and ask him why he had done this and she wanted a public apology to clear her name.

The 'Maria incident' created much gossip, and I soon realized that the girls in the research group considered Maria a 'slag' and responsible for the sexual harassment. At the group meeting on 30 June, I raised this issue and asked them to define for me the characteristics of a 'slag' and how it was used in the school. Immediately there arose a discussion about Maria, as to whether her behaviour was that of a 'slag' or whether she was naive. All the girls, with the exception of Annmarie (to whom this kind of harassment had happened the previous year), blamed Maria. They argued that she had asked for it in the way she dressed, her make-up, the way she spoke, and the way she acted. Annmarie and I argued that Maria was not to blame at all, and that what Rani had done was a classic case of sexual harassment. Further I argued that the girls' behaviour towards Maria was also classic; the girl was being blamed and the boy was exonerated. This confrontation however did not make any difference to their position.

During the last weeks of the summer term, and in the wake of the incident involving Maria, the classroom observation ceased for my role in the school changed. I was anyway ready to abandon the participant observation strategy by this stage because of the problems already discussed, but now I found that I did not have time to visit the classrooms; my time was being used in a different way. Maria's experience led to a variety of people wanting to talk about and solve this problem (Maria, the research girls and teachers) and in addition I took on the role of counselling Rani every morning. The girls also wanted to discuss their own concerns as well as to tell me why Maria was a 'slag' and why they were not, as well as to chide me over my championing of Maria. But gradually a number of conversations developed in which the girls began to ask me some intimate questions about my life. I answered them all. This openness between the girls and me developed as they realized I was prepared to answer questions that other adults might not. At this stage the office was constantly engaged with girls discussing a variety of topics, mostly to do with sexuality.

The penultimate week of the summer term was Book Week. In many respects I had become integrated into the school community by this time and Mike Stroud asked me to organize a session for girls only. I asked a group called The Raving Beauties to come to the school because, as feminists, they would be able to give the girls in the project another dimension to the feminist perspective I was arguing. The Raving Beauties presented a range of feminist inspired poems and these prompted a discussion on slags and sluts. The Raving Beauties asked the girls to write their own poems using the very words that were usually used to denigrate women and then the poems were read extravagantly, loudly and with pride. The Raving Beauties had provided an alternative forum for feminist debate which had the effect of consolidating some of my arguments.

In the last week of term the Head of Year and I had planned an assembly for all the fourth year students in which I was to give a talk about sexual hararssment, and Mr Morrison was to tell the students that a grievance procedure existed which was to be used if anyone felt sexually harassed. At this meeting also a public apology was read out by Mr Morrison on behalf of Rani, apologizing for the sexual harassment and the defamation of character. The incident of sexual harassment had interested a number of teachers and during the summer holidays I helped write a sexual harassment policy for the school. At the last meeting of the term I asked the group if Maria could become a member of the project. There was a long discussion on this and finally, with much persuasion, they agreed. The term ended on 18 July.

Autumn Term

The research programme was resumed in the second week of the autumn term with a group meeting followed by individual interviews. Because by this time two of the data collecting strategies, the participant observation and the girls' diary writing, had been abandoned, I asked the girls at the first meeting what other activities would help produce data (see Appendix 6). A suggestion was made that we should go away for a few days together. They found the schedule at school prohibitive, and they wanted an uninterrupted period to talk and discuss various issues. To these ends I organized a weekend at Stansted, Essex, in an ILEA house.

In the meantime two further incidents had the effect of dramatically facilitating the progress of the research. First, on 8 September, I was harassed in the local swimming pool and returned to school angry, feeling 'touched', and needing to talk about it. Apart from the librarian, Liz Armitage, and the library secretary, I told all the girls who came to see me that day. One of them was Collette who said that a similar incident had happened to her. Her experience involved a boy two years older than her and someone she knew.[2]

The second incident, which had even more far-reaching consequences for the research project, was the attempted rape of Annmarie West on 12

September, at 6 o'clock in the evening, as she took a short cut through an alley on her way home.

This case was recorded in detail, both in diary form and with the tape recorder. 'At 9.00am, Mrs Turner (a senior mistress) and Annmarie appeared. Annmarie was looking very pale and withdrawn. Mrs Turner asked if I could spend some time with Annmarie. When the teacher had gone Annmarie whispered in a very small voice that she had been raped. I put my arms around her and took her into my office' (Diary, 16 September 1986, p. 104).

Annmarie had been attacked by a man who had managed to partially undress her and attempt rape, before he was disturbed (Int., 16 September 1986, p. 1). He had not succeeded in raping her. After the attack Annmarie went directly home but no one had been there so she had had a bath, washed her clothes and gone to see a friend. At this stage she had told no one. The first person she told was her boyfriend, Gary, the following afternoon. He suggested that she tell her mother which she did on Sunday evening. Her mother took her to the doctor the following day and then to the police station where they remained for several hours making statements and being cross-examined. At one point Annmarie was left with a police officer who suggested to her that the rapist had been her boyfriend, someone she knew, or that she was lying. This upset Annmarie and she swore at the police officer. She withdrew her statement and Mrs West and Annmarie left the station. The next day at school she told a senior teacher, Edith Taylor, who was apparently not supportive. Within a few hours of Annmarie telling me a number of girls in the school knew. One of them was Collette. Her reaction was one of frustration and outrage on two counts; firstly that a girl should have been attacked in this way, and secondly for the effect that rape had on the lives of other girls.

On Wednesday 17 September Edith Taylor came to see me after the morning break, to tell me that 'she felt Annmarie was lying'. I said that whether Annmarie was telling the 'truth' or not, she would have my support for this was what she needed now. Annmarie suddenly appeared. We all talked together. Mrs Taylor suggested that Annmarie should go to her next class, because she had to 'pull herself together', 'life was hard', that she had to 'put up with it' and continue with her studies, or she 'would never get ahead in the world'. I said that Annmarie could stay in the library if she felt like it. Collette suddenly entered my room without knocking, crying and shouting that it had not been her who had told others than Annmarie had been raped. She was very angry and was swearing loudly. 'Mrs Taylor was obviously bewildered that a) I allowed students to speak to me in this fashion, and b) to use words like "shit" and "bloody"' (Diary, 17 September 1986, p. 107). She tried to take control of the situation but the students took no notice of her and finally she left, looking angry and 'put out'.

At 3.10 on the same day, Alex knocked on the office door. She told me that there were many rumours in the school as to what had happened to Annmarie, but that she had guessed. When I asked her how she had guessed she didn't answer my question, but said that Annmarie would 'never get over it'. I was surprised at the conversation, and asked 'why?'. Alex told me that she had been nearly raped as a 10-year-old, that she hadn't spoken to anyone, that this man had been known to her (as a neighbour), and that he had attacked her. She had not told her mother or father because she had been crossing a waste piece of land near her home from which her parents had banned her. She felt it was her fault, and that her mother would be cross for disobeying her (Diary, 17 September 1986, p. 108).

There were now five girls who had disclosed sexual incidents: Carmel, Maria, Collette, Annmarie and Alex. A week later another girl was attacked. On Monday, 30 September, Jenny was waiting in the library in the morning. She asked if she could see me and said that she had been attacked by two men in the underpass near school, the previous week, and that they forcibly held her, touched her and threatened to rape her. She had escaped by biting and kicking and had come to see me both Thursday and Friday but I was not at school. She had waited until Monday, and told no one else (Int., 30 September, pp. 1–7).

During September and October my time was spent talking with all the girls, mostly on a one-to-one basis, but sometimes in twos or threes. Sometimes I was asked to play a parent role and visit the hospital, the eye specialist, and other agencies with them. This I did. The other main activity was the group meetings, which provided a focus for the week as well as a management forum for keeping the girls up to date with various school events. By this time many of the girls were coming to see me regularly and therefore missing lessons, and problems were arising from various teachers. (One letter was sent directly to Mike Stroud, my 'mentor': 'Dear Mr Stroud, Carrie Herbert has had Alex B. and others out of my class REPEATEDLY. During the last year Alex, Collette and several other pupils have missed nearly half of their . . . LESSONS. Arrangements have not been discussed with me in advance and I really do object to the way all this has been arranged.') This issue was never adequately resolved, but flared up occasionally and needed individual chatting to particular teachers. However, as the information the girls were giving me was confidential and sometimes traumatic for them, I did not want in any way to hint that they were disclosing unwanted sexual experiences which they needed time to discuss in detail. Some were to do with the girls' experiences of being frightened by men. Zaheda had been and still was harassed by men on public transport (Int., 17 September 1986, p. 2), Chanel had been accosted by a man who asked questions and tried to take her hand and lead her away when she was a little girl (Int., 9 October 1986,

p. 8), Linda had been chased by men in a car (Int., 9 October 1986, p. 7), and in addition to their own accounts they talked about other women and girls they knew who had been attacked or raped.

At the beginning of November the girls and I went to Stansted. The girls organized the timetable and one of the activities, which they themselves initiated, was a visit to another school to interview 15-year-old girls about the incidents of sexual harassment in their lives. I arranged with a local girls' comprehensive school in Hertfordshire for this to happen. Over the weekend the girls transcribed the tape recordings they had made, and began to analyze their data. The most significant part of the weekend was the discussion on Saturday afternoon. A general conversation began about the kinds of unpleasant experiences we had had with men. Seventeen incidents were discussed, initiated by Carmel who made public the sexual attack on her by her cousin, disclosed to me in April. The other nine girls described incidents which included men exposing themselves, masturbating in front of them, following them, chasing, propositioning, and asking for dates.

One girl, Zohra, came to see me at the end of this meeting and asked if she could speak with me. She had visited me on a number of occasions in the previous six months and I knew her well and I knew her background. We had had many in-depth conversations, some of which had entailed me telling her intimate details of my own personal life, but here at Stansted Zohra told me how as a 6-year-old she had been given some money and taken by an old man up to a flat, where he had penetrated her vagina with his fingers (Int., 13 November 1986, p. 1). The last dislosure came from Zaheda, also at Stansted, immediately after Zohra's talk with me. Zaheda told me that her brother, who was eight years older than her, had made her play with his genitals, when she was 5 or 6. Her older sister had refused, but Zaheda had not been able to.

Out of a total number of thirteen girls in the research group, seven had been sexually assaulted, and all the girls with the exception of Lucy and Ashley (neither of whom attended the Stansted weekend) had reported an unpleasant experience which had involved a man's or men's or a boy's unwanted sexual advances.

The last few weeks of the research project, between returning from the weekend and Christmas, was spent in debriefing both the girls and myself. We had all become extremely close, and the kind of research which had transpired meant that we all knew more about each other than most other people.

The research project itself had raised some major ethical dilemmas, and because of the unorthodox methodology revealed some extraordinary disclosures. (Throughout the nine months at the school, I was approached by a number of other people, both men and women, teachers, parents, other students and friends on the school who were interested in the project. Within that period five women, three students not involved in the project, and one man disclosed to me that they had been sexually abused as children, or sexually assaulted as adults. One woman teacher who came ostensibly to talk about Zohra to tell me how much more confidence she seemed to have in the lessons, suddenly disclosed that she had been raped herself a few years ago, and described the effect it had had on her life. It seemed that as a result of simply raising the issue, providing a sympathetic environment which acknowledged the existence of these problems and providing an understanding listener, other people also had the opportunity to disclose incidents similar to those disclosed by the girls). The disclosures had been of two distinct kinds, those made public, and those kept private. In the next section the private disclosures and the public disclosures will be discussed in detail in conjunction with the way in which the methodology was forced to change in order to accommodate this.

Notes

1 Data are taken from a variety of sources and they will be signified as follows: field notes: FN; my personal diary: Diary; group meetings: GM; private interviews: Int.

2 The various attacks will be described but the details are edited out. Many of the girls' descriptions involved considerable intimacies. My decision as a researcher and feminist to withhold these details was taken on the following grounds: protection of the girls' identities; reduction of erotic material; a belief that the details would add nothing of academic relevance to this book.

Chapter 7

Two Public Disclosures

Maria's Silence

Maria's experience with Rani, and her subsequent reaction and treatment, are excellent examples of the way in which pressures are exerted by particular people in society which inhibit girls and women from discussing their unwanted sexual encounters. An analysis of the episode involving Maria demonstrates how two factors maintain the silence: the fear or guilt which women feel and the suppression or distortion of particular information by others. In addition to these factors there is the ability that society has to enforce and maintain silence through a variety of strategies effectively making practices such as sexual harassment invisible or 'normal'.

Maria was initially silent about her sexually harassing experience because Rani had the influence to intimidate her, not only preventing her from talking, but actually frightening her sufficiently to stop her from attending school. Threatening to tell the school community that she was a 'slag' because she had 'slept with him', were adequate incentives to keep Maria silent and ensure that her side of the events remained invisible, at least for a while. Maria never explained why she chose to disclose initially to another girl. However once she had disclosed the chain of events is clear.

Maria came to school twelve days after the incident and spoke to Annmarie, a member of the research group. Although there is no substantive evidence to claim that it was Annmarie's raised consciousness (brought about by the discussions we had had in the group meetings and individually) that labelled Rani's behaviour 'sexual harassment' and persuaded Maria that it would be advantageous if she went to an 'understanding' teacher, Annmarie and I had discussed unwanted sexual attention and the part women were seen to have played. Annmarie had received both verbal and physical sexual harassment the previous year and we had talked about her feelings at her second private interview. At the time of Maria's disclosure it so happened that Annmarie was beginning to question her role in the events which led to her harassment, a point which becomes clear from the following extract.

> 'Carrie: "Is there anything else you want to discuss from the last transcript?"
> Annmarie: "Well I have been thinking about the way I might have provoked the boys, I mean without – you know – well I could have done, I mean the fact that I hang around the boys quite a lot."
> Carrie: "Do you think women provoke rape?"
> Annmarie: "No."
> Carrie: "Why not? I mean what happens if they are wearing a sexy little number and walking through a park at 2 o'clock in the morning? Aren't they asking for it?"
> Annmarie: "No. There's no law about what women can wear, and we can go where we want to."
> Carrie: "Well, why do you think you have provoked people to touch you?"
> Annmarie: "Well, it's not what I wear or nothing, maybe it's to do with the fact that I hang around with the boys . . . maybe they thought I was asking for it."
> Carrie: "So that gives them the right to touch you, does it?"
> Annmarie: "No, it doesn't." ' (Int., 11 June 1986, pp. 7–8).

There is no doubt that Annmarie knew the term 'sexual harassment' from her previous personal experience, and this, together with our discussion which had shown that I thought women were not 'provocateurs', may have helped Annmarie persuade Maria to seek help.

When I first spoke to Maria my diary records that 'she was shaking, nervous and seemed a little overwhelmed'. During that first meeting I reassured her that I would believe everything she said, that such episodes were by no means unusual, and that I would be able to help her understand and cope with her feelings about the experience (Diary, 24 June 1986, p. 63).

The effect the sexual harassment had on Maria was that she was initially silenced and unable to tell her parents, the teachers who were on the school trip, or her friends. Maria's reasons for not disclosing earlier were: she didn't want her parents told because they would be worried; if she told Mr Morrison she felt he would not believe her; and she thought the incident was trivial.

Maria's life was further upset because of the rumours which Rani had threatened to (and did) spread about her sex life. Maria saw these as a slur on her character, and therefore would not come to school. The consequences of this action are numerous. Fear of reprisals, or a repeat request from Rani, or a sexual attack and taunts, frightened this girl and curtailed her access to education. For a student to miss seven days of lessons because she was afraid of verbal abuse and defamation of character was not a trivial issue, but was an indictment of the way in which girls have learnt to suppress their feelings and silence themselves. Silence is chosen as the viable alternative for two reasons: firstly, because in the past their experiences may have been denied or trivialized; and secondly because they have witnessed others receive disbelief, hostility and blame for disclosing. Both these treatments warn girls from making public incidents of unwanted sexual attention or sexual interference.

The consequences for Maria which arose from the defamation of her character were lack of confidence (as shown in her nervousness about disclosing), anxiety arising out of having a 'bad' name (as shown by her absence from school), losing peer respect (as made clear by the girls in the research group), and missing out on specific school work (seven school days). All of these, I argue, if not dealt with appropriately, would have the ability to contribute negatively in the long term to Maria's social and academic development.

The second aspect to this case was that Rani's interpretation of what happened was taken as 'the truth' by most of the students involved in the incident, or who knew about it. They were quite able to believe his story which cast Maria in the role of a 'slag', as was told to me by Annmarie.

> 'Carrie: "And do you know what it was that Rani put around the school?"
> Annmarie: "He said that Maria had asked him to fuck her and he had gone outside."
> Carrie: "He actually used those words?"
> Annmarie: "Yes, and then he told Maria to go outside because he wanted to fuck her and Maria said 'O.K. you can fuck me'."
> Carrie: "And is he saying that he did or didn't?"
> Annmarie: "I don't know . . . But he's making up all these lies saying that people have raped her . . . " ' (Int., 1 July 1986, p. 4).

Rani had had the influence to persuade many others, boys and girls, that he was blameless and that Maria's actions had made her a 'slag'. If a woman or girl is sexually harassed it is her part in the incident that is questioned and it is her character that is scrutinized. The infringement on the part of the male is largely regarded as 'normal' behaviour, and certainly in this incident Rani was cleared by his peers and Maria was considered the culprit. Because of the roles that women and girls are expected to play, and the preoccupation with female virginity and purity, a girl's reputation is easily destroyed if rumours of the kind Rani perpetrated linger. For Maria and many girls the right image was important and, as I came to realize, it was the individual girl's job to protect her own reputation, for others would not do it for her.

Silence or distortion of facts are used by both men and women alike and help to confirm the stereotypes of masculinity and femininity. For Maria, much of the perpetuation of the idea that she was a 'slag' was promoted by the girls, as I found from the individual interviews and the group meetings. At an interview with Collette on 26 June I asked her what she knew about Maria, Rani and the incident because I had heard rumours from Annmarie that Maria was not the 'innocent' party, and that she had deliberately implicated Rani.

> 'Collette: "I know a lot. First, all my group think she's a slag: slag, I stress that point. I don't think she is a slag."
> Carrie: "What do you mean your lot? Who do you mean?"
> Collette: "Carmel, Alex, Chanel, [plus five others not involved in the research], they all think she is a slag, because when she first came to this school she was very free with herself, and then she went out with this guy."
> Carrie: "Is this hearsay or fact?"
> Collette: "Because I've talked to her. She went out with this guy and he asked her to sleep with him. She said 'no'."
> Carrie: "What do you mean being free with him?"
> Collette: "That she is given to letting the boys have their own way."
> Carrie: "What do you mean have their own way?"
> Collette: "She felt around . . . 'felt around' means just to let the boys feel you up . . . it means private parts. Maria wasn't sexually harassed, that's the whole point, she was rather naive about the whole thing."
> Carrie: "You mean she wanted it?"
> Collette: "Yes, she's a very naive girl. . . . It was naive, in the fact that she didn't mind, she didn't encourage it or anything . . . when people see her, whether they are boys or girls, they always say 'slag' " '
> (Int., 26 June 1986, pp. 1–3).

Collette's interpretation of Maria's behaviour was clearly influenced by the way society 'normally' interprets such cases. She argued that Maria was a victim of her own immaturity and naivety but interpreted this as an indication of loose morals. By apparently allowing boys 'to have their way', Maria had openly flouted the tradition that girls must preserve their own virginity. Because she had apparently allowed boys to 'feel her up', she had no right to protection or to a claim of sexual harassment. In Collette's opinion the way in which Maria made friends with boys had courted abuse and Rani's approach had been well within the expectations of males, given her casualness about relationships. This was consistent with how women and girls are forced to remain silent, for Collette found no transgression on Rani's part. His behaviour was acceptable, a 'normal' way for boys to operate so that responsibility for the unwanted sexual attention lay with Maria. It is clear to see from this example how it is possible for girls to be silenced by such an interpretation.

One of the ways in which this silence can be subverted is to confront and challenge the status quo. With Maria's sexual harassment case this was done in two ways. Firstly, through direct interaction with Maria and telling her that this happened to many women, by offering comfort, by providing practical support, by dealing with the matter as an important issue, by believing her interpretation and by showing her that something could be done about the perpetrator. As a result of Maria's disclosure to me and to a senior teacher, steps were taken to investigate the truth of this incident. Consequently the other girls saw the senior teacher's efforts to resolve this issue fairly. Rani's father, Mr Etal, was called in for an interview and Rani was instructed to attend four sessions of one-to-one counselling. Later, Maria asked to see Rani with a friend of hers and me, to ask him why he had done what he had done and to get an apology. She wanted both a private apology and a public vindication that he had lied and been responsible for spreading libel. Both were forthcoming for Rani apologized to her in the research room and also wrote a public apology which was read out at a Fourth Year assembly on 15 July 1986, organized specifically on the topic of sexual harassment. All these actions led Maria to reassess her part in the incident as well as provide a vicarious experience for others in the group.

The second way of confronting the status quo regarding sexual harassment was to challenge the research girls' attitudes directly, for as long as the girls continued to regard Rani's behaviour as acceptable, it would be impossible to document incidents of sexual harassment by male teachers, for this too would become 'invisible' through normalization. I realized the extent to which the girls in the group confirmed Collette's opinion of Maria in a meeting on 30 June.

> 'Carrie: "Now one of the things I want to discuss today is the whole area of why some women and girls are called 'slags'. How do you get the label? But the first thing I want you to do is to write down your definition of a slag."
> Carmel: "I'll just have to write down 'Maria' . . . " (general laughter).'

The girls wrote down their definitions and then shared them. Throughout the discussion that followed Maria's name was often used as a reference point for a 'slag'.

> 'Carrie: "Now you keep bringing up Maria's name" (groans from everyone) "as a slag. What are some of the characteristics of a slag and to be called a slag what do you have to do?"

Chanel: "Wear bright red lipstick."
Collette: "Yeah, terrible taste in clothes."
Ashley: "It's the way she acts."
Carrie: "But in what sorts of ways."
Carmel: "The way she walks, the way she talks. She's openly inviting people to come and talk to her, and she openly admits that she's got four boyfriends . . . at the same time. A boy said to her 'do you want to come to my house because I want to lick you out?' " [To 'lick a person out' means cunnilingus.] "And she said 'yes', and then she goes 'what does it mean?'."
Annmarie: "No, she came to me and said that these boys have been saying things and she doesn't even know what they mean."
Ashley: "Well she should have" [known what they meant before saying 'yes'].
Annmarie: "No, look she's got boys who go down her house. Like Jeremy knows where she lives . . . and has the cheek to go round saying, 'I've got binoculars and I can look at her getting undressed' . . . "
Carmel: "No, no, if she'd told those people in the beginning to go and fuck off . . . "
Annmarie: "But she never knew what they meant, so how is she supposed to?"
Carmel: "So someone says, 'can I lick you out?' and you go and say 'yes'. If someone came up and said something really suggestive, you'd say 'yes'? . . . "
Annmarie: "Listen people will do different things, right. I certainly wouldn't say 'yes', whether I understood what they said or not."
Carmel: "Well she should have said 'no' until she knew what they meant. Then she should have said 'I will come back tomorrow when I have looked up what it meant' . . . "
Collette: "Maria is terribly naive in her way of thinking . . . "
Carmel: "Oh rubbish . . . she just acts naive. Anyone who is naive wouldn't go out with as many boys. Look somebody comes up to you in German and says something in German and looks you up and down, wouldn't you tell them to 'fuck off?" ' (GM, 30 June 1986, pp. 1–6).

From this extract it is clear who the girls regard as being responsible for the harassment. They accused Maria of being a 'slag' on two counts and thus responsible for the attention. Firstly, because she had acted like a 'slag' before the incident in Shropshire, she was considered responsible for the sexual harassment, and secondly, irrespective of the fact that Rani had decided to be a 'virgin minder' and taken it upon himself to 'teach Maria a lesson', Maria's naivety and misunderstanding were ignored in preference for the interpretation (which matched the usual interpretation) that in fact she was a 'slag'.

The accusation that Maria had numerous 'boyfriends' and slept with them was not born out in the later interview that I had with Maria.

> 'Carrie: "You said earlier that you had a boyfriend here, is he still at the school?"
> Maria: "He wasn't at this school."
> Carrie: "Have you had a boyfriend at this school?"
> Maria: "Yes, I think."
> Carrie: "What do you mean, I think?"
> Maria: "Well, yes I did. He wasn't my boyfriend, but I think he was actually my first boy I went out with."
> Carrie: "The first boyfriend you went out with from here or ever?'"
> Maria: "Ever."
> Carrie: "Is he still in the school?"
> Maria: "No, I think he left."
> Carrie: "What do you mean, you think he left?"
> Maria: "I mean he left."
> Carrie: "What's it like to have a boyfriend, is it different in England to Bulgaria?"
> Maria: "Oh yes. You see I was very surprised here because I had friends in Bulgaria, and some of them had boyfriends, and in Bulgaria there isn't such a thing as 'can I go out with you?' Here I don't think you can go out much with boys when they say, 'can I go out with you?' Because I tried to have a lot of friends, but I realized that most boys wanted to not be friends, but . . . go out with you and want sex. . . . Some of them aren't like that. I do have some boyfriends here, but I become very sad when all of my friends [boys] ask me [to have sex]. I had a boyfriend here called Jeremy, and I was talking with him sometimes, but now he asked my sister out, because I said 'no' [to sex], and 'no' to another one, and so on and so on. There were other boys like that . . . I don't know, probably I don't have much experience. What do you think about it when they say 'can I go out with you?' It means what? Does it necessarily mean you become their girlfriend? . . . It's very hard, you see, I'm trying to explain those things to me to make it clear. . . . Because that boy asked me out . . . and I said 'yes', and he went to me 'that means you should be my girlfriend, does that make it clear to you?' And I [thought] just for the experience, I think it might be a useful

experience, if I go out with him, because that was my first boyfriend. So I went out with him."
Carrie: "And what happened?"
Maria: "One day he asked me to hold his hand and then to kiss him. And I said 'no', and it wasn't very successful really."
Carrie: "Where did you go?"
Maria: "Well the first day was a museum, then I think it was a cinema, and then it was a gallery. I think it was a Rembrandt gallery . . . I'm not sorry that it happened [the breakup], otherwise it would have gone further and further . . . otherwise he would probably have said 'could we have sex?' And I would say 'no', so he would probably leave me" ' (Int., 8 July 1986, pp. 3–6).

Furthermore the claim that Maria had understood Rani's colloquial request for sex was not substantiated in the later interview for I noticed a capriciousness in her use of English. One comment in particular would have been detrimental to her reputation if misunderstood. I asked her about the difference between having boyfriends in Budapest and London.

'Maria: ". . . . . Last year in the summer (in Bulgaria), there was a boy who just wanted to see me. I went once with him (sic) and he said 'here is my 'phone number, if you want to you can 'phone me, and I'll see you again, we can just speak and we can meet'. But it doesn't mean of course sex" ' (Int., 8 July 1986, p. 4).

The term 'went with', in the vernacular the girls used at this London school, meant 'to have sex'. Yet clearly here, Maria meant it in the literal sense. Although I have no evidence other than this to substantiate my claim, I believe that if the girls had asked her questions as to her behaviour with boys she may well have answered in this way, thus apparently confirming her promiscuity.

However, what was clear in the meeting was the strength of the argument that clearly saw Maria as the provocateur and Rani as the maligned party. One of the messages that I was being given was that girls who stepped outside a code of ethics which operated in that school (and maybe others) left them open to deserved abuse. There was a code of behaviour for girls which if followed would serve as a protection against sexual harassment. If one behaved in a certain way, boys would 'respect' you and thus not harass you. Maria had, according to the girls, shown contributory negligence and had 'asked for it'. The girls had learned that it was a girl's duty to demarcate the terms of a relationship with a boy if one's reputation was to remain intact. Maria had evidently not done this, her reputation was apparently ruined and she was culpable.

To have condoned this 'standard' interpretation, as already pointed out, would only make the data collection on sexual harassment more problematic, for the girls would be reluctant to disclose. Allowing an attitude to prevail which blamed the girl for the sexual harassment would perpetuate the silence. Towards the end of that meeting I challenged their beliefs with an alternative perspective. However it must be realized that this challenge was not premeditated for although it was in my repertoire to confront particular issues, when, where, what and how were largely spontaneous. I had introduced the idea of there being double standards which applied to girls and boys with regard to sexual experience, the difference in the number of sexual partners allowed and how virginity was viewed very differently depending on one's sex. The girls had found these issues matched their own experiences and had actively contributed to this part of the debate. Then I introduced a discussion on how women and girls collaborate in the perpetuation of these double standards and thus in the control of women.

> 'Carrie: "The thing that is bothering me, and I don't know how to say it because I don't think you will understand me, is that men use words like 'slag' to keep women pure and chaste and in our places. Boys call girls 'slags', and girls also call girls 'slags', because that keeps the girls in their places too. So if you call Maria a 'slag', she is supposed to conform. She is not supposed to wear these things and those things, and she is not supposed to sleep around, and she is not supposed to have three or four boyfriends. But you are doing the work of boys. You are being conned by boys to control the girls, and in fact you are becoming the police force of those boys. You keep saying she is a 'slag' and there are double standards going on because boys are allowed to do these things that you are not allowing the girls to do" ' (GM, 30 June 1986, p. 7).

The discussion developed:

> 'Collette: "Look I think this is really pointless talking about it because we haven't got Maria here to tell us if she went out with these boys or not."
> Carrie: "But does it matter?"
> Alex: "No not really."
> Annmarie: "It's not you lot that's going out with all these boys, why should you worry?"
> Ashley: "We are not worrying."
> Carrie: "Yes you are, you are all putting a label on Maria, making her something – we all know what a 'slag' is now and it's not a nice term – and you are all perpetuating . . . "

Collette: "But listen, if there was an equivalent of slag in the male, we would call some boys . . . "
Carrie: "But there isn't."
Collette: "Exactly, that's how we think. You say we do this because we don't mind boys screwing around, and we do mind girls sleeping around. Well we do mind boys sleeping around, but there is nothing we can call them apart from shithead or bastard."
Carmel: "I see what you are trying to say" (looking at me).
Carrie: "What am I trying to say, help me."
Carmel: "She's saying that what's happening is that the girls are getting labels, and that boys are doing the same, but they are called something sweet for it. But the girls are being called slags for it, and that they are being called slags by both [boys and girls]" ' (GM, 30 June 1986, p. 9).

There is evidence here that one of the girls, Carmel, was beginning to understand that there was an alternative way of viewing the world and this was clearly an effect of my intervention. Such changes in perception are not easy to pinpoint, but here Carmel was beginning to articulate the existence of double sexual standards for women and men.

Despite my arguments and alternative interpretation most of the girls held that it was Maria's fault that she had been sexually harassed and that Rani's behaviour was reasonable. According to the girls' standards it was the girl's job to defend her virtue. Boys were expected to 'ask', to 'try things on', to see how 'far they could go' with a girl, and girls were expected to say 'no' and be the purveyors of chastity, as was evident in Rani's written statement quoted in the previous chapter. Overall the research group felt sorry for Rani, believing that Maria had deliberately wanted to get him into trouble (GM, 30 June 1986, p. 13). However they were now being exposed to an alternative analysis and despite their arguments and justifications I maintained that Maria was a victim of sexual harassment which was apparently hidden and suppressed, resulting in her initial silence. This perhaps set the scene for change in the future, for when the next disclosure became public the reaction from the girls was surprisingly different.

Annmarie's Silence and Suppression

The second public disclosure was made by Annmarie nearly three months later. Here again, as with Maria's sexual harassment, the attempted rape brought to the foreground the forces which typically silence women and girls. Interestingly though they were not nearly so powerful or effective.

Certainly they did not silence or suppress Annmarie (after the first twenty-four hours), and although she did feel 'dirty' she did not feel in any way that the attack had been precipitated by her or that it had been her fault, even though others thought it was. Similarly the girls in the research group were not only dismissive of the way others interpreted the incident, but they were critical of people who were confused about who was the true culprit.

Annmarie made her story public in two ways. Firstly she told her boyfriend, her family, and the police, and secondly she told various girls, teachers and me at school. These groups of people fell into two clear categories: those like her boyfriend, the police officer and a senior teacher who saw that in some way it was Annmarie's fault, and the girls in the research group who were clearly supportive of Annmarie and were angry about what had happened as well as angry about how she was treated. The way in which the girls responded was in direct contrast to how they had reacted to Maria.

Maria's experience had classically shown how women are often regarded as having 'caused' or 'aroused' men's sexual response. Whether the assault is in the form of indecent touching or rape, responsibility is transferred to the victim and often rests on her previous reputation. A woman's innocence is diminished if it can be shown that her clothes or behaviour were provocative, the time and location were isolated and thus unprotected, if she was sexually experienced or if she knew the assailant. All these factors help to remove from men full responsibility for their actions, transferring blame to women.

Annmarie was on her way home wearing school uniform which consisted of a grey pleated skirt, white blouse, navy blue cardigan, black shoes and white socks. She needed to catch two buses, changing at King's Cross, but as her connection had already gone she decided to walk rather than wait another twenty minutes. There were two ways to go: via the road, which was longer, or cutting through an alley behind St Pancras station into a housing estate. She had often walked this way before because it was much quicker.

Annmarie was a sexually inexperienced 15-year-old schoolgirl in uniform when she was attacked at 6 o'clock one September evening at the end of the rush hour. The circumstances suggest that by virtue of her appearance, the location and timing of the attack, Annmarie should have been exonerated from blame. Interestingly her innocence was accepted by one group and questioned by another. I shall discuss these two perceptions separately. Those people who questioned Annmarie's role in the attack, implicating her, or who trivialized and dismissed the attack as unimportant were her boyfriend, Gary; her mother; a policewoman; a senior teacher; and her brother. All these were influential people in this girl's life.

Annmarie spent the Saturday after the sexual attack at a friend's flat. Gary, her boyfriend of a few weeks, was there too. In the afternoon, he and his friends were watching television when Annmarie asked him to go with her into the hall, because she wanted to talk to him. Gary's initial reaction implied that he was not interested, the attack was unimportant and that he was too busy to want to listen.

> 'Annmarie: "I would have expected to get some support off of him. I mean being the first person I actually did tell, I would have thought he would have given me some support, but he didn't, he just 'blanked me' " ['blanked' was used to mean to be ignored, or to be stared at defiantly] ". . . a plain old blank, a couple of words and then 'and don't call me out like that again people might start to suspect something', and that was it."
> Carrie: "What do you mean 'don't call me out again'?"
> Annmarie: " 'Cos he was sitting down with all the others, and I just said to him 'I want to tell you something'. And that was it. I got him to come out, and he had a go at me after"' (Int., 8 October 1986, p. 2).

Later that evening she spoke to Gary again about the attempted rape.

> 'Annmarie: "Well he blanked me the first time, absolutely blanked me . . . and then I was talking to him again in the evening . . . and he was very supportive and kind in the evening, well not very supportive, but he was a little bit more understanding."
> Carrie: "What would you have liked him to do?"
> Annmarie: "I think I would have liked him to . . . just give me a shoulder to cry on, that is all I wanted" ' (Int., 8 October 1986, p. 3).

Annmarie told her mother on Sunday evening, forty-eight hours after the attack, at Gary's suggestion.

> 'Annmarie: "I was crying a lot and she [her mother] said, 'stop crying it's not going to help matters' and she said, 'I'll take you to the doctor's in the morning' . . . I said to her [a counsellor at the Rape Crisis Centre] that I really did feel dirty, and she said I was most likely to feel dirty for ages . . . I mean my Mum keeps saying 'you're not dirty, so stop saying it, and stop having all those baths' " ' (Int., 16 September 1986, pp. 6–8). A few days later Annmarie told me that her mother had said: ' " 'Stop complaining and stop talking rubbish'. It upset me an awful lot." ' (Int., 24 September 1986, p. 1).

The response that Annmarie received from her mother was initially one of concern, but as the days passed she became less tolerant of Annmarie's need to wash repeatedly, and denied her the right to cry or talk about her experience. She wanted Annmarie to forget the incident, be silent and suppress her feelings. Annmarie found an outlet for her need to talk at school and in particular with those in the research project.

Annmarie's experience at King's Cross Police Station was not dissimilar. Both she and her mother were interviewed by a variety of officers, and the response she received was one of intimidation, disbelief and trivialization.

> 'Annmarie: "She [a police officer] was nice to me while my Mum was there, but then afterwards she was more or less calling me a 'slag' and a 'whore', and telling me that I was lying, and that it was my boyfriend . . . she was really having a go at me. . . . They took me and my mum into a room and got us a cup of tea and coffee. Then this policewoman, Doreen, started talking and she was really nice, and then my Mum went out and she said 'are you sure this happened, are you sure you're not lying?' "
> Carrie: "Did the policewoman say to your Mum would she leave the room?"
> Annmarie: "No. . . . Doreen was going to take my Mum, and one of the blokes was going to stay with me. But I said 'no way'. Coppers they might be, but there was no way [I was going to be left with a man]. So they put Doreen in with me and she was a right cow. I wish I had taken one of the blokes instead. She was really horrible, she kept saying to me 'are you sure? Are you going around flirting with all these blokes? Was I too scared to tell my Mum?' " ' (Int., 16 September 1986, pp. 1–7).

Annmarie came to school the day after her interview with the police. She saw a senior woman teacher and told her why she had been absent from school and what had happened. Once more Annmarie was made to feel that the attack had been one in which she had taken an active part but Annmarie would not accept this interpretation.

> 'Annmarie: "She [Mrs Taylor] had a go at me. She told me when I go out I should clip (sic) my fingers and wake myself up because I'm always in a dream or a daze, and that I should have known better than to walk down that alleyway. I mean from King's Cross I've been doing that same route for about five years, one doesn't change it just like that." ' (Int., 16 September 1986, p. 2).

About six weeks after the attempted rape Annmarie told me that she was having difficulty with her brother Shane, who not only trivialized the attack but made the assumption that once violated a woman could be 'used' by anyone. ' "My little brother yesterday he said to me, we were just having a laugh, and he said to me, 'come on Annmarie, how do I rape you? What is it like? Tell me!' And I slapped him." ' (Int., 31 October 1986, p. 1).

The reactions of some of the girls in the research group were in marked contrast to those of Annmarie's boyfriend, family and the police. Given that they had severely chastised and blamed Maria twelve weeks earlier for her part in the sexual harassment incident, there had been a change in their attitude. They were very supportive of Annmarie and understanding of her feelings and declared that she had not 'asked' for it and that she was a victim of an unprovoked attack.

Collette's reaction in particular was markedly different as can be seen by these two examples. When Maria had been sexually harassed, Collette had come in on one of the preliminary counselling sessions and had asked what had happened. When one of the girls had finished telling her she turned to Maria accusingly and said, ' "Did you do it [have sex]?" ' (Diary, 24 June 1986, p. 66). I had answered sharply that she would hardly be making it up, and that we were here to support her, not to cross-examine or doubt her. This had extended into a discussion on why girls should want to 'make up' stories and what kudos there would be in fabrication.

In Annmarie's case Collette's attitude was very different. Whether this was as a direct result of my reaction twelve weeks earlier is not clear, although I would argue that Collette had become more aware of feminist attitudes towards such issues as rape, from being a member of the research group. Collette came into the office when Annmarie and I were discussing the attempted rape and Annmarie told her what had happened. With great indignation and tears in her eyes Collette railed: ' "I can understand you [Annmarie] being scared and upset and angry, I don't think anyone has the right. I think everyone has every right to walk down that alley and I think it is absolute bullshit when people say to you, 'don't walk down alleys and don't go out at night' . . . you shouldn't have to think that someone might come up and rape you".' She continued more angrily at the injustices imposed on women. ' "What gets me is, O.K. don't walk out at two o'clock in the morning in a park, that's obvious, but come off it, what have we got to live . . . for. More and more every year our lives are becoming smaller and smaller, our days are becoming shorter and shorter. . . . Sure I could stay out late after work as long as I take a taxi home. . . . Look it's not fair, we should have a right to live. Men don't have to suffer all this . . . with rapists. It's just not fair anymore. It's ridiculous." ' (Int., 16 September 1986, pp. 14–16).

Carmel was also angry when she heard about the teacher's reaction to Annmarie and this too was a very different attitude to the one she had shown towards Maria. ' "Did you hear what Mrs Taylor said to her? Mrs Taylor said to her that she was 'asking for it'. A person who has been raped, four days later, someone tells her that she has been 'asking for it'. Isn't that bitchy?" ' (Int., 23 September 1986, p. 11).

Maria's reaction was one of sympathy and concern for Annmarie's future relationships. ' "I'm trying to think how I would feel if I was raped. How would you feel towards men? If you were too sensitive you might not want to marry any more because at that age you are still very young for such a thing. You might feel depressed and afterwards when your husband or boyfriend is making love to you, you will connect it to the person and you will see his face, so you will just hate men, and you might think they will all rape you." ' (Int., 20 September 1986, p. 2).

Alex came to me on the afternoon that Annmarie's attack became public, and told me that she had guessed what had happened from rumours she had heard and the way Annmarie had looked. She said that this type of attack was serious and that girls did not get over it quickly, if at all. In the conversation Alex showed her concern from a position of 'knowing' what it felt like and could empathize with Annmarie's predicament.

The attitudes of the people who blamed Annmarie were consistent with the attitudes of people who are unaware of the way in which particular incidents can be interpreted to favour the 'normal' or 'male' interpretation rather than an interpretation from a female perspective. Because of the way in which society depicts women and men, women who are sexually attacked are viewed as provocateurs and men who are the assailants as having 'normal' sexual urges. The girls in the group had begun to realize the way in which silence and suppression control women, but to what extent their sympathy or change in attitude was due to the research project and its intervention in their lives can only be guessed at.

These public disclosures had two consequences vital for the research. Firstly, the fact that they were public forced me to 'practise' my political stance rather than just 'preach' it. I supported the two girls, Maria and Annmarie, verbally and practically in the face of teacher, parent and student opposition, insisting that they should be treated sensitively, not be blamed but be cared for, given sympathy and acknowledged as 'survivors'. This precipitated the second consequence. The vindication that I had accorded Maria, and the vindication accorded Annmarie by both the research group and me gave other girls, who had similar incidents to 'tell', the assurance that we would believe them, that we would not blame them, that they were not unusual and that we would listen, understand and support them.

I would therefore argue that the public disclosures were central to giving other girls the courage to speak about their experiences. It is also my contention that because of the nature of the research, and in particular the political perspective and the methodology adopted, an environment had been created in which the girls realized that they would receive different treament from that which they had received or learnt to expect when, or if, they had disclosed in the past. It is my belief, also, that the girls' attitudes towards perpetrators and the women involved in these incidents changed, because of a reframing of the perspective which they had previously held. Once they would have perceived the girls' behaviour as 'asking for the treatment' and the boys' behaviour as being normal and typical, but now they were beginning to regard the boys' actions as aberrant and to view the girls as having behaved appropriately. It was this change in attitude which enabled the girls to talk about their experiences at Stansted in a way that would have been impossible six months earlier. Finally I believe that by making these cases public within the group, girls who had experienced unwanted sexual attention could see that they were not unique but one of larger group of females who had been subjected to such experiences.

Chapter 8

Seventeen Public Disclosures in One Afternoon

The girls in the research group had asked for a weekend to discuss 'women's issues' without the interruptions that occurred in school. This had been their own idea and together we had planned a three-day 'holiday' from the school. For the Saturday afternoon we had arranged a group discussion. I had decided that the topic would be the difference between sexual harassment and other sexual attacks because of the confusion the girls were having with these names. For example after Jenny had told me about the attempted rape on her in the underpass near school by two youths, she said, '"Was that sexual harassment, what happened to me, because I didn't know?"' (Int., 30 September 1986, p. 1).

However, the plan for the discussion that I had envisaged did not materialize. As the discussion developed the girls began to give different examples of unwanted sexual attention they had received in their childhood and adolescence. Some had a few to tell, some only had one. It was interesting that in this relatively public forum the girls felt that it was acceptable to talk about these incidents without fear of being blamed, made to feel 'dirty', promiscuous or 'used'.

The following extract is taken from the discussion at Stansted. The disclosures began when the discussion turned to how frightened the girls were of the threat of rape.

> Alex: 'When I read in the newspaper about rape, you know the first thing I look at is the area.'
> Linda: 'When I walk down the street late at night, you don't see me wandering down, turning here, turning there.'
> Carmel: 'You should see me when I've been to extra maths . . . I would rather come early [to school] than stay late. I'm so scared I don't want to take that kind of risk.'
> Zaheda: 'Yeah, well I'd rather go a mile a different way home if

it was brightly lit, rather than dark streets.'
Collette: 'Yeah, rather than risk it.'
Carrie: 'Hold it. Four people in this room have been sexually abused, attacked or assaulted . . . some of them it happened to when, according to some, they were walking down places they shouldn't have been.'
Carmel: 'I think if we all put our hands up, those who have been sexually abused, because I think it would make us all more comfortable with each other.' (A few girls raise their hands.)

At this point I became concerned and anxious. I did not want any pressure put on the girls to disclose a private experience in a public forum and I wanted to assure them that I would not break any confidence.

Carrie: 'Well it's up to the people to do it if they want to, I — er — well it was told to me in confidence and there is no way I will . . .'
Carmel: 'I think I will trust you lot all enough to tell you that it happened to me.'
Collette: 'Yes, go round the room.'
Carrie: 'No.'
Collette: 'And those who want to tell can tell.'
Carrie: 'No.'
Carmel: 'But I'm saying that I trust the people here enough.'
Carrie: 'If Carmel wishes to tell people that's fine.'
Carmel: 'But it would make us more comfortable with each other.'
Collette: 'The people who have got their hands up want to tell, it's in confidence.'
Carrie: 'Sorry, I thought you wanted everyone to divulge their personal life.'
Collette: 'No.'
Carrie: 'Go on then.'

It was then that I began to hear incidents which had happened to the girls, most of which had not been disclosed before. These extracts are in order, but in the original were interspersed with questions from the other girls requiring more details, or in some cases a discussion about how the attacked girl managed to recover. For ease of presentation these digressions have been omitted and all the cases have been numbered to assist in the discussion which follows this extract.

(1) Collette: 'I was walking home at about 4 o'clock, and there was this guy from our school, and he was on his bike, and he started talking to me. I didn't think anything of it . . . he had the advantage, he was bigger than me, and he walked me to the door, and then

he came up to me and felt me up. Then he said, "I bet you liked that". And I said, "I hated it, go away". As he was going he said, "do you want a date?", and I said "fuck off, I don't want to know". I felt so dirty, and weak at that point.'

(2) Carmel: 'It happened when I was really young. I was in [country], but the thing is I don't remember who it was. It was a kind of cousin. I was only about 6 or 7. He lived in a kind of, well he lived with my mother's sister, so he must have been a cousin, but he wasn't their son. I don't know, he just abused me, but I don't remember it. Sometimes I think it might have been a dream, because I sometimes don't remember anything. The only thing I ever remember is that he used to take us in a room, and he used to say he was giving us a present. But I do remember that I didn't like what he was doing. That's just about it, but from then on, sometimes I do remember, because sometimes I bolt if a guy comes near me. . . . But it doesn't affect my life. I don't think about it. . . . But the only time I think about it is when I'm with Carrie. . . . Before, I talked to my sister about it, it was like as though I had a mental block, because I can't remember what happened, all I can remember is that it happened. But it's as if I don't want to remember. For years I just totally forgot about it until my sister mentioned that it happened to her, but not in the same way. She was about 16.'

At this point I decided that I needed to change direction and to stop the conversation. I felt some girls might be pressurized into disclosing when they didn't want to.

Carrie: 'Right this is actually how we started the conversation, but I want to get on and look at the films.'
Collette: 'No we want to hear other people's experiences.'
Linda: 'But they may not want to say those things.'
Chanel: 'I think you should leave it now.'

However, some of the girls were obviously not interested in seeing a film and so they continued with the disclosures. In retrospect this over-ruling of my wishes was indicative of the relationship we had together. Although I was an adult, a teacher and twenty years older than the girls, a situation had developed in which they had autonomy. As they knew what they wanted to do, my voice suggesting change was disregarded.

(3) Zaheda: '. . . I hate being alone at bus stops, because nearly always I get approached by somebody, and you know, it's the hand on your leg, and when you say "go away", you're really nervous,

especially in areas like near our school. They can tell I am really nervous. When I get on the bus my Mum says never go upstairs, but you can't always sit downstairs when it's packed. Yeah, and its happened to me downstairs as well, so I put my bag next to me, so nobody can touch me up, but that doesn't stop it. I mean they are always trying to feel me up and what do you do, scream and shout and get off the bus? I just think nobody is going to believe me.'

(4) Alex: 'Well I was on the bus and there was this man sitting across from me and he kept looking at me, and whenever anyone looks at me I get a bit nervous and I laugh . . . I had my folder in front of me, and I was peeping over it, right, and he kept nodding his head, and I thought to myself, "he's a bit weird". I sneezed, right, and the next thing he was unzipping his trousers and masturbating in front of me. . . . He had this little boy, his grandson or something sitting next to him [indistinct] . . . a man and a woman got on the bus and sat sort of near him, and I got up and told her . . . and she looked at him, and he went red, and he quickly put the child on his lap.'

Carrie: 'Well we have lapsed into the gross end of sexual harassment, and fairly explicit sex on buses. Actually that happened to me when I was 7 on a train with my brother.'

(6) Jenny: 'I remember I was at my friend's house and I must have been about 5, and this man come (sic) and he said he was the gas man, and he had his card and everything to show, and I'm in the kitchen talking to my friend, and he said, "come here", to my friend, so she went up to him . . . and he undid his trousers and pulled down his briefs, and then he was fiddling with his penis, and then all this squirt thing came out . . . and afterwards he started laughing.'

(7) Collette: 'My Dad, he had this friend, and I hated him. I hated the sight of him, and he always used to come and say, "aren't you beautiful".'

(8) Carrie: 'When I was little, I used to stay with a friend of my family, Mrs Gray, and her husband Mr Gray. He was a great churchman, very religious, and she was very moral and strict. Mrs Gray was fantastic, but Mr Gray was an absolute creep. He had a piano and he would get me to sit next to him, and then he would rub his hand up and down my leg. I don't think my parents would have believed me, and I just didn't have the guts to tell them.'

This prompted Carmel to return to her experience and tell more.

(9) Carmel: 'I'm sorry, but I couldn't tell my parents. I couldn't tell my sister. When I stayed with some people, who were friends with my father, and apparently he did it to my sister, and she wouldn't lie about something like that. I know if I told my Dad [about my abuse] he would be so disillusioned.'

Yet again I tried to draw the conversation to an end and began to sum up.

Carrie: 'Right, so now the number of people who have had a nasty sexual experience before the age of 16 has risen.'
Linda: 'I think everyone has had some nasty experience.'
Carrie: 'No, you haven't, Chanel hasn't, Zohra hasn't.'

(10) Zohra: 'I have.'
Carrie: 'Oh!'
Collette: 'Do you want to share it with us?'
Zohra: 'No.'
Carrie: 'That's all right, you can if you want to.'
Zohra: 'No, not now.'

(11) Fitti: 'I have been propositioned, but I got out of the situation as fast as I could . . . I was fairly new to the school, and I was going under the underpass, and this stodgy middle-aged man came up to me and said "hello darling, would you like to come home with me?" But the thing is if you come out of the underpass you can see the police station, and I just felt [safer] and when I got far enough away I said, "I don't know what's wrong with you, you must be a stupid pervert." I mean I don't look as if I'm of age, and I kept shouting out stuff like that to him when I was far enough away, and I knew nothing could happen to me.'

(12) Carmel: 'The problem is you always get propositioned . . . I was about 14 or 13, and I was in Oxford Street, and there was a guy who kept following me around and he came up to me and he said, "excuse me, have you got the time?", and I said "no", and I kept walking, and then he said "excuse me, but I would like to make love to you", and then he said, "excuse me, I think you are beautiful", and I said "excuse me, I've got a bus to catch" and I ran' (everyone laughs).

(13) Carmel continued: 'And you know those little things that stick out at a bus stop, I was sitting on it and reading and this car pulls up, and I am used to people saying "oh I know your Dad", . . . and they always give me a lift home. And this chap sort of went'

(beckoning with index finger) 'and I thought it must be one of my Dad's friends, but I didn't recognize this guy . . . and he just looked at me . . . and he sat there for five minutes, and I was sitting there getting scared . . . and he just went away.'

(14) Annmarie: 'I was walking home and this bloke started to follow me, and I hadn't even noticed him until he came up to me and started talking to me, and then he started to put his arm round me, and I said, "oh just go away", and I went on walking, and he said, "can I walk you to your house?" And I said, "just go away I am not interested", and then he started trying to hold my hand, and he was trying to kiss all up my hand, and I just said, "go away".'

(15) Alex: 'I was sitting at the back of the bus, right, and a man was sitting over there, and I think he quite liked me. Where I get off the bus is a long way from the beginning, and I thought this man should have got off the bus a long time ago, because he was on the bus before me, and when it got to my stop I got off and looked behind me and this man was with me. I crossed the road and this man kept looking at me, and I walked on. I was scared at first, but I didn't want him to see where I was going, and then I lost him.'

(16) Collette: 'We were walking along and this man in a big car came past and he goes really slowly, and he unwinds the window, and he starts to proposition my friend, and he says, "come on girls, come in the car, come on, come on". And he followed us, like halfway up the road. My friend was saying "come on, come on, let's run", and he was saying "come on, come on, come on girls". Finally, we just did a double take and ran.'

(17) Linda: 'Well one day we went to Hyde Park on the boats, and we were rowing the boat and we said, "oh we had better get back because the time is up", but we just couldn't row it, and at the end we thought we needed some help. So there was a man in another boat, and we said "could we tie our boat to yours, and could you help us?" So he did. And then when we got back to where you park the boats he said "Wait, wait I want something from you", and we just started running.'

The anecdotes emerged in a way that is reminiscent of a word association game. There were words or phrases that triggered the girls' memories and as such a pattern can be seen to exist. Thus Collette's (1) and Carmel's (2) initial discussion as to the need for 'honest' disclosure precipitated these two experiences. Then Zaheda (3) opened the area of sexual harassment with her experiences on the buses and was followed by both Alex's (4) and my (5) disclosure of not just sexual harassment on public transport but men exposing themselves and masturbating. This triggered Jenny's (6) memory of her experience of a man masturbating in the privacy of a home, making connections with Collette's (7) recollections of her father's friend and my (8) experience of Mr Gray. My admission that I was unable to tell my mother prompted Carmel (9) to return to her inability to tell her parents and the added penalty of disillusioning her father if he knew the truth. The disclosure from Zohra was only foreshadowed and was disclosed later in private. This will be discussed in the following chapter. Fitti's (11) declaration of being propositioned in the street alerted Carmel (12, 13) and Annmarie (14) to offer their similar stories, and this in turn reminded Alex (15), Collette (16) and Linda (17) of their experiences of being chased.

The majority of these disclosures had been of the common type, that is unwanted sexual attention that affects many if not most women. This is not to imply that the experience is in anyway less traumatic for the girl at the time, but to indicate that they felt confident in sharing this experience because of its frequency. On the other hand girls who had been subjected to the least common type of abuse still felt that their contribution was not appropriate for a public forum. Alex who had disclosed in September that she had been raped as a 10-year-old did not find the environment conducive for sharing her experience, and Zohra, although signalling that she had been attacked, was not prepared to disclose publicly, neither was Zaheda.

In order that the girls could talk about the incidents they had experienced a challenge had to be made which would successfully confront the normal interpretations of these behaviours. The strategies by which incidents of this kind are usually made unproblematic is by silencing the girls and women with a variety of techniques, or by suppressing or distorting the information. Through the weeks and months prior to the Stansted weekend this challenge, via intervention, had clearly been achieved for here were the girls describing a plethora of incidents which confounded the statistics and contradicted the comfortable view that most adults have of childhood. The girls had been able to articulate experiences because the perspectives with which people usually describe these incidents had been shifted, giving the girls confidence in their own blamelessness for the unwanted sexual attention.

One issue, however, which must be discussed is that of the validity of these disclosures. Were the girls lying? By lying I do not mean the kind of lie which is told to escape punishment, to avoid blame or to gain possessions. The untruth to which I am referring is the exaggerated tale or the fabricated experience. Was it possible that the girls were 'telling stories' which in their innocence and youth they thought would 'help' me in collecting data? Were the seventeen cases disclosed at Stansted nothing but a large-scale charade on the part of the girls to outdo one another? Were they competing against each other as to how bad an experience they could describe which would set them apart as sexually 'experienced' in the eyes of their friends?

I challenge this line of thinking for five reasons. Firstly, despite popular myth, there is no kudos for a woman or girl in making up stories of this kind. Women who report incidents of sexual harassment are often open to more severe discrimination and victimization than if they remained silent. From the conversations I had with the girls, prior to the Standsted weekend, they were aware of the stigma attached to violated women and girls as well as the further unwanted attention many received as a result of telling others. They were assured of an intact reputation if they remained silent, and knew of their vulnerability if they disclosed. One example of this was Jenny who was reluctant to tell anyone outside the research group of her attack in the underpass on 26 September 1986, for she believed that she would receive greater hardship.

> 'Carrie: "Why don't you want people to know?"
> Jenny: "I wouldn't mind telling the sexism group because you have to tell them all your problems, that's what the group is about, but I wouldn't like my name mentioned [outside the group]."
> Carrie: "Yeah, but why?"
> Jenny: "No, because some people would just laugh at me, right?"
> Carrie: "Yes".
> Jenny: "And they might think someone is going to do it again."
> Carrie: "What do you mean?"
> Jenny: "Well before, this girl got raped and she told her friends and she asked me to go and tell the [others] and I went around and told the [others] for her because she didn't even come to school for about four weeks. And one boy said, when the girl came back, he went up to the girl and said, 'I would like to do it [rape] to you'."
> Carrie: "Right."
> Jenny: "So that's why, do you see what I mean?"
> Carrie: "Yes. So now that you have had it done to you, you think they might come up to you and say 'oh you like being sexually harassed', and they might make a joke about it."
> Jenny: "Yes that's the way the boys in this school think".' (Int., 30 September 1986, p. 4).

Jenny's fear of reprisals was a common feeling, for disrespect or repudiation for girls who admitted to these attacks was frequent. Maria had been badly treated in the school once it was known that she had been sexually harassed. Annmarie's disclosure had also prompted condemnatory comments and abuse from particular sections of the community, namely, the police, her family and some teachers. Advertising the fact that one has been sexually assaulted is an open invitation for further harassment. Surely then it was not in Annmarie's best interest to disclose such a fabricated tale? The solicitations of the group would have been poor compensation for the treatment she received. Fabricating tales about sexual experiences does not promote a girl's image though it may for a boy.

Perhaps it is because men are expected to boast about their sexual exploits that it is believed that women have the same predisposition. However the difference for women and men is that for one of the reputation is enhanced, for the other the reputation is diminished. The girls knew this when they were discussing the word 'slag' (GM, 30 June 1986) and the issue of double sexual standards was raised.

The second reason why I refute the argument that the girls were fabricating the tales is the significance of the incidents they chose to tell in public and those they chose to suppress. For example, Jenny had the chance to describe in detail the incident of the attack in the underpass if she had wanted self-aggrandisement, for she had suppressed the actual details to the girls at the time (26 September 1986). The reason she chose not to describe this attack, I suggest, was that it was sexually intimate and thus demeaning, frightening, and recent, and Jenny was outside the school gates when she should have been in class. In Jenny's mind there was some fear that she would be found guilty even though I had emphasized her innocence. The incident she chose to reveal (6) was a case of exposure in a friend's kitchen and clearly shows a 'little girl's' description of masturbation. I believe she chose this incident because time, maturity and the degree to which one's intimacy is violated, play a part in the confidence to disclose. I have already argued that women and girls are more likely to be exonerated from blame if their innocence can be established. As a 5-year-old 'innocence' is usually granted automatically. A child is not even slightly culpable in a case of a strange gas man masturbating whilst on a call, whereas in the underpass incident Jenny's culpability would be less easily dismissed. Also I suggest that the gas man's actions were not so intimately intrusive for Jenny as the recent attack. Further, time plays a part in the healing process and after ten years Jenny could view the masturbation with more detachment than she could the incident of a few weeks ago.

Another girl who chose not to make a more 'exciting' episode public was Alex (4). Alex had spoken to me after Annmarie's attempted rape and had told me her experience, but in the forum at Stansted she chose to report an incident I had never heard before. Why? I believe that, like Jenny, Alex decided that the incident on the bus was 'safer' to describe and more in keeping with the level of other disclosures than the rape she had experienced as a 10-year-old. The man on the bus did not actually touch her and therefore this was not an intimate intrusion on her body, as was the earlier attack. Unlike Jenny, time had not for her distilled the former experience, but like Jenny she chose to share the sexual assault which was more frequently experienced by other women and in which she was less culpable by common standards.

In the light of these disclosures I conclude that if the girls had wanted to fabricate incidents and to lead me on they would have offered their most dramatic experiences. Alex and Jenny remained quiet about their sexually intrusive attacks, as did Zohra and Zaheda. These last two girls' private disclosures will be analyzed in the next two chapters.

The third reason why I found the girls' disclosures credible is that of the continuum of frequency as described by Kelly (1987). If the girls had been fabricating it is reasonable to assume that the tales would have grown more sexually explicit and horrific as the afternoon continued. In fact the incidents became more mundane and less frightening. Kelly (1987, p. 52) argues that the continuum on which sexual harassment can be located is not decided by trauma, for this is an individual assessment on the part of each victim, but on frequency. Thus those incidents which happen regularly are gathered at one end of the continuum, whilst those that are less frequent are gathered at the other. As the afternoon developed the incidents which were discussed moved from the more indecent, and thus the less frequent, to the less indecent, the more 'normal' and the more commonplace. The experiences of this group are consistent with the findings of Kelly (1987, pp. 46–60) and Hanmer and Saunders (1984) all of whom argue that most women have experienced indecent exposure, touchings, attempted assaults, but fewer have been raped or sexually molested.

The fourth reason for my belief in these incidents is the nature of the data forthcoming. On a macro level I had been explicit about the kind of data for which I was looking throughout the research: the sexual harassment of these girls by male teachers. At a micro level the afternoon discussion at Stansted was for me to make a distinction between sexual harassment and sexual assault. In addition I had organized a number of films which would emphasize the point I was making through narrative and documentary evidence. When the girls had initially begun to tell me about their sexual experiences, although I did not spurn their disclosures, I did not tell them that this was not what I wanted, because it was not my intention to document examples of this kind. Neither did I encourage them to disclose these incidents, in fact I tried to silence them. Carmel, Maria, Collette, Annmarie, and Alex had all spontaneously disclosed their experience of indecent incidents prior to the Stansted weekend. Carmel's disclosure was as a result of my challenge to her perception of rapists, Maria and Annmarie were victims of attacks, Collette told me of her indecent assault by a boy after I told her of my incident at the pool, and Alex's story came immediately after Annmarie's attempted rape. I was not looking for the kind of data with which I was presented. If the girls had wanted to 'please me' they would have fabricated stories about Mr X, the English master doing 'y'.

On a deeper level, and the fifth reason why I believed the girls, was that I knew from my readings, from my own women friends, confirmed by the other people in the school who had come forward voluntarily to tell me of their unwanted sexual attacks, that sexual abuse and assaults were common. That eight girls out of thirteen had had experiences on the infrequent end of Kelly's continuum, and that all had experiences of some kind of unwanted sexual attention did not surprise me.

I now wish to turn to the question of why it was that the girls chose to reveal incidents in their lives, which for many of them had been silenced for so long, why also did they choose to make them public, and why did they all emerge on this particular Saturday afternoon? There are a number of issues here to do with methodology in general and in particular, reciprocity, demystification, naming, trust, devolution of power through sharing and the developing of group skills. Furthermore I believe that location of the discussion and the research which we had conducted at the local school the previous day, had changed the atmosphere and dynamics of the group. I shall look at each of these issues in turn.

It had been my intention to be reciprocal with the girls, not only sharing my experiences if necessary, but also in actively engaging them in discussions, presenting my viewpoint from a feminist perspective and thus often challenging their perceptions. I had decided to follow Oakley's advice and to answer any questions the girls might ask, which in itself could involve naming and the introduction of new concepts, perceptions and understandings. Throughout the weekly group meetings these changes in the girls' perceptions had taken place slowly, sometimes coming to a crisis, for example with the discussions on 'slags' and the workshop with The Raving Beauties. More often such change was gradual, some girls' understandings changing more quickly than others. There is little direct evidence of the process of change: the sharpest contrast can be seen in the girls' response at the beginning of the research in April, and the understanding and insight they displayed towards the end of the project.

The process by which the girls changed was partly attributable to the way the research methodology adapted. Talking in groups about women's issues, and bringing examples of how other women experience life, helped the girls to see that their experiences were not unique. I had shared particular intimacies with the girls: my experiences; my feelings as to how I was treated at the time; the way in which society saw my behaviour; and the way in which topics such as relationships and sexuality were more easily discussed now than when I was 15. I also discussed how vulnerable girls and women were without knowledge and how important it was for them to have an understanding of their sexuality in order to be in control of their lives.

One of the ways in which the closeness had developed was to do with the way the research methodology had allowed the girls to make decisions about when they came to see me. Although a few had taken advantage of this situation in order to avoid particular lessons regularly, the system had proved to be very successful. The girls were not 'called in' to talk when I was ready, but came and 'talked' when they had something to say. This was unusual in a research project for interviews are usually determined by the researcher's need to collect data, rather than the respondent's desire to offer data.

It had been necessary to establish a group in which members would trust one another, as well as allow each person to feel that they could contribute. Talking in a group is a learned skill and the first two sessions demonstrated that the girls were inexperienced in group work, so it was necessary to build communication skills. I did this by having group discussions, showing the girls how to share time, how to avoid putting each other's contributions down, how to encourage others to participate and how to listen actively, respond positively and support contributors if necessary. All these would have been impossible in a larger group but are skills that can be achieved in a group of this number.

It was also imperative that these skills be learned in order that statements could be made and discussed but not ridiculed. As most of these girls were used to mixed groups it was important for them to re-learn how to contribute in an open debate. Further it was important to be able to offer support in a group when participants disclosed feelings or concerns. During the summer I had taken time to teach the girls these group skills and this helped them develop their communication abilities. Thus when the girls began to disclose intimacies about their childhood experiences, the support and concern from others was evident. Not one girl put another down, ridiculed, disbelieved (at least publicly), ignored, trivialized or dismissed the individual experiences.

One of the functions of the group was to help the girls describe feelings and attitudes which up until now they themselves had had ignored, dismissed or trivialized. I have already given evidence of the need for this in the labelling of certain concepts such as 'double standards', and the naming of particular behaviour such as 'sexual harassment' and 'sexual assault'. Naming actions meant that they could be identified. I had shared some examples that I personally had experienced. This gave the girls examples of tangible incidents to which they could relate. When I disclosed to them I tried to describe my feelings about the ambiguity for women of feeling responsible yet knowing that one had in no way been provocative. The sharing of my experiences had reduced the importance of age difference and experience between us, and this had helped develop a non-hierarchical research group.

Two further factors which could account for the numerous disclosures at Stansted were the location and the research the girls had conducted on the Friday afternoon. Going away from home to an environment where we could discuss issues without fear of interruption was in itself conducive for disclosures to be made. Any group of people 'isolated' from their immediate family and friends is drawn together. We had built up a good rapport within school, but over the weekend the relationships developed and strengthened. The visit to a local rural girls' comprehensive school on Friday afernoon had also been instrumental in helping the girls identify as a group in an environment where they were strangers, in the minority, and yet were the 'experts' in what they had come to do. In London, whilst setting up this weekend, one of the girls had had the idea of collecting data on the sexual harassment of girls in schools by male teachers. They wanted to replicate our research project, to see whether other girls were subjected to this unwanted sexual attention. To these ends they decided to form pairs, to interview three or four students per pair with prepared questions and a tape recorder. The London girls in their interviews found that they had the same problem as I had had. When they asked the participants whether they had been sexually harassed they found that some girls did not understand the question. It was therefore necessary for the 'researchers' to 'tell' the interviewees what it was they were looking for. Once definitions had been given, the girls at the rural comprehensive school were able to give examples of sexual harassment that either they or their friends had experienced from some of the male staff members.

The afternoon at the rural school was extremely important for a number of reasons. Firstly I realized that the research group girls were very articulate in describing sexual harassment and they were able to locate in another setting the very behaviour for which I had been looking. This drew me to conclude that, as they could identify sexual harassment, my lack of data at the London school was not from their inability to identify it and it gave me satisfaction to think that it was not happening to any great extent in their own school, for this was what my own observations had revealed. Secondly, I believe that the methodology which the research team used in this school, i.e. that of deliberate and condensed intervention, had not distorted the information or contaminated data. Some of the participants had been sexually harassed, some not. There could have been little reason for these girls to have fabricated incidents. Thirdly, having conducted the interview, the research girls were upset by what some male teachers had done to some of these girls. In one of the reports made after the tapes had been transcribed, Linda and Chanel wrote: 'There are only four male teachers in the school, but even knowing they are surrounded by women still doesn't stop two of them from constantly sexually harassing the girls. They do things like pulling the back of bras of the girls, lifting up tops, making comments like "what a big girl you've grown to be". Wendy said: "I was wearing trousers, I was in the lunch line, Mr H. came along and with a tray he was holding in his hands, he swung it up between my legs and then said, 'you're lucky it was only a tray', and then walked away". Wendy told me she told her mother who took no notice. When we asked why they didn't do anything they said, "it happens all the time to all the girls, nothing would be done about it, I'm sure the teachers know about it". To them it was so frequent that they thought nothing could be done about it. We told them that if they wanted we could try and do something. We told them that in our school it didn't happen, but if it did it would be dealt with straight away. As soon as they thought they had a chance of doing something about it they got'really exitted (sic)'. For the girls to have had yet more exposure to the fact that many women and girls are subjected to unwanted sexual attention, gave them more incentive and confidence to disclose in the public setting later on in the weekend.

I have described in this chapter only those incidents which were disclosed publicly. I have suggested that the methodology which I used to gather data had developed to such a degree that relationships, confidences and private experiences which had been silenced for years were able to receive a hearing. An environment had been created in which the girls were supported and believed, and in which a different perspective was provided in order that a different sense could be made of particular incidents. The incidents which were disclosed privately and which will be discussed in the next chapter were however of a different sort.

Chapter 9

Private Disclosures

This chapter will present two disclosures which were told to me in private. They were different from the public disclosures in that the incidents happened when the girls were much younger, the assaults were all of a physical nature (i.e. the infrequent end of the spectrum), and the girls had told very few people, if any at all. One of these three private disclosures was apparently as a direct result of Annmarie's attack, for Alex disclosed on the afternoon the attack became public. Zohra's private disclosure did not fully emerge until the weekend at Stansted, although there is evidence of her turmoil long before the story unfolded.

Alex

The second private disclosure was that of Alex. Alex came to the research room late on the afternoon of the day after Annmarie had told me of her attack. She knocked at my door at about ten past three. At that time Annmarie's attack had not been made public, although all the girls knew 'something had happened', because I had been unavailable all day. It was not surprising then when Alex told me that she had heard a rumour that Annmarie had been attacked. I asked her if she believed it. She answered definitely. The degree of certainty with which she replied prompted me to ask why she was so certain. Without hesitation she said that girls or women who suffered such attacks rarely recovered. Once more I prompted: How did she know this? Her answer was to describe the rape she had suffered as a 10-year-old. (The recording of this disclosure was taken the following day. Even though she had had a few hours to think about what she had told me her description is not edited because it shows anxiety manifested through repetition, detail and self-accusation, common in the other girls' accounts.)

> 'Alex: "It was a cut through from my friend's house to our house, and if you didn't go through there you had to go all the way round on the main street, and as it was kind of late I just ran across . . . [a big open field]. I knew the man, but not to speak to, but to see him, and I was running across the field, yeah I must have been running, and you know he called me, and I knew I saw him everyday, and my Mum saw him everyday, and everyone saw him everyday, so I didn't think anything. And I went over to him, but it's so long ago I don't remember it, but I must have gone over to him and I think – well there were people in his house as well, there was a party or something, but I don't know what was going on, but there was a noise coming from his house, and he was sitting outside the house on the grass bit, and he called me over. So I went over, but I didn't actually go up to him, because I'm really someone who is cautious, I wouldn't go straight up, I always stay a distance away. . . . And I sort of went over to him, but I didn't actually go to him and he said something but I wasn't really listening because I was thinking about the time. I always think about the time, and it was time to go. So I turned round and he grabbed me from the back, yeah he grabbed me from the back and had me on the floor." ['Had' in this context means rape.] "I don't know how I got up, I don't know how I got up anyway, I just can't remember. And I went home, and I didn't say anything to anyone, and all my Mother said was, 'how did you get home?' and I said, 'I took the long way round'. I couldn't tell her I took the short cut because she would have killed me, and from then on I wouldn't even leave the house unless someone was with me."' (Int., 17 September 1986, p. 2).

Prior to this disclosure I had been glad that Alex had come to see me, for a social visit, or so I thought, for it was nearly the end of school. 'Chats' were not often recorded, as this one wasn't, for the girls and I would talk about a range of topics not relevant to the research, but crucial for building friendship and trust. Friendship and trust had been established with Alex, and we had had prior conversations, one in particular, when she had explained to me some of the colloquial usages of words and phrases found in her school (Int., 15 July 1986 and 5 September 1986). And it was to her I turned on this afternoon for some 'saneness', in a day that had been sad and traumatic and difficult.

I was also feeling disturbed by Annmarie's demeanour regarding the attempted rape. I had written in my diary that 'the whole day was very confusing, with Annmarie oscillating between almost crying, looking very withdrawn and subdued, to her talking animatedly about her boyfriend (who had "blanked" her) and how she wanted to have a relationship with him and perhaps marry him' (Diary, 16 September 1986, p. 104). The other disturbing characteristic of her disclosure was the way in which she had sometimes smiled when she had described the attack. The next day I wrote that 'she smiled and looked coy' (Diary, 17 September 1986, p. 106).

It was to Alex, as one of the most mature young women, I turned to ask if she felt any disquiet with the incident as described by Annmarie. In retrospect I realize that I too was a victim of the common societal interpretation of an attempted rape. I was sceptical of the attack; I thought that Annmarie wanted attention especially from me, and would certainly receive it if she claimed she had been raped; I felt that the story of the attack did not 'ring true', because Annmarie was not displaying what I considered 'appropriate behaviour' for a sexually assaulted person. Barry (1979, p. 40) records just this situation when she describes the rape paradigm and how society judges the innocence of a raped woman. 'Her victimisation is proven or disproven on the worth of her word, the test of her character, the chasteness of her past sexual life, the mode of her dress, the glint in her eye, and the smile on her face.' And I was just as culpable, judging Annmarie on the chasteness of her look, the glint in her eye and the grin on her face. It was only latterly, from an article by the Sheffield Rape Crisis Centre in SMASH, the Sheffield Men Against Sexual Harassment publication, that I learned that women can talk about their rape in as many different ways as there are women: they can be silent, withdrawn, hysterical, angry, apologetic; they can cry, laugh, smile, shout, whisper or talk rationally. Each way of disclosing is as valid, if disconcerting, as the other.

However, Alex had a more implicit way of 'knowing'. She could tell a person who had had a similar experience to herself and was in no doubt that Annmarie was 'telling the truth'. She told me that she had guessed before she was told anyway, and that Annmarie would never get over the attack. The way in which Alex recognized in Annmarie the same or similar symptoms, understood the fear, the pain, the vulnerability, and the guilt, prompted her to come to confirm Annmarie's experience and to disclose her own assault.

Alex's sense of guilt and her feeling that in some way she was responsible for the attack had echoes in many of the other girls' disclosures. Zohra had taken the offered money and had felt guilty; Collette felt she had encouraged a schoolboy to walk home with her and the boy had then touched her genitals (the term she used was 'fingered'); Jenny had been out of school when she knew she should have been in class; Annmarie had taken a short cut which she knew to be dangerous and now Alex felt guilty about her disobedience.

This feeling of guilt is one that is often felt by those who have been sexually attacked and is a very effective way of silencing the attacked person, supressing information and thus inadvertently protecting the assailant.

The first disclosure from Alex was not recorded because of the haste and unexpectedness with which the disclosure came. This however raises an ethical question for researchers. The tape recorder was set up as it always was, although a new tape would have needed to be found, opened and loaded. The dilemma is as to one's role. As a researcher it is in the interest of the research to record all incidents which are pertinent to the research. Even if one is caught 'off guard' it would have been possible to have stopped the conversation whilst I organized the recording. However, where do research needs become displaced by the need to respond as a friend, to listen because one really cares about the person and her problem rather than because the disclosure constitutes 'good data'? This problem was one with which I was faced with Zohra. Her disclosure, to be described shortly, occurred in the dormitories at Stansted. To have asked to record that personal trauma would have been to show insensitivity and impropriety. Therefore one of the ways in which I circumvented this dilemma was to ask the girls at some later stage to talk to me again with the tape recorder. This gave them the opportunity to reflect on what they had said and to repeat their story in a less emotional state after the initial shock of disclosure had passed. Being a researcher then brings conflict between the need for 'proof' of data, and the humanitarian sensitivity required when dealing with issues of this kind. I believe it was the needs of the girls at that time that took priority and to these ends Zohra, Alex, and some of Annmarie's disclosures were not in the original but were restated.

Zohra

In the first interview I had with Zohra on 29 April 1986, she talked to me about the problem of arranged marriages which as a young girl in her culture and religion she would be expected to have. Initially I thought that Zohra's anger was connected with the dual life many girls in her position are expected to play. Many find a tension between their family traditions and values and those of the culture in which they are living. Her friends at the school were able to go to discos and parties and have boyfriends, as well as being allowed freedom at weekends to shop, go to cinemas or meet friends for a drink. All these social interactions Zohra was denied.

> 'Zohra: "In my religion I'm not allowed to have a boyfriend till I'm married. I have to have my marriage arranged, but I'm not having it arranged. I'm meant to have it arranged, but I'm not going to."
> Carrie: "How do parents find a suitable husband?"

Zohra: "Well they kind of think of someone from a relative, you know. But I don't want anyone from my relatives, I want to choose my own. . . . Even though I'm not getting it arranged they have to see the man. In an arranged marriage you don't even speak to him. You don't even know him. Like my cousin, she had it arranged, she didn't see him and when she got married he was ugly . . ."' (Int., 29 April 1986, p. 5).

I wondered why she should want to tell me about these traditions in such detail although I supposed this was how she interpreted the topic 'women's issues'. So I listened to her anger and fear, unaware that there were other issues to which she was alluding and that once she had built up enough confidence and gained enough information and we had established a trusting relationship, she would talk more freely. The process took over six months.

During the first interview and in my efforts to find out how much each girl knew about 'women's issues' it was clear that Zohra was rebelling against the traditional role that her parents expected her to play.

'Carrie: "Would you call yourself a feminist?"
Zohra: "Yes."
Carrie: "What does that mean to you?"
Zohra: "Well I don't go telling everyone."
Carrie: "No, no that's alright, I won't tell anyone."
Zohra: "No, I mean I don't tell, 'oh I'm a feminist you know'. It means to me that . . . I believe in women. I am a girl you know and I have to grow up. My Mum believes I have to grow up to be like her, but I don't want to, I want to have it my own way . . . and feminists they are like that. I would like to get to know other people [feminists] really, not men, because I mean I do not just like men, I just like women."' (Int., 29 April 1986, p. 10).

At the next interview on 9 June, Zohra told me about the extended family in which she lived. In the home there were Zohra's mother, her father, two younger brothers and two younger sisters, her father's aunt who was in her late 60s and largely responsible for many of the domestic chores and with whom Zohra had many arguments, a female cousin of 20 and her prospective husband, who was also a relative. It was during this conversation that I realized Zohra was being put under pressure to get married.

'Zohra: "Every time people come to my house they're always talking about me, you know, 'give her to my son'. They treat me as though I'm some piece of money . . . They say 'I can't wait for Zohra to grow up so I can give her to somebody' . . . And I'm always saying to my Mum, 'why are you talking about me. I'm too young to know about this sort of stuff', and she says, 'oh I'm only joking', and I say, 'well don't joke about it' . . . When people come they are always saying, 'Zohra's growing up' and they talk because they have got sons, and they say, 'if you are going to give her away, give her to my son'. I hate that stuff."' (Int., 9 June 1986, pp. 3–4).

In the second interview we had again returned to the issue of arranged marriages and I asked Zohra how long she had been against the idea.

'Zohra: "I don't know. When we were young they [her parents' friends] used to come and joke about it. I don't know when, it just happened."
Carrie: "So you have been thinking about it for some time, it just hasn't happened?"
Zohra: "No I've been thinking about it."
Carrie: "What, before you were 13?"
Zohra: "I don't know, because then I didn't know about marriages."
Carrie: "Why?"
Zohra: "I didn't know about marriages, marriages and sex and things like that then. I did know about periods and thinks like that, but I didn't know about sex, until my cousin told me that when you get married and on the day of the marriage, you know, and I go 'what, are you joking?' That's when I knew."' (Int., 9 June 1986, p. 5).

Throughout all the interviews I had with Zohra she often talked of the way in which her parents tried to make her conform either by imposing a variety of threats, by using the reputation of the family as a lever or by using the religious teachings as a control. Zohra resisted the restrictions, at least theoretically if not in practice.

'Zohra: "My Mum keeps saying how you should respect men, but I don't go her way. I don't like men. I mean when they were young they used to respect men . . . but now everything has changed and so I don't believe in that stuff."' (Int., 29 April 1986, p. 1).

'Zohra: "I said to him [her father], I'd like a car when I grow up and he said he thinks it's bad for girls to drive, and he keeps giving me bad looks. I don't care."' (Int., 29 April 1986, p. 3).

'Zohra: "They say to me 'look at the other girls doing work in the house . . . why can't you be like that?' . . . But my Mum is always bringing up the subject, 'if you do anything wrong and people talk about us you will find yourself going back to . . . and staying there'."' (Int., 8 September 1986, p. 2–3).

Zohra's mother also did not want her staying away from home. A school trip was arranged for the students to go to Germany but Zohra was not allowed to go. Her mother said, '"'If you get there you might go with a boy, because you know you can't have sexual intercourse until you are married. You can't lose your virginity'. So they think I am like that but I keep telling them I'm not."' (Int., 29 April 1986, p. 7).

She told me about an incident of a man in a car, and the effect this would have on her parents if they knew.

> 'Zohra: "The other day on Saturday, I can't tell my parents right, but I was going down the market, and this man in his car came past and because I can't see very well he waved at me. I thought he was one of my cousins, and I went back and he stopped the car and he was saying to me 'come in', and I was saying 'but I don't know you'. But imagine one of my cousins who saw me, they would probably say 'oh Zohra's a bitch, she's hanging around', so I'm scared . . . if they found out I don't know what would happen."' (Int., 8 September 1986, p. 3).

During the last part of the summer term Zohra left to go on holiday with her parents back to her own country. Although we had short conversations, and I met her in the group meetings, it wasn't until September that we had another long private discussion. Once again the conversation returned to arranged marriages. This time Zohra chose to tell me in great detail her culture's ceremonial wedding traditions.

> 'Zohra: "We have three days of weddings, one on [for] the bride, one on [for] the bridegroom and one together. She goes in the car to his house and on that night when we all go to sleep they have it [sex], and I don't like it, because I don't want people to know about me, because you know they are virgins and they have blood and they keep showing it to all the women. I don't want women knowing about me, I think it's disgusting. If I was ever to get married . . . I would have three days and then on the third day I would go and leave and they would have to wait for the flipping blood, they won't even see it because I don't want them to know about me."' (Int., 8 September 1986, p. 11).

The concern that Zohra had with the ritual defloration and the subsequent showing of blood prompted me to intervene and challenge the myth that all girls of 15 are technical virgins. According to Nawal El Saadawi (1980, p. 28), a medical doctor, the hymen varies in texture, size and consistency from one girl to another and some girls have been 'provided by nature with an elastic hymen which does not bleed on the first night of marriage'. I gave Zohra this information telling her that many girls may not be able to 'prove' virginity technically for the hymen could have been non-existent or so fragile that it tore in the normal course of childhood.

> 'Carrie: "But you don't always bleed."
> Zohra: "You don't? That's if you're not a virgin you don't bleed."
> Carrie: 'You don't always bleed, some girls do and some girls don't."
> Zohra: "Well I've always known that . . ."
> Carrie: "I didn't."
> Zohra: "Well, I've always known that virgins bleed, 'cos they are always showing it in my country. So I don't know."
> Carrie: "Well I would like to know, I mean it is quite reasonable for the girl to be a virgin, and they have sex on that third night but she doesn't bleed. I would like to know what they do then."' (Int., 8 September 1986, p. 11).

Zohra was very much aware of the consequences for a bride who was unable to prove her virginity. (She told me this information after the first draft of this chapter had been written in June 1987). 'If you were not a virgin on your wedding night you were put into a bag or sack, and then wrapped up and thrown in the river. Other times they would put you in a sack and put knives in you.' The retribution for brides who have lost their virginity is emphasised by El Saadawi (1980, p. 26), for 'a girl who does not preserve her virginity is liable to be punished with physical death, or moral death, or at least with being divorced if she is found out at the time of marriage.' When Zohra talked about this issue she became very agitated. The transcript shows her anxiety in the incompleted phrases and her ungrammatical sentences which I have not edited.

> 'Zohra: "They say, the parents, they might, well I don't know what they might do, but they will say she had it off with another bloke or something like that, and the marriage (sic) might get divorced and she still stay with her parents, but her parents, now she's not married and they will think, I don't know what will happen then, but she will get into trouble . . . because they think if you don't bleed that means you are not a virgin and you have had it off or something."
> Carrie: "But that is untrue, I mean you can be a virgin and you can have sex for the first time and you may not bleed."'

Immediately after this discussion I realized that Zohra was looking more anxious. I assumed that she had somewhere else to go as she kept looking at her watch. She said that she didn't have to leave and so I asked if she was upset by the content of the conversation. She said that nothing was wrong. However, I pursued this line and asked if she was anxious about questions I might ask her.

> 'Zohra: "No I don't feel anxious, I will answer anything, and I like talking to you, Carrie, because I know you're not going to tell anyone and I feel free to answer. But I don't have any problems. Well I do have some, but I do tell you about them. I'm not even allowed to tell my cousin some of the things I've told you. So I'm not anxious or nervous. I may seem a bit fidgety, but I am always like that."
> Carrie: "Have you got any questions you would like to ask me?"
> Zohra: (lowering her voice) "No."
> Carrie: "Well some of the girls come in here and ask the most extraordinary questions."
> Zohra: (again with lowered voice) "No I don't have any."
> Carrie: "And sometimes I think, 'how am I going to answer this question?'."'

In this last extract Zohra established a number of factors. Firstly she told me that she trusted me not to divulge any information she might give me. Secondly she told me that I was the person with whom she shared her most intimate secrets, even above her cousin. Finally she told me that she had given me information that was highly secret, information that her family would not like to be divulged. Presumably if I could be trusted to keep this information to myself, I might be trusted with further information. However, at the time of this interview I received no more information from her, for after asking if she had any questions she suddenly said:

> 'Zohra: "Was it hard on the first night, you know, I mean having it [sex], did you ever have it? 'Cos my cousin had it and I haven't asked her how it feels, 'cos I want to know how it feels, you know, I'm scared you know, I really am."' (Int., 8 September 1986, p. 12).

I then told Zohra my first experience of sexual intercourse. She had asked me a straight question and she wanted a personal response. According to Laslett and Rapoport, quoted in Oakley (1981, p. 44) this was 'interactive research'. The principle of hierarchal relationship is not adhered to, rather an attempt is made to generate a collaborative approach to research by engaging both the interviewer and the respondent in a joint enterprise. Oakley (1981, p. 42) herself had formed intimate relationships with the women in her research into childbirth, and 15 per cent of the questions asked of her were to elicit her experiences or attitudes towards the issue of reproduction. For Zohra to have been able to ask me this personal question indicated that a relationship of sufficient trust, honesty, and equality had been established.

When Zohra left the interview room, I did not foresee that the information I had given her about sexual intercourse was to prove to have been exactly what was necessary for her to make a vital connection. It wasn't until the weekend at Stansted that she signalled that there was more to this conversation than I had anticipated. I have already quoted the extract in which she publicly declared she had had a 'nasty sexual experience before the age of 16', but that she was not prepared to discuss the details in that forum.

After the group meeting at Stansted she asked to talk to me. There was no recording of her disclosure, for it happened where she found me, without a tape recorder, standing in the dormitories of the hostel. However, on our return to school we discussed the incident again and I asked her if I could make a recording. (The extracts are taken from that interview which was made on 13 November 1986, and then amended by Zohra in June 1987).

> 'Zohra: "I was about 4 or 5 and I was playing downstairs [in a courtyard]. I was living in Oakwood Court, and I was playing with my little sister and her friend. And this man [a stranger] came up to me, who I didn't know at the time, he smelled of beer and he had, you know when you drink your veins show, and he gave me some money, and he took my hand without me answering . . . When I showed it [the money] to my Aunt, it was foreign money, it wasn't actually even money, but I didn't know because I was so small . . . So he took me up the stairs [into the block of flats], I didn't even have anything to say . . . and there were these black people coming, and he hid me behind the wall, because I still remember it, and then he picked me up and put his fingers up [my vagina]. Oh God, I didn't know what happened to me. I was dizzy. I just gave her [my Aunt] the money, she was wearing a long kaftan dress and trousers underneath. She got the money and threw it at me and said 'that money doesn't work here'. I was asleep on a sheepskin rug and my Aunt was sitting beside me. Whenever I wanted to go to the toilet I had to use a baby's pot, and you could see, whenever I did, it was blood."' (Int., 13 November 1986, p. 1).

The way in which Zohra described her story was full of contradictions as to whether she was guilty or blameless. The overtones of self-accusation and rationalization were present as she talked. Although she had taken the money he had given her, presumably as a bribe or for payment, it is as though she rationalized that it wasn't really payment or a bribe because the money had no value. Had the money had currency would she have considered herself a prostitute? When the assailant took her hand she didn't say 'yes', she didn't say 'no'. Here I believe that she felt she should have cried out or put up a struggle. Because she didn't, she blamed herself and consequently justified her actions by emphasizing that she was so young and that she didn't understand what was happening.

It is fairly clear to see how a woman or girl can be made to feel that an attack of this kind is not to be talked about, and how silence and then suppression make the incident invisible. The case of Zohra's attack is no different in the way it has been suppressed from the attacks made on Annmarie, Maria or any of the other girls in the group. The difference between Zohra and the others is that she had to carry the burden of her non-virginity until her wedding night, for then her lack of 'technical' proof, irrespective of the assault, would be realized.

I wish now to look at the forces which have allowed this incident to remain silent and just a nightmare in Zohra's mind. Firstly I shall discuss Zohra's great-aunt, who I shall call Aunt Reham, a woman in her mid-50s at the time of the incident, but now in her late 60s. Aunt Reham had been married and widowed and was living with her brother's family under impecunious circumstances. Her role in the family was that of cook and as they ate traditionally, much preparation was necessary for nine people, including the daily baking of bread. Aunt Reham had had her own children and so it can be assumed was aware of sexual matters. Also from what Zohra said it can be assumed that she was a traditionalist, upholding her culture's standards and attitudes. Her arguments with Zohra were to do with Zohra's flouting of the traditional behaviours which she felt were appropriate for a great-niece in this culture.

Aunt Reham was often left to childmind, especially in the early days of the family's arrival in London, for both Zohra's parents went out to work. When Zohra was attacked Aunt Reham was responsible for the child's welfare and was the only adult around. Although Zohra cannot remember whether she told her aunt what had happened, she said:

> 'Zohra: "But she saw the blood and everything like that, but I don't know whether she knew what it meant."
> Carrie: "And she didn't say anything?"
> Zohra: "No. I remember my Mum and Dad . . . they came in and she was saying, 'look at your daughter, she's sick' or something, that's all I remember."' (Int., 13 November 1986, p. 1).

Whether Aunt Reham knew what had transpired when the 4-year-old was found vaginally bleeding, can only be conjecture. If she did not know, one wonders why a doctor's advice was not sought at this stage, or at least the parents made aware of the bleeding. However if she did know it is clear enough to see why she chose to silence Zohra and to keep the truth from the parents herself and to tell the parents on their return that Zohra was only 'sick'. (From the way Zohra's virginity had been protected by her parents, for example when she wanted to go to Germany with the school, it is probable that they were not told of the attack.) From what Zohra had said about the rituals and traditions in her culture's life, virginity, or at least an intact hymen, was regarded as being of prime importance. To have been in charge of your nephew's eldest daughter and to have neglected your duty so that a man could violate her, would have had serious consequences. There would certainly be serious consequences for the little girl anyway, for her value, purity and thus marriageability had been destroyed. If this attack were to be made public Zohra's life would be negatively affected. There would be shame for Zohra, shame for the family and possible ostracism for both from the community. There would be little chance later of a 'respectable' marriage for Zohra with the result that she might have to remain unmarried and thus a financial burden on the family.

It is clear, however, that if Aunt Reham did understand what had happened she would have been caught by pressures which militated against disclosure for what she may have considered 'Zohra's benefit'. Her position was tenuous as a 'dependent' in her nephew's home and family, for her presence was based on charity and goodwill. What would be the consequences for her if she admitted to negligence and declared that her great-niece had been violated by a stranger? As Zohra was an object made valuable by men for her worth as a virgin, so too did Aunt Reham have worth for the male community, as a preserver of female chastity. She had failed in this task and to have disclosed her negligence would have been to have lost her security within the family. As an outcast woman in a foreign country she would have been destitute. She had no English, was not a skilled worker and she was aging. Women of her culture were not expected to work outside the home, thus preventing them from gaining competence in their adoptive language or an understanding of the new culture in which they were residing. Aunt Reham was a dependent on male power, manifested here through her dependency on her nephew for her livelihood. Return to her country of origin was unthinkable.

Collusion by women in other women's sexual violations is reasonable in a society in which women have little institutional power. Zohra's silence can be understood for it is likely that fear, threat, blame, trivialization or disbelief were elicited and imposed. All these would effectively silence a 4-year-old for a while and later as she grew up and became aware of her culture's traditions (even if she did not fully appreciate what had happened), she would choose to remain silent by her own volition, as she apparently did for many years.

Then why did she choose to disclose to me? I believe there were three main factors: the environment, the publicity of Annmarie's and Maria's cases, and the intervention technique incorporated into the research methodology which gave licence to provide new and relevant information. Firstly, I had deliberately set up a research environment which was built on sharing, trust, non-hierarchical decision-making and open questioning. This had provided Zohra with the confidence to ask me, in private, a question she was not confident to ask others. Her question about sexual intercourse was deliberate; she needed information. The information I gave her unwittingly was consistent with Oakley's 'no intimacy without reciprocity'. If I had sidestepped that question not only would I have not been truthfully sharing the research project as I intended, but more importantly I would have not been giving her the information she needed in order to connect her past experience with the forthcoming reality of a traditional wedding celebration. 'No intimacy without reciprocity', then, is one important factor in this methodology, and 'no information without knowledge' is another.

I have already discussed in detail the second point in the previous chapter, that of the way in which the publicity of the disclosures made by Maria and Annmarie created an atmosphere in which the girls felt 'safe' to disclose. I had given proof of my concern and commitment to women and girls who had been attacked in providing support for and recognition of the trauma they had suffered, as well as openly vindicating the girls' behaviour whilst arguing that the boys and men had to accept full responsibility. I believe that this last argument was important in the decision many of the girls made before disclosing.

The third factor was the role of intervention. Here I gave Zohra the missing piece of her jigsaw puzzle. She knew what had happened to her, she knew it had to be kept a secret, but she didn't know why. She also knew about the blood on the sheets and the importance of virginity. What she did not know was that virginity is predicated on the existence of a hymen, and that it is the tearing of the hymen that produces the necessary evidence. Once I had described for her the act of sexual intercourse, she could make the connections herself. Once the connection had been made the burden, I suspect, became too much for her. Zohra had to check out that the link she had made was correct. Her disclosure was as a result of my intervention. Intervention here means my input of information rather than a clear challenge to the progress of conversation as was seen in Carmel's case, where I challenged Carmel's notion of the average rapist. For Zohra then this methodology was conducive to breaking the silence in two ways: firstly by providing her with the appropriate information, and secondly by setting up an atmosphere in which she could safely disclose an incident which would have meant her ostracization from her family and wider community.

Chapter 10

Zaheda

I now wish to turn to the final disclosure, that of Zaheda, who, like Zohra, chose to wait until Stansted to talk about her experience of sexual abuse. Up until this time Zaheda had only disclosed incidents which had been of the frequent variety, and she had had many of these including being touched by men on the bus and train, approached by men in the swimming pool and propositioned while she waited for the bus (Int., 17 September 1986, pp. 1–2).

Following the 'public disclosures' at Stansted, Zaheda asked to speak with me. I suggested making a drink and it was whilst we waited for the kettle to boil that she began her story. This section was not recorded, for reasons similar to those previously discussed in Zohra's case. However, when we made the tea we went to a little room where I recorded the rest of her disclosure. This extract has been edited because there were interjections not relevant to the case which might have identified the family.

This disclosure was the only case of assault by a family member I came across. The perpetrator was Zaheda's 14-year-old brother, Hassan, the objects of his unwanted attentions, his two sisters, Rukeya and Zaheda who were 8 and 5 at the time.

> 'Zaheda: "I can just remember the room and my sister, and my brother there, but now I can't stand being in the same room . . . I can't hear him talking in this, I can just remember something like musical statues, and 'you can touch me and you do this'. And we used to do it, and I think, well it seemed quite natural. I mean I didn't seem to be worried about it then, I suppose something triggered it off later on and I started thinking about it . . . He didn't do anything to me, well I don't think he did, I don't know he may have done. I know we never took our clothes off. Well he did but I didn't, so I think that's all right. I can cope better knowing that I didn't take my clothes off. You know sometimes he would pretend he was going into the bathroom and turn the light on and get ready there,

> and then go into our room which was next door and say 'touch this' [his penis] and all that. And my sister would say 'go away, go away', I don't know, I didn't feel ashamed or anything. I didn't think it was wrong, well I was too young I suppose."
> Carrie: "And what do you think now?"
> Zaheda: "I don't think it was wrong because I didn't have any say in it. He was bigger anyway, if I had said 'no' he would have forced me anyway."' (Int., 9 November 1986, p. 9).

Zaheda's disclosure of her brother's unwanted sexual attention had been triggered, according to Zaheda by 'those programmes about what happens in families' (Int., 9 November 1986, p. 1). It was in September and October 1986 that the topic of the sexual abuse of children began to become public and programmes began to appear on television, and it was to these that Zaheda was referring. Esther Rantzen's television programme initiated a children's help telephone line and the public began to be educated about the seriousness and frequency of this social problem. For example, the Childline 'phone number was clearly advertised on public transport and children who were involved in sexual abuse were encouraged to call for help. Zaheda was aware of this new interest in a subject that she had experienced as a child and it was a television programme that had helped her make the link between her reality and the theory of sexual abuse in the home. It was this connection in conjunction with the research project's topic that created the right environment in which Zaheda could disclose.

When I asked Zaheda if she had thought of ringing Childline she replied: 'No, because I thought they might think I was stupid, if I didn't really know whether it had happened.' (Int., 9 November 1986, p. 7). Her confusion as to whether it had happened had been present throughout the disclosure with statements such as: 'But I don't know whether it did happen or not, I'm sure it did though' (Int., 9 November 1986, p. 1), and her allusion to the fact that it may have been a dream. I tried to reassure her that her experiences were real.

> 'Carrie: "Let me tell you I believe you one hundred per cent and I know it is not a figment of your imagination."' (Int., 9 November 1986, p. 8).

Disclosures which had contained an element of 'I don't know whether it really happened', or 'I can't remember the details', had arisen before. The first disclosure, in April, when Carmel had told me of her experience with a friend of her father's, had been curtailed, suppressed or forgotten. Alex too said she could not remember certain parts of the experience, for example how she got away, Zohra's experience was described in the simple phrase, 'he put his fingers up', and now Zaheda was saying that she didn't know whether it had been a dream. The act of suppressing the experience, or of 'forgetting' the details, is not uncommon.

Constance Nightingale, an incest survivor who recently made a television programme (*The Nightingale Roars*, broadcast on ITV on 13 June 1988, 10.35pm, producer Jane Henriques), described how for over forty years she had 'forgotten' that she had been continually sexually abused by her father. Her memory was reawakened when she read some of her sister's poetry and found that her sister too had been abused. For the four girls who had been sexually assaulted as young children, suppression of the incident had been a well-kept secret. Recalling the incident after eleven years in Zohra's case, after eight years for Carmel, after six years for Alex, and after nine years for Zaheda was difficult for two reasons. Firstly, the incident was deeply buried and had never been talked about before because of the consequences that revealing the incident would have entailed. The consequences, whether they be in the form of blame, fear, reprisals, or ostracism, result in the victim remaining silent. Secondly, because they did not want to believe the details of the incident, because the experience had been particularly intimate and traumatic, discussion of the details, even to me, could have been too embarrassing. I did not ask for details, and they did not willingly provide them. Perhaps it was because Annmarie, Jenny and Collette had all been recipients of unwanted sexual attention in the recent past that they could furnish extremely detailed accounts. These girls either couldn't remember, or couldn't give away the details.

When we left Stansted, Zaheda was in very high spirits, which I believe was a result of sharing the secret burden she had carried for ten years. On the train home she led some of the girls in a loud, rousing and continuous rendition of 'Girls just got to have fun' (Cyndi Lauper, 1984, CBS Records) much to the amusement of the other travellers.

Two years later and just before the final manuscript went to print the girls who had been involved in the research read the final draft. Zaheda was one of the girls who responded. 'I read your book . . . it's really very powerful and strong with a definite message of how women are secretly undergoing so much silent torture . . . I want other people to read your book and if they're experiencing sexual abuse, to feel that they are not alone, that they can recover and feel happy with their lives like me. Thanks to you I am now a happy teenager free from any dark secrets, my secret was a big burden which was hard to carry, but you helped me to understand all the facts, to bring it out into the open, and know that it couldn't have been my fault at all' (personal communication, November 1988).

I have already discussed in Zohra's case the way in which a girl's experience can be negated and trivialized or ignored by other women. Zaheda too had this experience. Following a television programme on incest which Zaheda had watched, her sister returned from work and saw the last few minutes. As the two girls prepared for bed Zaheda tried to ask her sister if she remembered anything.

> 'Zaheda: "I was thinking, 'how am I going to say it to her?', and then I said, 'you saw the ending of that programme didn't you?' and she goes, 'yeah', and she said, 'you're always watching them aren't you?', and I said 'yes'. And then I said, 'what would you do if you were married and that happened to one of your children?'. I said something like that, and she knew there was a question behind it, and she goes, 'what do you mean?' And I said, 'do you remember anything?' And straight away she said, 'no, what do you mean?' And I said, 'look I want to ask you something', and she said, 'no, I don't want to know, I just don't want to know. If I've forgotten then that's fine, I don't want bad memories brought up'."' (Int., 9 November 1986, p. 3).

Clearly her sister, Rukeya, could remember the incidents too, but unlike Zaheda she was not in an environment in which she could voice her opinions in safety. As a 19-year-old she had suppressed the unwanted sexual attention and was frightened or humiliated or embarrassed by the memory. Further she may have had added guilt that she had been unable to protect her younger sister at the time, or as the elder sister that she hadn't told her mother and so when confronted by her 15-year-old sister she continued to refuse to discuss the abuse. Interestingly, the experience was not denied, just silenced once more.

This case in particular brought up an ethical problem which became theoretical rather than practical, but is one that must confront researchers continually. It is the dividing line between observing confidentiality and acting as a professional on behalf of a minor, a person under the age of 16. When Zaheda told me about her brother's unwanted sexual attention she also told me that the trouble had recently recurred because she was now, after a few years of being abroad, living back in the same house with him. Hassan was at that time 24 years old.

> 'Zaheda: "I am just uneasy with him [Hassan] . . . I still think he likes me . . . You see sometimes I'm sitting watching the television, and I'm nervous anyway because he is in the room and I don't know, first of all I thought perhaps it was because I was watching to see if he was watching me and I was exaggerating it, and I was watching television, but he could be watching me, and I would turn round like that" (indicating a sudden turn of the head) "and he'd be there

> and he would suddenly go like that [look away]. And if I am in the kitchen he'll come into the kitchen and then I will go out and then in a short while he will follow me."' (Int., 9 November 1986, p. 7).

From the beginning of the research project I had maintained that whatever the girls said to me would be confidential. I would not disclose their stories to anyone else who could identify them. They realized that the research would probably be written into a book but I had promised that all the names would be changed, locations altered and family idiosyncracies obscured in order to protect them, as well as the school's name and their family identity. It must be remembered however that the research was initially concerned with the sexual harassment of these girls by their male teachers. Although this could have uncovered some material which may have been problematic, I had not anticipated that I would discover any illegal sexual relationship between a girl and a teacher.

With the project's change in focus, I was in an area which was clearly on the edge of finding cases which entailed moral danger if not criminal practices. Yet my original promise to the girls was that their disclosures would retain anonymity, even if the details of the case were published. Here, in Zaheda's case, was the situation of a 15-year-old living in a house in which a man of 24 might decide to practise what he had practised at the age of 14. My dilemma was: where did my responsibility lie? with Zaheda to keep her secret, or with the law to protect a young girl? As it was, in this particular case the immediate danger was averted, for her brother, within a few weeks, moved out of the family home into a flat of his own. But what if one of the girls had told me about an on-going incestuous relationship with her father? In theory I would have maintained the confidentiality I had assured the girl at the onset of the project. To have done otherwise would have been to flout the girl's trust in me and to gain data under false pretences. However I would have counselled the girl to speak to a person who had experience in this area, a social worker, a teacher, or a doctor.

How did the Silence Work?

There were many different strategies used to silence both the girls who were actually attacked and also the women and girls like Aunt Reham and Rukeya who were involved by default. These controls, as we have seen, are varied, and more than one can apply to any situation.

For Alex, Zohra and Jenny the factor which kept them silent was that they believed they were guilty. Taking an 'out of bounds' route home, accepting money, and being out of school during lessons, meant that each believed that in some way they had 'asked for' the treatment and that it was therefore deserved. If they 'told' they thought they would be punished not only for the violation but also for the accompanying misdemeanour. The consequences for each of the girls manifested itself in a lack of confidence sexually, a fear of going out, a mistrust of men and a realization that 'normal' sexual relations with future husbands or boyfriends might be difficult.

Although Alex, Jenny, Aunt Reham and Rukeya were silenced by guilt they were also silenced by fear, as were Carmel and Maria. Jenny and Maria feared that if they disclosed to anyone that they had been attacked they might be open to further abuse and attack. It was also important that they suppressed the information in order to retain a 'good' reputation. Carmel and Alex were frightened of their parents' reactions. Carmel said that she would not tell her father that she had been attacked because 'if they had believed me . . . I think my Dad would have probably killed him' (Int., 29 April 1986, p. 19), and because of the country in which she was living at the time she meant actual murder, not a euphemistic use of the word 'kill'. Alex did not tell her parents because she thought her mother would be angry with her. Aunt Reham must have been frightened both for herself and for Zohra. There was the fear that she would be blamed for allowing Zohra to wander away from her protection, and the fear that Zohra's future would be ruined for lack of technical virginity. Rukeya may well have been frightened of the repercussions such a disclosure would have for the family, as shown by her treatment of Zaheda (Int., 17 December 1986).

Zaheda remained silent because she wasn't sure it had happened, and like Carmel she offered her story with the proviso that it may have been a dream. In addition Zaheda wanted to protect Hassan from being discovered for she believed that he had led a very difficult life. His father had died when he was a baby and he been brought up with his mother and a stepfather with whom he did not get on. Further, according to Zaheda, Hassan had been discriminated against by this man as a young child and had felt rejected and unloved. Zaheda wanted to protect him from any more harm and consequently remained silent. Protecting either the assailant or one's family from knowing what had happened was one reason that both Maria and Jenny gave for not telling their parents, for they did not want them worried or upset.

Another factor which guaranteed silence was that of not being believed. One of Maria's reasons for not asking for help was that she thought the teacher would not believe her version of the incident. Annmarie was not believed by a number of people, including the police and a senior teacher, as well as by me, though privately and only temporarily.

Trivialization also silences girls and women who have been sexually attacked or assaulted. Annmarie's boyfriend thought her attack was unimportant and 'blanked' her. Maria did not initially want to report her sexual harassment because she felt it was unimportant.

The inability to name the attack as an attack also kept some girls quiet. Carmel did not make the link with her cousin's attack until she realized that male friends and family members can sexually attack girls. Jenny did not know what to call the attack she had received, and it was information that Zohra needed to name her assault and to begin to understand its implications. Zaheda too needed the television programmes to 'trigger' her thinking, and then the appropriate forum in which to articulate her experiences.

Finally shame was a further force which kept girls from talking. Like the guilt and the concern with their reputation, shame was feared by many girls if they disclosed. Zohra and Zaheda in particular felt ashamed of what had happened and that was one of the reasons, I believe, for the length of time it took for them to disclose. Carmel's shame manifested itself in her reluctance and inability to disclose details of her attack.

Each person I have cited here had more than one reason to remain silent, with the exception of Rukeya (Zaheda's sister) and Collette. These two are interesting cases because they do not conform to the pattern into which the others fitted. However I believe there are reasons for this deviation. Rukeya remained silent and denied her experience perhaps because she did not have access to an environment like that provided by the research project. Her reaction of angry denial to disclosure was the same as many women's and indeed probably that of the girls in the group, had it not been for the awareness process in which they had been involved. Collette on the other hand felt no shame, guilt, fear, and neither did she think she had dreamed it, nor was it unnamed for her. Partly I believe that this was to do with her home environment, for she was the girl who came into my room on the first day and declared that she and her mother were both feminists. Collette had in many respects already confronted the issue of silence and suppression and had decided not to accept these as controls. When the boy sexually molested her she immediately told her mother and her tutor. She was believed by both and action was taken towards the offender.

Keeping incidents of sexual abuse, sexual harassment and any other unwanted male attention hidden and silent is to tacitly accept that nothing can be done and that these practices are 'normal' male behaviours. Challenging the 'normality' of the attacks, sharing the cases we had experienced, discussing who was really to blame, and for each girl to reach the understanding that she was not responsible, was to begin to break down the silence and suppression which had controlled and isolated the girls, hidden the practices, and normalized the behaviour.

There were two girls in the research group who did not disclose any incident of sexual harassment or sexual interference. These two girls, Ashley and Lucy, were the only two students to whom I did not get particularly close and with whom I did not share many of my own intimate experiences. It was these two girls, and Maria (her father refused permission), who did not come to Stansted and therefore did not partake in the public disclosures at the general meeting. It can only be speculation as to why these girls were 'unique' in the group, and one reason may have been that they had not experienced any unwanted sexual attention. However, the reason could also be that we, they and I, did not get close enough for them to have trusted me adequately, or to have lost the inevitable embarrassment brought about by talking about such issues. Perhaps they did not find the environment of the research group and the individual interviews or chats conducive for disclosure. But there may have been a further reason for their failure to integrate at an individual or group level. These two girls were both white and 'cockney' born and in this way were unique in the group. All the others were not born locally, and I believe that this affected the dynamics of the research group. Had there perhaps been a shift in the balance of power between the cultures? Although the majority of the school were by no means white anglo-saxons, this was the dominating culture reflected in the teachers' nationalities, most of them being white, English born and middle-class. Was it that the group united against the representation of the white anglo-saxon protestant ethic, and in this way were able to reject Ashley and Lucy? It is impossible to tell, but what was clear was Lucy and Ashley did not get as close to me as the others, they did not become an integral part of the group, they did not come to Stansted and coincidentally they left school the term that I left, disillusioned with the fifth year, the course and education. Lucy went to be an apprentice hairdresser and Ashley went to childmind for one of her mother's friends.

Chapter 11

Female-controlling-practices

Presented with data such as I was (which had stemmed from a research project designed to document examples of sexual harassment by male teachers) I began to ask myself how normal or abnormal was it that out of thirteen girls four had been subjected to attempted or actual rape, and four had experienced a range of other sexually intimate attacks. Was the use of women or women's bodies such an unusual occurrence? Was it a new phenomenon that women and girls were subjected to this kind of oppression?

In order to place the attacks in a theoretical context I began to call the type of behaviour used to oppress women 'female-controlling-practices'. The female-controlling-practices which I had inadvertently discovered when talking with the girls had been varied and for many each had experienced a variety over many years. What did the female-controlling-practices have in common? Firstly, the women and girls on whom they were perpetrated were usually silent about the experience. They told no one and found it very difficult years later to talk to me about their attack. Secondly, because many female-controlling-practices are ignored as problems and are often regarded as 'normal' and 'typical' male behaviours, girls learn that their experiences, however unpleasant, are indeed unremarkable. Thirdly, the girls had no way of describing their experiences, for the language we have at our disposal does not easily take account of these experiences and there are no actual words to describe what happened. For example there is no specific word which describes what happened to Zohra which would differentiate her experience from that of Zaheda. Fourthly, the female-controlling-practices enhanced men's lives in a variety of ways: through sexual gratification as in the case of Hassan; through sexual perversion as in the case of Zohra's atttacker; through intimidation as used by the two men who attacked and assaulted Jenny: through ego boosting as displayed by Collette's assailant; and through asserting one's power and popularity as in the case of Rani who sexually harassed Maria.

In order to locate the theory of female-controlling-practices in a wider and more comprehensive context I decided to look at other ways in which women had been oppressed throughout the world and in different cultures to see whether the theory could be applied to other practices. I decided to take the two customs, Chinese footbinding and African female genital circumcision and to analyze these practices in terms of the theory of female-controlling-practices. It will be argued that both came to be regarded as 'normal' and 'typical' customs, that women remained silent about their suffering and pain, that both practices enhanced men's power and sexual gratification whilst decreasing women's chances of health, independence and happiness.

Chinese Footbinding

Footbinding was widely accepted and practised among the upper classes in China for a period of a thousand years. Walker (1983, p. 319) stated that this 'strange erotic custom . . . even exerted some influence on Western Europe where women were often praised in romantic literature for having the tiniest feet possible.' The crippling of the Chinese girl began at the age of 5 or 6 and was commonly justified in terms of femininity for future marriage. The smaller the feet, 'lotus hooks' or 'Golden Lotuses', as they came to be called, the greater the potential for a prestigious marriage. In fact, access into court concubinage or high society life was dependent upon having tiny feet. Prager (1983) has written a short fictional story about footbinding which provides a historical insight into the operation itself as well as presenting the reader with an understanding of the cultural pressures which predispose a 6-year-old to accept the crippling process. The need to satisfy society's ideal of beauty is seen to be inculcated early into this child's psyche.

A 6-year-old girl, Pleasure Mouse, is placed in a chair and bound arm and leg with leather thongs.

> 'The footbinder took hold of the child's right foot, and leaving the big toe free bent the other toes beneath the foot and bound them down with the long silk cloth. The women . . . watched the process intently. She then took a second cloth and bound as tightly as she could, around the heel of the foot and down again . . . with the result that the heel and toes were brought as close together as they could go, and the arch of the foot was forced upward in the knowledge that it would break, restructure itself and foreshorten the foot. The last binding was applied beneath the big toe around the heel, pushing the appendage up and inward like the point of a sickle moon. When

> the right foot was done the footbinder bound the left foot in the same manner . . . retrieved the tiny shoes . . . and . . . forced her bound feet into the shoes.
> '. . . [T]he footbinder untied the leather thongs and released [the child's] arms and legs. [The child] screamed. She looked down at the tiny shoes on her now strangely shaped feet and she screamed . . . She jerked towards her mother and screamed [again]. The women held her up. "Walk", they chanted altogether, "you must walk or you will sicken. The pain goes away in time."
> '"In about two years' time", crooned the courtesan. [The child] hobbled two or three steps. Waves of agony as sharp as stiletto blades traversed the six year old's legs and thighs, her spine and head. She bent over like an aged crone and staggered around not fully comprehending why she was being forced to crush her own toes with her own body weight' (Prager, 1983, pp. 33–36).

An alternative to life with crippled feet was death. Once the feet had been bound the girls were 'offered' an escape from the ordeal. Prager's story reveals this choice, for when Pleasure Mouse collapses with pain she is asked '. . . Do you wish to stay on earth, or do you wish to come with me? . . . You can be a constellation, a profusion of stars in the summer sky . . . or you may choose to stay as you are. It is your choice Pleasure Mouse' (Prager, 1983, p. 36). The 6-year-old chooses life rather than death.

Footbinding was, according to Walker (1983, p. 319), a life-long torment and one 'that slowly broke bones and deformed the flesh until the full beauty of the atrophied three-inch lotus hooks were achieved. Many women died of suppuration and gangrene before the desired effect was complete.' The crippled women were considered 'immeasurably charming' by reason of their vulnerability, their suffering and helplessness. Once the footbinding had been completed the women had to keep their feet tightly bandaged forever, for to let them spread would cause even worse pain. To many Westerners, footbinding was imagined to be the harmless and painless controlling of the foot's natural growth creating a perfectly formed but miniaturized foot. In reality, Dworkin (1974, p. 103) claims, they were 'hideous . . . odiferous, useless stumps.'

Mary Daly (1978, p. 261) found that the 'Golden Lotus', the maimed feet, were meant to resemble vaginas and were considered by men, according to a 'Lotus Knower' (Daly, 1978, p. 138), to have seductive characteristics used as instruments for male sexual arousal. Walker (1983, p. 319) wrote that 'Chinese poets sang ecstatic praises of lotus feet that aroused [men's] desire to fever pitch'. Daly (1978, p. 143) also revealed that men enjoyed squeezing the stumps to the point of causing acute pain, smelling them, biting them and whipping them, stuffing them in their mouths and having their penises rubbed by them.

Contemporary research and writing on Chinese footbinding (Daly, 1978, 1973; Dworkin, 1974, 1981; Prager, 1983; Walker, 1983) reveals that the 'aesthetic' and subsequent 'marriage' justifications which normalized this practice were unfounded. However the belief that only women with lotus hooks would be chosen for high-status positions by wealthy husbands perpetuated a practice which in reality served men's sexual interest. Bound feet provided men with erotic pleasure whilst severely curtailing a woman's way of life and creating a dependent, immobile, readily accessible sexual object.

With the social revolution in the 1920s came the need for women to enter the labour force. The 'normal' and 'typical' practice of footbinding became regarded as abnormal; the tiny 'lotus hooks', which Daly (1978, p. 138) said had been seen as objects of 'fascination and bewilderment for centuries', were suddenly disparaged. Daly (1978, p. 143) wrote that it seemed that 'males were able to change their aesthetic standards for female beauty when their politics required this.' Certainly an altering of a thousand-year view which regarded deformed feet as 'typical', to a view which held the same practice as 'aberrant', highlights the insecurity of the social justifications once the social conditions in which they were performed changed.

African Female Genital Circumcision

Official estimates of genital circumcision made by the World Health Organisation in 1979, according to Steinem (1983, p. 300), were that it had been performed on seventy-five million women. It is practised extensively in Africa and the Middle East, and according to the Minority Rights Group (MRG, 1983, p. 3), endangers 'their lives and their health.' The practice of genital circumcision falls into three main categories as described by Hosken (1982, pp. 26–28):

(i) Sunna Circumcision: Removal of the prepuce and/or tip of the clitoris.
(ii) Excision or Clitorodectomy: Excision of the entire clitoris with the labia minora and some or most of the external genitalia.
(iii) Excision and Infibulation (or Pharmonic circumcision: see El Saadawi, 1980, p. 40 for further discussion on this type): The excision of the entire clitoris, labia minora and parts of the labia majora. The two sides of the vulva (which may be scraped first) are fastened

together. A small opening is left so that urine and menstrual blood can be passed.

One form of circumcision, known as infibulation, is described by M.A.S. Mustafa, and recounted in the thesis of Dr A. David (cited in MRG, 1983, p. 3), entitled 'Infibulation en République de Djibouti'. 'The little girl, entirely nude, is immobilised in the sitting position on a low stool by at least three women. One of them with her arms tightly around the little girl's chest; two others hold the child's thighs apart by force, in order to open wide the vulva. The child's arms are tied behind her back or immobilised by two other women guests. The traditional operator says a short prayer . . . . Then she spreads on the floor some offerings to Allah, split maize, or in urban areas eggs. Then the old woman takes her razor and excises the clitoris. The infibulation follows: the operator cuts with the razor from the top to bottom of the small lip and then scrapes the flesh from the inside of the large lip. This nymphectomy and scrapings are repeated on the other side of the vulva. The little girl howls and writhes in pain, although strongly held down. The operator wipes the blood from the wound and the mother as well as the guests, "verify" her work, sometimes putting their fingers in. The amount of scraping of the large lips depends on the "technical" ability of the operator. The opening left for urine and menstrual blood is miniscule. Then the operator applies a paste and ensures the adhesion of the large lips by means of an acacia thorn, which pierces one lip and passes through into the other. She sticks in three or four in this manner down the vulva. These thorns are then held in place either by means of sewing thread or with horsehair. Paste is again put on the wound. But all this is not sufficient to ensure the coalescence of the large lips; so the little girl is then tied up from her pelvis to her feet: strips of material rolled up into a rope immobilise her legs entirely. Exhausted, the little girl is then dressed and put on a bed. The operation lasts from fifteen to twenty minutes according to the ability of the old woman and the resistance put up by the child."

On the marriage night the abnormal vulva graft and reformed vagina have to be slit on one or both ends with a sharp scalpel or razor or dagger, so that the male organ can be introduced (El Saadawi, 1980, p. 9; MRG, 1983, p. 3). Daly (1979, p. 169) writes that intercourse must be frequent hereafter, to prevent the scar reknitting. If divorce or widowhood occurs some women are restitched to ensure chastity. El Saadawi (1980, p. 9) writes that on remarriage the process of widening is repeated and today, according to Koso-Thomas (1987, p. 1), practices of this severity proceed unabated in rural areas, towns and cities.

The types of circumcision practised seem to be as varied as the different countries or cultures which perform them. Some societies perform the operation on babies as young as a few days old, some at about 7 years, and others shortly before marriage (MRG, p. 3). In most cases however the ritual is conducted when the child is between the ages of 3 and 9 as in the case of Nawal El Saadawi (1980, pp. 7–9).

> 'I was six years old . . . [t]hey carried me to the bathroom . . . then suddenly the sharp metallic edge . . . cut off a piece of flesh . . . I screamed with pain . . . it was like a searing flame . . . I saw a red pool of blood around my hips . . . I wept and called out to my mother for help. But the worst shock of all was when I . . . found her standing by my side.'
> Nawal El Saadawi's personal experience of circumcision led her to describe this practice as a 'barbaric procedure'.

Jomo Kenyatta devotes a chapter in his book *Facing Mount Kenya* (1938, ch. VI) to defending the initiation ceremony of boys and girls in the Gikuyu tribe (the spelling can be either Gikuyu or Kikuyu), for in his view the practice 'is regarded as the conditio sine qua non of the whole teaching of tribal law, religion and morality.' The chapter, however, predominantly describes the girls' initiation; for the boys he details only a two-mile race 'to a sacred tree . . . which they have to climb and break top branches' (p. 140).

The operation on the girls, on the other hand, renders them physically unable to walk for eight to twelve days. Yet according to Kenyatta, 'the clitorodectomy is a mere bodily mutilation' (p. 133). Kenyatta's understanding and description, by necessity second-hand, is in sharp contrast to that of El Saadawi, mentioned earlier.

> '. . . [A] clean cowhide . . . is spread on the ground . . . The girls sit down on the hide, while their female relatives and friends form a sort of circle several rows thick. No male is allowed to go near or even peep through this cordon. Any man caught would be severely punished.
> '. . . Her sponsor sits behind her with her legs interwoven with those of the girl, so as to keep the girl's legs in a steady, open position . . . [ice cold] water is thrown on the girl's sexual organ, to make it numb and to arrest profuse bleeding as well as to shock the girl's nerves at the time, for she is not supposed to show any fear or make any audible sign of emotion or even to blink. To do so would be considered cowardice and make her the butt of ridicule among her companions . . .
> 'A woman . . . takes out from her pocket the operating Gikuyu razor . . . and in quick movements and with the dexterity of a Harley Street surgeon, proceeds to operate on the girls . . . At the time of the

surgical operation, the girl hardly feels any pain for the simple reason that the limbs have been numbed and the operation is over before she is conscious of it' (pp. 145–147).

One of the reasons for the continuation of clitorodectomy as a ritual, according to Kenyatta, is that it serves as a way to remember particular years. 'The history and legends of the people are explained and remembered according to the names given to various age-groups at the time of the initiation ceremony'. The abolition of the 'irua', Kenyatta argues (p. 134), would destroy the tribal calendar system.

The tradition of genital circumcision, however, seems more likely to be perpetuated through social pressure, for Kenyatta (pp. 132–133) states that '[n]o proper Gikuyu would dream of marrying a girl who had not been circumcised'. In fact semi-detribalized Gikuyu who married uncircumcised girls were forced by their parents to 'divorce the wife married outside the rigid tribal custom and then marry a girl with the approved tribal qualifications. Failing this, they [would] have been turned out and disinherited.' It would seem that marriage as a way of life without the necessary surgery was an impossibility. Parents, unwilling to have either themselves or their children ostracized, would conform to the local tradition.

Kenyatta in his book is adamant that Gikuyu circumcision has no long-term effects, nor does harm to the women in the tribe. Yet there are contradictions to his claim. Coote and Campbell (1982, p. 232) recognize that to remove the clitoris is to remove a woman's centre of 'erotic pleasure'. The memorandum prepared by the Mission Council of the Church of Scotland in 1929 leaves no doubt as to the severity of the operations imposed on the girls. The paper (cited in Hosken, 1982, p. 154), reads: 'This operation comprises cutting away the inner and outer soft parts lying around the birth canal . . . The result is the replacement of much of the normal elastic tissues of these parts, with an unyielding ring of hard fibrous tissues. These parts are highly sensitive and the cutting causes great agony. The following . . . have been seen . . . in the Kikuyu (sic) Province . . . Infection of the bladder with danger of spread up to the kidney, sterility owing to impossibility of sexual intercourse . . . [D]uring childbirth . . . the hard fibrous ring . . . hinders . . . stretching so that delay, especially in first births, leads in some cases to the death of the child.'

The difference in attitude and understanding towards this operation is symbolized in the two different descriptors used: genital circumcision or genital mutilation. From the reports made by organizations such as the Mission Council of the Church of Scotland, this operation was considered a mutilation, was extremely dangerous to a girl's health and life, and a barbaric tradition. Moves were made in the 1920s and 1930s to get the Kenyan

Government to abolish the custom. Led by the Duchess of Atholl the attempt 'was an utter failure' (Hosken, 1982, p. 155).

Current writers on the issue of 'genital mutilation' as they call it, Barry (1977), Daly (1978), El Saadawi (1980), Hosken (1982), the Minority Rights Group (1983), Steinem (1983), and Koso-Thomas (1987), are all explicit about the detrimental effects it has. The reasons or justifications for the perpetuation are multiple. Koso-Thomas (1987, p. 5) lists them as being: maintaining a higher degree of cleanliness and good health; the belief in the aesthetical appearance; prevention of stillbirth in primigravida (woman pregnant for the first time); promotion of political and social cohesion; prevention of promiscuity; improvement of male sexual performance and pleasure; increase of matrimonial opportunities; preservation of virginity; and enhancement of fertility. According to Koso-Thomas (1987) none have any real scientific or logical basis (for a detailed discussion on the reasons for the perpetuation of circumcision see Koso-Thomas (1987), 'Female Circumcision' and Hosken (1982, p. 5) states 'the mutilation . . . is not for . . . protection, but is basically a political move to render women powerless and helpless due to their isolation and physical impairment, thus they are easily controlled and exploited by men.' Further she claims (p. 161) that there is no doubt that 'it serves as the underpinning of polygamy, and assures absolute male sexual domination.'

The Similarities between the Female-controlling-practices evident in Footbinding and Genital Circumcision and those found in Sexual Harassment

I have shown how footbinding and genital circumcision are practices which serve to control those people on whom they are performed. In what ways are these practices and their consequences similar to the sexual harassment (here I use the term sexual harassment to cover the broad spectrum of unwanted sexual attention which was experienced by the girls in the research group, sexual attention which ranged from being chased to being raped) experienced by Zohra, Zaheda, Alex, Carmel, Collette, Maria, Annmarie and Jenny? I believe there are a number of significant similarities.

Firstly, there is the control at a cultural level. Footbinding and genital circumcision illustrate the way some societies treated particular groups within their own culture, and, despite the negative consequences for those people, how the customs were generally regarded as 'normal' and 'typical'. Sexual harassment is condoned as 'normal' and 'typical' behaviour in our society and for centuries has been regarded as an acceptable way to treat women. In fact it could be concluded that sexual harassment in some forms is a custom and a tradition in Western society. Touching women, wolf-whistling, making passes and sexual innuendoes are not treated with contempt as aberrant, rather they are shrugged off as 'normal' and customary ways in which men relate to women. It is interesting to speculate whether in other cultures such as China or Africa this kind of Western behaviour would be considered aberrant?

The second control is of a physical nature. Chinese footbinding and genital circumcision controlled women's bodies in a number of ways. Although both dealt with anatomically different parts of the body, both were similar in that they lessened women's ability to be independent. The major and direct controls of women were those of health and mobility. It was difficult for Chinese women to walk, and as Prager (1982, p. 23) describes, carry a baby for nine months, or give birth easily, for according to Daly (1978, pp. 137–141) compressing the feet resulted in thickened thighs and misshapen ankles. Even if an upper-class woman wanted to be active it would have been impossible given her disabled feet.

For the women in Africa who have been circumcised one of the major controls is that of continual ill-health throughout their lives. In the Hosken report (1982, p. 166), a midwife argues that circumcision can result in brain-damaged babies or stillbirths, because of the abnormal delay in the second stage of labour as the hardened scars prevent the perineum dilating adequately. For some women during childbirth, the circumcised orifice results in a rupture of the internal divisions between the vagina and the rectum, leaving her to 'continually dribble urine and faeces' and so to be ostracized by family and society. Koso-Thomas (1987, pp. 10–12) writes that the women she interviewed were unaware 'of what a feeling of wellness [was]'. African women are unaware that their ill-health which negatively controls the quality of their life is as a result of the circumcision.

Clearly the sexually harassing experiences had had an effect on the girls too. Although physical ill-health was not a major factor it could be argued that there were other less tangible controls which reduced their freedom and autonomy. Zohra's life, for example, was circumscribed by the thoughts and fears of her wedding night and the ultimate truth which would be revealed. Carmel was afraid to stay late at school, Collette of coming home at night, Alex of visiting her friends after dark. These fears successfully curtailed their social activities, controls seldom placed on boys. For some, such as Maria, there was the added control of not wanting to return to school after her experience of sexual harassment and thus missing out on lessons. Another consequence for the girls was their fear of being able to conduct a satisfactory sexual relationship with male peers. Zohra was emphatic about not having a sexual relationship with a man to the extent that she was prepared to run away to America on her wedding night. Alex too was frightened of the effects her experience would have on future sexual relationships. Carmel was wary of becoming involved with men and Maria felt that such an experience could be recalled once one was married and expected to have intercourse with one's husband. What is interesting is that like the African women who do not understand that their ill-health is a direct result of circumcision, neither do many women in the West realize that their lack of freedom to walk the streets at night or go to public bars is a direct result of male aggression.

The third direct control arising from these practices was the division it created between the women themselves. Establishing an atmosphere of distrust and fear effectively isolates and maintains control of women whilst giving more power and authority to men. A division between women had been effectively created because of the way in which these practices had developed in China and Africa. Even though the operations clearly benefited men and were detrimental to women, women had become engaged in the perpetuation of the actual operation. This twist, whilst allowing men to benefit in a variety of ways, also exonerated them from any of the direct 'blame'. In examining some of the evidence available it is clear that tension and distrust is fostered amongst the women and girls. One example is El Saadawi's (1980, p. 8) first-hand account of finding her mother responsible for her circumcision. 'But the worst shock of all was when I looked around and found her [my mother] standing by my side. Yes it was her, I could not be mistaken, in flesh and blood, right in the midst of these strangers, talking to them and smiling at them, as though they had not participated in slaughtering her daughter just a few moments ago.'

In Prager's story (1983, p. 27) the mother was aware of the possible consequences her actions might have for she had bound her elder daughter's feet and as a result their relationship had deteriorated. The mother did not want this to happen again so she engaged the services of a footbinder.

Experiencing sexually harassing behaviour can have similarly divisive effects on women and girls as well as promoting power and solidarity amongst men. If we consider Maria's experience, she was ostracized by the girls in the research group because it was felt that she had asked for her harassment. She had 'let down' the female side of society by acting in a way that was considered 'provocative'. I have already described how the girls found it hard to see Rani as the culprit and the protagonist. Our society encourages women and girls to align themselves with the male perception of what has happened, thus creating a situation in which women who do not conform are marginalized by other women. This creates distrust and isolation. Men on the other hand benefit from using sexual harassment for it furthers their control over women and their power, as Mahony (1985, pp. 50–53) and Farley (1978, p. 33) demonstrate.

Because girls are often led to believe that it is only 'loose' women who get attacked, they are reluctant to share their experiences because of what others might say. This isolates the victims in their own world, for they cannot share their burden. By perpetuating the belief that women have to behave in a particular way and by regulating those who don't through criticism, ostracism and contempt, women are successfully divided as a group.

Isolating women from each other not only encourages distrust and fear but also allows a hierarchy to develop. Women who support the male system and 'police' other women have more authority, bestowed on them by men. Koso-Thomas (1987, p. 1) shows how many African women too perpetuate their own oppression, for they are supportive of the traditional patriarchal demands. They 'organis[e] groups which mete out punishment to non-conforming women and conduct hostile campaigns against passive observers'.

One of the features of both the Chinese and African cultures was that a mother was forced by social pressures into continuing these female-controlling-practices, for she was unable to allow her daughter to go 'free' from footbinding or circumcision. This fourth control restricted adult women for if they had refused to perpetuate the tradition, their daughter would have been ostracized and despised and remained unmarried and consequently financially destitute. Thus a mother was caught in a double bind. If she performed the operation herself or was involved in the preparation, she risked damaging her relationship with her daughter, while if she refused to allow the operation to take place her daughter's adult life would be ruined.

Adult women in our society are caught in this double bind too. Why did Annmarie's mother want her daughter to forget about her attempted rape? Was she embarrassed by what others might say or think? Did she believe that in some way her daughter had been responsible for the attack? Whatever the reason was, Annmarie was angry, disappointed and frustrated by this attitude and felt that her mother was isolating her and trivializing the incident. This resulted in Annmarie becoming emotionally more removed from her mother. Similarly both Zohra and Zaheda became isolated from the women who could have helped them talk about their fears. Aunt Reham and Rukeya both refused to discuss the incidents.

All these women were behaving in similar ways to African and Chinese women. By perpetuating the silence about female-controlling-practices the practices could be continued. The result for the women and girls involved was that they felt isolated, marginalized and unable to talk about what they had experienced.

The fifth similarity between all these female-controlling-practices is the long and far reaching effect they have all had. By taking these two extreme cases it was possible to see how ideologies about feminity and masculinity developed and when considering sexual harassment, how these concepts are maintained. The mutilation of women in a way which ensured immobility and unwellness served to exaggerate differences between men's and women's physical capabilities. Women came to be desired for their immobility and their frailty, and men desired for their ability to provide and protect. Femininity was a constructed ideology, encapsulated in passivity, whilst the masculine image became encapsulated in action. With the feminine ideology came dependency and with the masculine ideology came power. The notions of masculinity and femininity became understood as natural rather than constructed.

The practices can be illustrated in the following equation, using footbinding as an example. Women with disfigured feet were considered beautiful and were revered. Therefore women aspired to have lotus hooks in order to belong to this category and were silent about the pain involved. However, once footbound the feet continued to be painful, resulting in immobility and subsequently enforced passivity. Eventually women became identified as naturally passive, helpless creatures and were considered desirable because of these traits. Bound feet thus became a requisite if a woman was to be regarded as sexually desirable. Footbinding was a 'normal' practice for 'normal' upper-class women. On the other hand, natural-footed, active women were identified with coarseness, peasantry and degradation. Upper-class Chinese women did not aspire to this category. Natural-footed women were regarded as 'aberrant'.

In many respects this equation is applicable to girls and women in the West. There is an emphasis on the image of women through fashion, hairstyles, clothes, shoes, and make-up which is 'packaged' and sold to women and girls. Girls who take these fashions seriously are considered feminine, and thus desirable. Girls who are not concerned with this image are considered, like Maria, to have bad dress sense and to be wearing unsuitable clothes. (Interestingly when Maria wore lipstick, a sign that she was following the feminine tradition, she was called a 'tart'). Girls therefore aspire to dress in a way that is considered fashionable and feminine. If they do this with success they are popular, if they fail they are ridiculed. But there are two points to be made here. Firstly, if they dress in a way that oversteps the mark of 'femininity' (wherever that mark may be) and dress 'provocatively' then they are blamed for their own attack. If on the other hand they wear dungarees, flat shoes and no make-up they are considered 'butch' and unfeminine. But if they dress in a way that is considered feminine and 'pretty' the chances are that they are not only wearing clothes and shoes that inhibit their free movement but they are wearing clothes that attract male comment. Tight skirts and high-heeled shoes may not be conducive to an easy getaway, but they are considered feminine.

As a particular kind of 'femininity' was created for Chinese women which only existed in those who fitted into the recognized mould, so it is precisely this situation which faces African girls who have not undergone circumcision or Western girls who refuse to cooperate as feminine models.

In all the practices described those affected were females, resulting in further female oppression and more male control. The continuation of all these practices depended on one important and common feature. For a variety of reasons, the women and girls remained silent about the actual experience as well as the real effect of their experiences. Silence is the sixth common feature which female-controlling-practices share.

The Chinese and African women who were subjected to these female-controlling-practices were brought up to suffer quietly, to put others before themselves, not to complain unduly of their discomforts, to accept the status quo and to underplay depression or distress. There can be no doubt, however, that for many years women suffered far more than 'mere discomforts' (Kenyatta's description of circumcision) from the mutilations imposed on their bodies and minds, which they were powerless to prevent.

Silence was a significant element in the London girls' lives before the disclosures. Alex had told no one of her rape. Zohra had been effectively silenced by her aunt. Zaheda had been denied discussion of her memories with her sister by Rukeya's rejection and dismissal of the subject. Both Jenny and Carmel had remained silent. Silence seems to be a common denominator in female-controlling-practices. When Annmarie and Maria had tried to break the silence by talking some people had ignored or disbelieved them, or had transferred the blame for the attack to the victim.

The fact that many of the girls found themselves in positions where they were not believed or where they were blamed as having been responsible for their own attack not only silenced the girls but must have had an effect on how they perceived themselves. The disjunction between how they remembered the experience and how they were told to perceive it inevitably results in confusion and distortion. For example Annmarie was told to 'forget' the incident by her mother, the attack was trivialized by her boyfriend, the police officer told her she was lying, and the teacher indicated that it was her own fault.

The controls that I have just discussed could be described as primary controls. There are however secondary or indirect controls which female-controlling-practices construct. Immobility made Chinese women entirely dependent upon their men financially, socially and educationally. Knowledge, money and social acquaintances existed outside the domestic sphere and thus were only part of the male world. Upper-class Chinese women were excluded from these aspects of life. African women too because of their ill-health were dependent on their men. The experience of sexual harassment can have a secondary controlling influence too. In order that women do not get sexually harassed, for example in the streets or in the pub, they have two alternatives.

Either they remain at home, which has already been discussed, or else they go out in the company of a man or men. In this way a woman can consider herself relatively 'protected' from other males, because it is recognized that she 'belongs' and is the 'property' of another man.

The final point I wish to make concerns the hidden justifications for the perpetuation of female-controlling-practices. Disabling women, socially, physically or mentally, served and serves the male interest, for women are made increasingly dependent and therefore available for any demands, sexual, emotional or domestic, made upon them. The practices perpetrated on women by men and women, and the purpose for their existence, however, has often been disguised beneath a rhetoric of social justifications. An unacknowledged reason for footbinding, circumcision and sexual harassment was and is the provision these practices made for men's sexual needs. Deformed feet were considered erotic, constricted vaginas a guarantee of virginity, faithfulness and sexual satisfaction for the husband and likewise some of the cases described to me were evidently sexual in motive and gain for the assailants.

The female-controlling-practices of sexual harassment, footbinding and circumcision all are derived from similar sources and have similar outcomes: the need for men to preserve their power; the damage it holds for the female victims; the silence that surrounds the practices; and the distortion as to who is responsible.

Chapter 12

Societal-controlling-mechanisms

In the last chapter I have shown how female-controlling-practices have served to keep women in a particular position, *vis-à-vis* men, in various cultures and societies. The West is no exception. Now I want to extend this theory and to ask the question: If female-controlling-practices are an acknowledged phenomenon why are they continued? After analyzing the data I collected it is my belief that there are mechanisms which silence and suppress and thus undermine many of the problems and realities concerned with its existence. I call these societal-controlling-mechanisms.

In order to describe these mechanisms I will take the specific issue of rape, as a subsection of sexual harassment, and discuss firstly how it is a female-controlling-practice and secondly how societal-controlling-mechanisms perpetuate it.

Rape as a Female-controlling-practice

It is the aim of this section to analyze the characteristics of rape and to suggest that it is as much a female-controlling-practice as those discussed in the previous chapter, for it controls women's lives in a variety of ways. Even though rape is a condition that is not actively sought, but experienced by default, it holds common attributes to the practices discussed above. I suggest that there are two aspects to this issue; the potential that all women have for being raped, and the experience some women have of being raped. One is a collective fear experienced by many women, the other is an individual reality experienced by an indeterminate number of women. I shall take these separately.

Women's Potential for Being Raped

There are three issues associated with the potential for being raped that make just the threat of rape a control in itself: the fear of being raped; the beliefs about women's vulnerability; and the belief that women are complicit in their attack.

The fear of the potential of being raped, Brownmiller claims, is a 'conscious process of intimidation by which all men keep all women in a state of fear' (1975, p. 15). The fear of being attacked and raped is a problem many women carry with them through their lives. One of the ways in which this fear is perpetuated is through the constant reminders that various agencies, such as the police, give of the need for children, adolescent girls and women to be vigilant about strange men.

However, they are also taught that there are ways to avoid these traps. For example, by staying at home, by only going out with 'nice' boys or men, or in groups, by not going out with 'older married men', by not walking at night alone, or going to pubs, rough areas, or deserted parks, by walking only in well-lit streets, by wearing decent and respectable clothes, a girl or woman can save herself from attack. In order to live a safe life, women are encouraged not to lead a 'normal' existence ('normal' in this case meaning men's normality), but to curtail their movements because of what might happen to them.

Girls and women also recognize that, once raped, they occupy a different and negative position in society in comparison with women who have not had this experience, so they have the added responsibility to protect their own reputation which rape would ruin. In addition to taking precautions during leisure time and in the public sphere such as shopping, women frequently have to curtail their professional or working lives, taking jobs which do not involve 'dangerous' travel or unsafe environments which would put them 'at risk'.

The second aspect which leads women and girls to believe that they may be raped is the strength factor. Women and girls learn they are not as strong as men; they will not be able to fight off a would-be rapist so they are vulnerable. Statements such as 'I would be paralysed with fright', 'I wouldn't know what to do', 'I think I would die', all contribute to the belief that once attacked women have no chance. It is also maintained that fighting back can make the man more aggressive and angry, and that rapists are very large, strong youths, or are often black.

The belief, that women are unable to protect themselves, further curtails women's lives. This fear, however, is not necessarily founded on the truth, for rapists, like all men, range in size from large to small, from weak to strong. Peter Sutcliffe, the 'Yorkshire Ripper', is a diminutive man, with size 7 shoes and a 'soft voice' and had always been a 'mother's boy'; John Duffy, the 'railway' murderer and rapist, on trial at the Old Bailey in January 1988, was small in stature, not over five foot six inches tall and weighing probably nine and a half stone; Ian Brady, the 'moors murderer', and John Christie, the killer and necrophile, were not large, heavy men either.

It is generally true, however, that ordinary, untrained women and men have very different physical capabilities. It has been argued that this has more to do with gender stereotyping than potential. As Connell (1987, p. 85) writes, '[t]he social definition of men as holders of power is translated not only into mental body-image and fantasies, but into muscle tensions, posture, the feel and texture of the body. This is one of the main ways in which the power of men becomes "naturalized" '. In this way men are encouraged to take an interest in their fitness, strength and musculature but women are neither encouraged as much, nor given the same opportunity to develop their bodies. Yet if women were trained, the differential between men's and women's physical performances would be reduced. Nicholson (1984, p. 35), claims that 'the difference in physique . . . is exaggerated by the . . . different sorts of lives and [the] . . . different attitudes towards taking physical exercise'. He cites examples of trained athletes, and reveals that women's fastest running time, over an 800-metre track event, has improved by more than eighteen seconds over a forty-year period, whilst that of men has improved by only three seconds. Although men can still run faster, the gap between the fastest man and the fastest woman has been reduced considerably. In swimming the difference is even smaller. The world record set in 1972 by Mark Spitz for the 400 metres free-style was beaten ten years later by a woman. A woman holds the long-distance cross-English-channel swimming record. In Eastern European countries where women athletes receive much more encouragement the measurements of muscle power and lung capacity are much closer than in the West. These figures provide some challenge to the myth that women are always weaker, more passive, and incapable of self-defence or putting up an attack against a would-be rapist. (Evidence which would help to dispel this argument would be very difficult to collect, for there is no research or accumulated evidence that I can find of women who have successfully beaten off attackers. Having more examples of women who fight, and making this publicly known, would help to contradict the 'rapeable woman' syndrome). The social attitudes which support women's vulnerability help rape become a successful female-controlling-practice.

The third aspect affecting the potentiality for being raped is the myth that women who don't want to be raped can't be and as a result some women who are raped are held responsible for the rapist's actions. Judges have given lenient sentences to some rapists, believing either that the woman didn't take enough precautions to protect herself or that she incited the man's passions. Benn *et al.* (1986, p. 3) cite a case in 1982 when a 17-year-old woman was held partially responsible for her rape because the judge deemed her to have been guilty of 'a great deal of contributory negligence'. He claimed that in accepting a lift she had put herself at risk. The rapist was given a four-year sentence. In the early 1970s, Mr Justice Melford imposed a two-year suspended sentence on another rapist, who had also raped a young woman hitchhiker. In both these cases, the women were penalized for showing initiative and making their own choice of transport. By hitching a ride, they were considered at fault. If a woman is raped whilst hitching, it could be concluded that she 'asked for' it. Radford (1987, p. 143) cites a case where another woman was held responsible for her own rape. Here the husband, Mr Mitchell, used domination and force towards his wife, including ' "insistence" on sexual intercourse'. It was deemed by the judge to be a justifiable technique to keep a family from separating.

The fact that women are considered partly responsible for rape and the myth that those women who do not want to be raped won't be only succeeds in making rape, as a female-controlling-practice, more effective. For if it is believed that women are partially responsible, then it must follow that only 'bad' women are raped. If 'good' women do not get raped (and this is determined mainly by the women's compliance with society's advice to stay home or only go out with male protection) a divide is created. This division between different groups of women has, some may argue, been deliberately, yet artificially constructed. By artificially creating categories of 'angels' and 'whores', or between 'rapeable' and 'unrapeable' women, a division is created amongst women themselves. Women who believe that those who get raped have been complicit in their own attack have assimilated societal-controlling-mechanisms, enabling rape as a female-controlling-practice to have more strength and validity.

It seems, therefore, that some women are considered 'rapeable' either because it is thought that they put themselves in dangerous situations and as such deliberately 'ask for it', or they are made to believe they are too weak to defend themselves and therefore accept the attack passively. In this way women are constructed as 'rapeable beings' in this country, as much as the women in China and Africa were footbindable and able to be mutilated. For women who are subjected to either physical or psychological female-controlling-practices, the consequences are similar. Women are often encouraged to become dependent on men, whether for 'protection' from other men, or for sustenance, and because of the controlling influence of the fear of rape, some women may even have to curtail their potential earning capacity.

The Experience of Being Raped

I have discussed the way in which the fear of rape acts as a control even if the act itself has not been committed. I now wish to turn to the actuality of being raped, for here I suggest that the female-controlling-practice gains strength, because of the difference in perception, and consequently definition, that there is between women and men. I propose that the way in which women are considered 'rapeable' has to do with the way in which females and males perceive the act itself, for whether sexual intercourse is defined as love-making or rape depends to some degree on one's gender. As women and men experience sexual intercourse very differently, it is reasonable to suggest that the act of rape would be differently described by both parties.

A letter to the Editor of *The Village Voice*, Philadelphia, Pennsylvania, USA, 22 October 1979, provides an example of how one woman experienced rape. 'Forcible rape is not in any sense intercourse . . . the rapist repeatedly batters with his penis in the very delicate and sensitive features lying outside the vagina, causing the tissue to tear and to bleed. When the force of the thrusting eventually results in the penis entering the vagina, it enters usually no more than a few inches, and . . . the lining of the vagina [is] . . . ripped and torn' (Stanko, 1985, p. 34).

Male writers have a different perception. Ogden Nash is reported to have said '[s]eduction is for sissies; a he-man wants his rape', and Norman Mailer to have written '[a] little bit of rape is good for a man's soul' (cited in Russell, 1984, pp. 117–119). In Rhinehart's novel, *The Dice Man*, Luke's expression of his intention to commit rape, his advances and violence towards Arlene perpetuate the view that women are unconsciously wanting to be 'taken'. Rhinehart's description of rape is presented as the epitome of male-female sexual relations.

Research into male attitudes towards rape further points to the discrepancy in perception between men and women. In one survey Briere, Malamuth, and Ceniti (cited in Russell, 1984, p. 122), asked 356 American male subjects the following question: 'If you could be assured that no one would know and that you could in no way be punished for engaging in the following acts, how likely, if at all, would you be to commit such acts?' Among the sexual acts listed were 'forcing a female to do something that she really didn't want to do' and 'rape'. Sixty per cent of the male sample indicated that under the right circumstances (i.e. anonymity and promise of no punishment), there was some likelihood that they would use force, or rape, or both, against women.

Bromberg and Coyle's claim (1974) (cited in Schram, 1978, p. 56), that the average convicted rapist does not perceive himself as an aggressive man, either during or after the offence, helps clarify this point. Some rapists prefer to see their act as evidence of a sexual need, and they believe other men understand this motive. A rapist interviewed in *Men on Violence* (LWT Production 7 August 1988, director Nicholas Metcalf) felt that the rape he committed was due to his sexual frustration and lack of a suitable female partner. However it is not only men who believe this. Women, too, are brought up to believe that men, once sexually excited, are uncontrollable. As I have already argued, raped women are still seen as being complicit in their own rape, for it is to do with what they are perceived as having done, worn, said, not said, or been. They must take responsibility for arousing men's passions. Forced sexual intercourse can be reframed as a 'natural' male sexual drive, rather than a violation of woman. Whilst women are taught that rape is a 'normal' male activity, rape will continue to be a female-controlling-practice.

Rape as a violation of women can exist because the differences in perception are not clearly articulated in our society, nor are the different viewpoints considered having equal value and validity. Rather, it is the male perspective that is taken as the 'truth'. This one-sided 'truth' calls into question whether there is such a thing as an 'objective' or a 'subjective' reality of rape.

Rape is defined by describing the act in an 'objective' way from a particular position. This 'objectivity' is created by a social process which constructs a reality by defining as 'knowledge' what it sees as existing. Rape is not perceived by women and men as the same thing, in terms of experience or acts, nor in terms of descriptions, but the definition which is given more validity is that of the men, because of the controlling position they hold in society. Consequently the definitions that are in common usage must be regarded as only partial 'truths'. This is not to suggest that men or women are deliberately defining rape differently, or even providing a dishonest description, but that they arrive at their perceptions and understandings from different experiences, overlaid with the common societal framework.

It could be argued that there is no such thing as a category of 'being' free of social perception. For perception is a social construction, created by those who have had the authority to decide how things will be interpreted. Men have been in the position to force their view upon the world through having a monopoly on art, literature, politics, finance, technology, thought and all other institutions and consequently the majority of 'valid' perspectives are derived from the male standpoint, describing not only their world but that of women as well. MacKinnon (1983, p. 636) argues that '[t]he male perspective is systemic and hegemonic'. Although it must be recognized that the traditional male standpoint is not always every man's opinion, most men tacitly agree to it without considering it a particular point of view. This is one of the fundamental problems in defining rape. The view that what we 'see' is how things 'are' does not challenge the position that how things 'are' is a male-imposed awareness.

One of the traditional perspectives that exists in the controversy over rape is that women enjoy harsh sexual treatment and that they have an unconscious desire to be raped by their husband or lover or even, in some cases, by a stranger. (Nancy Friday's (1973) research into women's sexual fantasies gives examples of women who fantasize about being raped. Fantasies cannot however be directly linked with actual desire. It could be argued that many people have different fantasies, precisely because they are 'safe' daydreams. Friday (1973, pp. 108–109) argues rape fantasies in this way. 'By putting herself in the hands of her fantasy assailant, by making him an assailant – she gets him to do what she wants him to do, while seeming to be forced to do what he wants. Both ways she wins . . . Fantasy need have nothing to do with reality, in terms of wish-fulfilment'.) This erroneous belief was the linchpin of a gang rape in 1975 in Britain. William Morgan invited three friends to have intercourse with his wife at their home. He warned the men that she might put up some resistance, that this was part of her sexual enjoyment and they were to take no notice. That three men could engage in a gang rape, despite the woman's repeated protests, and still reasonably believe the husband's assurances that the wife was enjoying herself, makes plain the power that exists in rape myths. To continue to believe that rape is enjoyed by some women helps to maintain the status quo and 'normality'.

The 'normal' point of view makes sense of men's experiences and their interests, yet claims to represent the female perspective as well. Because it is the standard way of seeing the world, and is considered the 'rational' way of interpreting life, women are forced into accommodating this view too. Stanko (1985, p. 9) asserts that '[c]ast in a mould constructed within male-dominated society, women's experience of sexual and physical violation takes on an illusion of normality, ordinariness'. Consequently there are some problems for women in describing their lives in these terms for some, if not all, of their experiences are forced to fit a model which does not easily bend to take the female perspective. Thus some women live within a life of contradiction for at least some of their experiences. There are some women who accept and adopt the male standpoint, as we have seen in the Chinese and African cultures, and in the way some women consider raped women to have been complicit in their own rape. This is not uncommon, for women are rewarded for agreeing with 'societal' values, even at the expense of their autonomy. Having these attributes ensures that the woman will continue to 'enjoy' male protection, as long as she agrees not to challenge the dominant and 'normal' perspective.

Many people believe it is less traumatic to be raped by someone one is close to, than by a stranger. Yet I would suggest that this is a male-centred perception, rather than a woman-centred experience. Being raped by a stranger has 'advantages'. Firstly, the woman may well never see this man again. (Because, according to Schram (1978, p. 55), only 3 per cent of rapists are convicted and sentenced and, according to the London Rape Crisis Centre, as few as 25 per cent of raped women make a report, the likelihood of a woman meeting a rapist in court is slim.) Secondly, there is no emotional attachment to the attacker, he was not known before and there are no memories of happier days. Thirdly, the fact that the rapist was a stranger, and not a person she chose as her partner, relieves the woman of self-accusation. She can console herself with the thought that to the rapist she was 'just a woman'.

However to be raped by a man with whom one lives, whom one trusted and loved, with whom one may have had children, with whom one had at least some shared past, is, I would suggest, very traumatic. It calls into focus the woman's perceptions of the man she has 'chosen' to marry or live with, it raises issues about trust and loyalty, and it creates problems with naming. Wives are reluctant, and in some cases unable, to see their husband's unwanted sexual approaches as rape, for women have been raised with a perception of intercourse which has the male experience defining what is 'normal'.

The way in which society is defined, it can be argued, represents a particular male hegemony, manifestations of which can be found in the law and its enactment, the media and its presentation and the government and its policies. The dominant perspective of the world informed by this hegemonic masculinity is subscribed to by many, particularly powerful men for it serves their interests. Thus what constitutes the difference between rape and intercourse in the courts becomes a matter of deciding which perspective is taken as the 'true' one, often centring on the issue of force. The level of force, however, is determined by what men count as 'normal' sexual relations, not by how women perceive force. But there are further problems for what a woman experiences as intercourse may have been described for her by her husband as 'normal' sex and she may have no other experience on which to base her judgement. This results in women perceiving and describing rape, or at least unwanted sexual intercourse, as 'normal' sexual relations and therefore applying inappropriate naming which obscures reality. I would suggest that forced sexual intercourse in marriage is not exceptional, and reflects the feminine and masculine divide of gender roles.

As most women do not see coerced sex as rape neither do most men convicted of rape believe that they have committed a crime, rather that what they have taken as being 'normal' sex, a woman has exaggerated and named 'rape'. But as many men are systematically conditioned not to notice what women want anyway, there is the possibility that they may not understand the woman's communication patterns. Not only may they not recognize a woman's indifference or revulsion to sex as non-consent, they may even misinterpret the signs the woman gives and believe she enjoyed the experience. Some rapists even ask the victim if she liked what they were doing, if she would see them again, and when leaving tell her that they love her. Women engaged in unwanted intercourse, through coercion rather than force, use a variety of survival strategies; some may ignore the request, plead illness or indisposition, remain passive, begin another activity such as reading, or feign sleep. Men may take these signs as consent, or at least churlish acquiescence.

Women have had little opportunity to create their own descriptions for themselves. Spender (1980, pp. 179–80) writes that for women rape is 'an event which cannot be readily symbolised in our language, for the only name which is available names the experience as males see it, as it pertains to them, and there is a huge discrepancy between male and female experience of this event. The meanings of the dominant group are sufficiently inadequate for females to be completely false'. It is because phenomena such as rape have such an inadequate definition for describing the female perspective that some women, e.g. feminists, have begun to view the world in a different way and to challenge the one 'objective' way of looking. These women who find that their experiences just do not and will not fit within the male-defined 'rational' way of looking at the world, have made a new framework which puts at its centre female understanding. Challenging the given labels in the language, and changing the emphasis on female-experienced phenomena, may reduce the likelihood of rape continuing as a female-controlling-practice.

It must be recognized, however, that any new and different way of perceiving the world will not deliver a new unbiased objectivity. For the one which is informed by women is equally one-sided and equally different from that provided by men. Thus I am not arguing for one ultimate 'truth', but rather a way of explaining why women's perspectives need to be dealt with in a way which is comprehended and respected. The way which is often labelled the 'feminist' perspective is ignored or described as a polemic. Yet the purpose of a feminist critique is to give validity to women's and girls' experiences and to claim those experiences as the experience of women. Brownmiller's (1975, p. 18) definition of rape is feminist oriented. 'If a woman chooses not to have intercourse with a specific man and the man chooses to proceed against her will, that is a criminal act of rape'. Seen this way it is not so much what rape is, but the way it is described by those involved, which is significant. As gender bias prevails for everyone concerned in a rape case, the rapist, the woman, the jury and the judge, it is reasonable to suggest that judgement about the contested intercourse will be determined by those with the arguments which fit with the 'reality' of the world, as it is usually viewed, that is, from the male perspective.

If acts of unwanted intercourse are not labelled 'rape', but are 'normalized' (rather than seen as 'aberrant'), rape, and also the threat of rape, can operate within our society as a phenomenon that does not need discussing for it is considered an unremarkable or 'typical' occurrence which obscures its revelation as a means of continuing women's subordination. Further it seems that the true effect of rape on women is hidden by strategies of which one is an inaccurate assessment of the act which has suppressed the facts, hidden the women and girls who have been raped and underestimated the number of victims. Consequently raped women and girls believe that they are one of the 'unlucky' few, rather than of many. If acts of unwanted intercourse were given a female oriented definition, a different proportion of rape cases would emerge. Trivialization, incorrect naming, and different perceptions, resulting in silence and suppression, have had their effect in perpetuating a view of rape as 'typical', even 'normal', behaviour. It is to a consideration of how these operate that the second half of this chapter is devoted.

The Societal-controlling-mechanisms which Hide the Female-controlling-practice of Rape

Silence and suppression are fundamental to the survival of societal-controlling-mechanisms for I believe they distort the 'true' picture of rape. The two mechanisms are closely related although there are important distinctions to be made between them. Suppression is applied by others, both men and women, whilst silence is self-imposed. Firstly I will show how there have been cases of rape which have been deliberately suppressed. Secondly I will discuss the way in which the act of rape has been silenced through women themselves remaining silent.

I am not, however, arguing that the women and men using these two strategies, silence and suppression, have a free 'choice' as to whether they make public, or keep private, the incidents of rape. The societal-controlling-mechanisms are so subtle that, as I argued in the previous section, the 'normal' point of view (or male point of view) does not make them problematic and so they continue.

Suppressing Rape

Particular incidents of rape have been suppressed, through reanalysis and rewriting, resulting in a distortion of the true extent to which women and girls have been victims of unwanted intercourse and sexual abuse.

It is often thought that women and girls exaggerate, fantasize, or lie about the issues of sexual attack, sexual harassment, rape and incest. Freudian theory would appear to have reinforced this idea. It has recently been claimed by Jeffrey Masson (1984), psychoanalyst and projects director of the Freud Archives at the Library of Congress, New York, that Freud himself intentionally suppressed a key finding from his early work, concerning sexual molestation, or what he called 'seduction'. Basing his research on previously unpublished letters, Masson argued that Freud found irrefutable evidence as to the prevalence and reality of child sexual abuse. Initially Freud was quite prepared to accept that women's experiences of childhood sexual interferences were real, for in the paper he gave in 1896 to the Society for Psychiatry and Neurology in Vienna, 'The Aetiology of Hysteria' (cited in Masson, 1984, pp. 259–269), he declared 'the most important finding that is arrived at if an analysis is thus consistently pursued is this. Whatever case and whatever the symptom we take as our point of departure, in the end we infallibly come to the field of sexual experience. So here for the first time we seem to have discovered an aetiological precondition for hysterical symptoms'.

Freud's research was based on laborious individual examinations which had in most cases taken up a hundred or more hours of work. He concluded that the cause of 'hysteria' in all the eighteen cases he studied was a traumatic sexual experience. The traumas ranged from attempted rape and the witnessing of sexual acts between parents, to experiences which were 'astonishingly trivial'. Beneath every case of hysteria, he believed, was 'one or more occurrences of premature sexual experience'. Moreover Freud was 'inclined to suppose that children [could not] find their way to acts of sexual aggression unless they [had] been seduced previously' (Masson, 1984, pp. 269–277).

His paper was ignored or ridiculed by the other members of the Society. Later, after a variety of personal and professional problems, and according to Masson the threat from colleagues that if he pursued this line of thinking he would be ostracized from psychoanalysis, Freud reneged. His new analysis of his patients' experiences was that they were lying to themselves and to him. He developed a theory instead that the disturbing reports of childhood assault and sexual trauma were fantasies which the girl used as a defence against her own autoerotic experiences and her guilty wish to sleep with her father. Freud's capitulation resulted in his assertion, 'I was at last obliged to recognise that the scenes of seduction had never taken place and that they were only fantasies which my patients had made up'.

However it was not just a case of Freud disbelieving his patients. Even when he had irrefutable proof that the women were telling the truth (such as corroboration by another woman or a brother), Freud ignored this evidence too. Freud's deliberate suppression was maintained by his family and other eminent psychoanalysts after his death and up until 1982. This act of suppression has resulted in a belief that men, especially fathers and husbands, do not rape their daughters and wives. I suggest this view supported the publicly acceptable notion that rape was a rare occurrence, while fantasy rapes were common. In order to silence Masson's controversial claims he was dismissed from the Freud Archives, and was served a $13,000,000 lawsuit, for he had challenged the established view that women lie about sexual advances, the position which Freud, his family and friends had succeeded in maintaining.

The suppression of this evidence has had many consequences. The myth that women and girls lie about their traumatic experiences has resulted in women being at best dismissed, and at worst treated severely, in order to elicit the truth. Freud's 'findings' gave 'validity' and power to the superstition that women could never be trusted. Thus a 'truth', which contradicted the findings Freud himself gathered from 'laborious individual examinations', to use his own words, giving women and girls grounds for claiming their experiences were real, was deliberately suppressed.

The fact that little girls and women are not believed by their parents, family or friends, as a result of the myth that they lie and fantasize about sexual experiences, is one that can be readily found in many autobiographical and biographical works (Bell, 1976; Armstrong, 1978; Rush, 1980, p. 61; Allen, 1980; Spring, 1987). These have been published in the last few years in the wake of a reversal in beliefs, by some sectors of the community, about the truthfulness of accounts by women and girls about unwanted sexual experiences.

The suppression of evidence led, not surprisingly, to the view that many men on sexual offence charges were victims themselves of female ire and some men were subsequently exonerated. The inaccuracies which developed have become hard to dislodge. Alfred Kinsey, the American sexologist of the 1950s, contributed to the belief that old men were incapable of molesting children thus bolstering Freud's earlier claim and successfully subjecting more young children to silence and scepticism. Even today this myth has not been totally eradicated if one views the probation Judge Kenneth Cooke gave to a 61-year-old man with three previous convictions for sexual assaults and indecent assault. On this occasion he had sexually assaulted a 4-year-old girl (*Daily Telegraph*, 7 August 1987). It is interesting to speculate as to how much of the judge's sentence was influenced by the residual myths of little girls' dishonesties, and old men's sexual incapabilities, given powerful legitimacy by Freud and Kinsey.

I have given the example of Freud's patients, who tried to make public the fact that they had been raped, abused or molested. They were not believed, and the information was suppressed. There is another type of suppression of female experiences and that is of the rape of women in war. Rape in this context has been legitimated in several ways. Firstly there is the problem of the control of soldiers in a foreign country, for one commanding officer is often responsible for 500 men. Brownmiller (1975, p. 31) quoted General George Patton of the US Army as saying in the second world war, '. . . in spite of my most diligent efforts [to stop men], there [will] unquestionably be some raping . . . '. Secondly there is the tacit belief that a conquering army can take the 'spoils of war' which include the bodies of women and girls. Thirdly, there is the belief that men away from their regular heterosexual partner, be it wife or girlfriend, will become uncontrollable without regular sexual release. If local women are available there is no immediate problem. In cases where there is a shortage of women and girls, or there is a likelihood of the women infecting the men with venereal disease, it has been known for military brothels to have been set up and maintained by the occupying army. According to Barry (1979, pp. 70–71), women and girls are procured from around the world 'to stock military bordellos'. She cites Pouf, a brothel within the barracks of the French Foreign Legion in Corsica, where women were forced to 'receive 60 to 80 Legionnaires a day', until the situation came to light in 1977. According to a Legionnaire of fifteen years' service, the bordellos were set up by the military leaders. Brownmiller (1975, pp. 91–95) described how prostitution was introduced for the American military in Vietnam by degrees. Initially bars were set up, then massage parlours and a shanty town of brothels which ringed the bases, until finally women were accommodated in 'two concrete barracks, each about one hundred feet long'. Here they lived and worked servicing 'the four-thousand-man brigade. Each building was outfitted with two bars, a bandstand, and sixty curtained cubicles . . . '. The women who formed the stock for these brothels were displaced refugees. They were forced into this position because of their inferior status created by the war, and because they had lost their families, friends and homes. 'The American military, which kept its hands partially clean by leaving the procurement and price arrangements to Vietnamese civilians, controlled and regulated the health and security features of the trade'.

The suppression of rape during war can occur either through a country's deliberate attempts to conceal the large-scale rape of conquered women, or through the individual war correspondent's 'choice' not to write about individual incidents. Two examples of the deliberate suppression of large-scale violations are the cases of the Rape of Nanking, and the rape of more than a quarter of a million Moslem women in Bangladesh. In December 1937 Japanese soldiers invaded Nanking, China's capital city, and raped approximately 20,000 women and girls in the city during the first month of occupation. Top security instructions were given to commanders in the field to repress information leaking to the world press for they were aware that rape was an unconscionable crime under the Hague Convention. Some stories however did appear in foreign newspapers. Brownmiller (1975, p. 62) cites one of the violations suppressed by the Japanese commanders. '. . . At . . . . . we captured a family of four. We played with the daughter as we would with a harlot. But as the parents insisted that the daughter be returned to them we killed them. We played with the daughter as before until the unit's departure and then killed her'.

The rape of the women in Bangladesh, mostly Moslems, in 1971–72 went largely unreported. The Bengali government declared independence in March 1971, and troops from West Pakistan were flown in to quell the rebellion. During the fighting between 200,000 and 400,000 women were raped. In the aftermath thousands of illegitimate babies were born. It was rumoured that the raping was a deliberate conspiracy on the part of the West Pakistanis, to create a new race of Pakistani/Bangladeshi people. Neither the rape of the Moslem women nor that of the Chinese women were well reported; the suppressions were clearly successful.

Incidents of rape can also be effectively suppressed by individuals. Because rape in war is considered a legitimate male act, soldiers are given tacit licence to rape. Tacit behaviour is condoned behaviour and as such so unremarkable that rarely, if ever, were sexual violations of women considered newsworthy enough to be reported by war correspondents. Ignoring particular aspects of war results in reports which are only partially accurate. In this way certain aspects and manoeuvres are given primacy, others are marginalized. Death, fighting, and acts of bravery were reported with impunity; rape was unacceptable yet inevitable, normal, unnewsworthy and silenced through non-reporting.

Dan Rather, a CBS correspondent assigned to Vietnam in 1965–66, said 'Rape was not something that was foremost in my mind when I talked to people . . . My average story was shooting, shelling and bombing . . . I never did a rape story, and if you had been doing my job I don't think you would have, either. Everywhere you looked there was a horror and a brutality . . . My own limited experience led me to conclude that everyone who passed through a village did it – steal a chicken and grab a quick piece of ass . . . ' (Brownmiller, 1975, pp. 91–92). Peter Arnett, a New Zealander and Associated Press correspondent in Vietnam for eight years, also ignored the issue of rape even though he heard screams when interrogation units led women into the forest. His justification for silence was that '[t]he South Vietnamese are a private people and it was always done quietly' (Brownmiller, 1975, p. 89).

Rather's claim that everyone grabbed a 'piece of ass', and Arnett's comment that the South Vietnamese raped in private, are these men's way of suppressing the fact of rape in war. Death and killings were common, yet they were still reported. Rape of women was common, but this was considered unnewsworthy. Was this because it was considered a 'normal' and 'typical' way for soldiers to behave, or because it would be disloyal to print this type of story in the national newspapers back in the soldiers' home country? Whatever the correspondents' reasons, the fact remains that this type of rape was deliberately and effectively suppressed.

If particular aspects of life, and in particular rape, have been deliberately suppressed by men, this has an effect on women. Incidents that are deemed not to have existed, or are suppressed because they are so 'bad' or so 'normal', create for society in general, and women in particular, the impression that these incidents did not exist, cannot have happened and furthermore if you had had first-hand experience your experience was indeed wrong. I have argued that rape can be suppressed via large scale organizations or by individual people. Both forms of suppression result in a lack of information, leading to a lack of recognition, culminating in the absence of a problem. Suppression is an effective mechanism in the maintenance of social control.

Silencing Rape

Silence by women about rape is a self-imposed act, but not one, I would argue, that arises from free choice. The 'choice' women have does not come from a position of 'innocent until proven guilty', for disclosure is often overshadowed by women's awareness of the consequences disclosure would bring. It is unlikely that women will report incidents if they are fearful of being called a liar, if they fear they will not be taken seriously, if they think little will be done to apprehend the assailant, or if they fear the treatment they will receive will be counter-productive for them. The following examples reveal reasons why women may be reluctant to break the silence of rape.

In England in January 1982 there was a furore when a television programme showed how a woman who was claiming rape was treated by the police. Although a widespread condemnation of the programme ensued, this type of revelation did not help women see their reception at a police station as being a positive experience. Benn *et al.* (1986, p. 13) give an example of a police rape interviewing strategy found in *Police Review*: 'If a woman walks into a police station and complains of rape with no signs of violence she must be closely interrogated. Allow her to make a statement to a policewoman and then drive a horse and cart through it. It is always advisable, if there is any doubt about the truthfulness of her allegations, to call her an outright liar'. It seems that a woman is vulnerable to mistreatment by the police unless there is irrefutable evidence as to her innocence.

When a woman pursues a rape case through the courts, there are reasons to believe that she may receive unwelcome and demoralizing treatment at the hands of a judge or through the comments of journalists and press reporters. Among others, Judge Sutcliffe (cited in Lowe, 1984, p. 81) said of a rape victim's testimony '[w]omen in particular and small boys are liable to be untruthful and invent stories'. John Junor, writing for the *Sunday Express* (10 July 1988, p. 16) commented on a rape case in the leader column: 'Despite the shrill screeches of protest from feminist movements, and the angry demands for the removal from the Bench, the judge who sentenced a 22-year-old lorry driver to just one month in prison for breaking into a nurse's home and then trying to rape her defends his judgement as "absolutely fair". And I agree with him'. Junor describes the event and concludes, 'If a woman acts like a tart, should she be at all surprised if she is treated like one?'

Societal attitudes towards rape reflect the general opinion that experiences of rape should be kept private. No matter how 'innocent' the woman or girl, the prevailing attitude is that rape is a shameful and degrading experience. The less said to anyone, police, parents, husband or friends, the better. A woman who is raped can find herself ostracized by the society in which she lives, convincingly dissuading others from reporting their rape.

Married women are often reluctant to tell their husbands that they have been victims of a sexual attack. Wives who disclose sometimes find their husbands unable to cope with the situation for they fear that in some way she 'asked for it' or enjoyed it, or that she has been sullied; they may file for divorce. (In literature Thomas Hardy (1891, Ch. 35) took this exact situation and showed how Tess, the raped heroine of *Tess of the d'Urbervilles*, was deserted by her husband.) Women remain silent, then, for fear of ostracism from society, family and friends, and of mistreatment by the police and the law courts.

Many women are sceptical of the punishment that will be applied if the rapist is caught and prosecuted. The average sentence for convicted rapists, according to the London Rape Crisis Centre (1984, p. 27), is between two and four years. In 1980, out of 421 men found guilty of rape in England and Wales, only four received life imprisonment. Over 50 per cent received sentences of three years or under. The sentences given to the men who were responsible for the so-called 'vicarage rape' were considered lenient by some (*Guardian*, 4 February 1987, p. 12). In this case, three men broke into a vicarage, two raped a young woman, and all three assaulted the vicar and the young woman's boyfriend and burgled the house. Mr Justice Leonard sentenced the older man to fourteen years' imprisonment, but he had not been one of the rapists. The two younger men received sentences of five years each and in addition, one had to serve a further five years for 'aggravated burglary', the other, three years. The rapists received ten and eight years respectively, in comparison with the burglar's longer sentence. It is understandable that women decide not to report a rape attack and pursue it through the courts, if the result is that aggravated burglary accrues greater punishment than rape.

When rape is not treated seriously women tend to conclude that nothing will be gained from making a report. According to the London Rape Crisis Centre figures (1984, p. 27), 19 per cent of rapists are not immediately imprisoned. A Parole Board's decision in one case (*Daily Telegraph*, 14 January 1988) to release a convicted rapist who had only served a quarter of his sentence is evidence of the laxity shown towards some offenders. The man was given parole on three separate occasions and each time he assaulted or raped other women. In another instance a man was released by police after committing two rapes and went out and raped seven more times. The prosecuting counsel said there were 'good reasons' why the man was freed (*Guardian*, 3 March 1988, p. 3).

The examples I have given are some of the reasons why women decide not to report an attack. The London Rape Crisis Centre estimate that only 25 per cent of attacks are reported, and this may be an over-estimate according to Gies *et al.* (1984, p. 59). Answers in a questionnaire distributed in 1977 to 128 police surgeons, of whom five were female, showed that there was a wide range in the number of rapes believed to take place, compared with those reported. Two of the surgeons believed that every case was known and two others believed that only one in a hundred came to the attention of the authorities. I suggest that the number of rapes which go unreported is largely speculation but that the majority of rapes remain undisclosed, because of the pressures which encourage women to remain silent.

The myth which was given academic weight by Freud, that women lie, is not verified by women writers and researchers. Hall (1985, p. 22) claims that there is no evidence to show that women are prone to 'cry rape', indeed she argues that the opposite is true. Women continually make light of tragedies, downgrading the importance of their own experience. Hobbs and Wynne (*The Lancet*, 10 October 1987, pp. 837–841), two paediatricians, reported that 'children relate only a small part of the abuse they have suffered', and from Constance Nightingale's (1988) personal testimony it is clear that some girls who have been sexually abused remain silent well into adulthood.

Thus the attitudes endorsed by Freud have led women and girls to suppress their own experiences, because they are unlikely to be believed. The evidence in the last chapter documented the extreme pain, humiliation and oppression that women and girls suffered and yet were prepared to accept. Hall (1985, p. 25) claims that '[i]t is common . . . for women to absorb within themselves the pain of violent, degrading, and undermining assaults. If the assaults are by their husband or father, for instance, they may go on for years.' In another context Wendy Savage (1986, p. 21) wrote that women did not complain about the pain of childbirth despite the adversity they faced. The suppression of the suffering woman's experience, the myth that women 'cry wolf', and that little girls are complicit in their seduction, further encourages the victimized woman or girl to remain silent.

I have given examples to show how the police, the courts, the authorities, and the family and friends of raped women, actually use strategies which ignore female-centred and female-defined problems. These are the societal-controlling-mechanisms to which I have referred. The result of these practices is that the women turn to silence, rather than face blame, cross-examination, a 'bad' reputation, unkindness, trivialization, humiliation and scepticism.

The examples given were mainly of women who were raped by people outside their known environment. Rape by a man one knows is a different and more difficult issue again. I have already shown, in the last section, how men may not realize they are applying unwanted pressure, coercion or force to their wife or lover. I have already explained how the difference in perception can account for the discrepancy between the male and female definition of rape. I now wish to extend my argument to show that societal-controlling-mechanisms not only silence the women who are raped by strangers, but also silence women who are not necessarily aware that they too are victims of unwanted intercourse.

There is evidence that there are many more incidents of rape which are not recognized and therefore not named 'rape', which remain silenced and invisible for they pass as 'normal' and 'typical' marital behaviour. Rape in a long-term relationship often remains unchallenged precisely because women find it difficult to define unwanted intercourse by their lover or husband as rape. Kelly (1987, pp. 57–58) cites just one instance: 'I remember an occasion where he wouldn't let me go, and he was very strong. He pulled my arms above my head, I didn't put up much of a struggle. I mean I wouldn't have seen that as rape because I associated rape with strangers, dark, night and struggle. I didn't put up much of a struggle, but I didn't want to, so in a sense that was rape, yes'. Here it is clear that this woman does not readily equate unwanted sexual intercourse by her husband with rape, for rape by a husband in this country is not accepted as a problem, indeed it is deemed not to exist, for it is lawful according to the Sexual Offences (Amendment) Act 1976.

The problem associated with defining something which is not deemed to exist, which has no vocabulary to describe it, which has no legal status, with which some people do not agree, and which has no forum for discussion outside the relationship, all contribute to the isolation of women. Women's isolation and their inability to share or recognize the true significance of their experiences is a universal problem. Women in Britain in the 1980s, in relationships where their partner forces sexual intercourse on them, do not consider that they have been raped and neither do they regard themselves as recipients of a female-controlling-practice. Further, neither the raped nor the footbound wife realizes that the silence about the practices is in fact one way in which men can continue to have sexual satisfaction in a way that physically or psychically controls women.

Incidents of rape have been largely suppressed and silenced through a variety of strategies and by a variety of people. However there is evidence to show that attitudes towards rapists and the women attacked are changing. It is not so much through the work of individual judges, police officers, politicians or magistrates that change is happening, but by the pressure being exerted by women's groups, particular sectors of the general public, trade unions and the influx of television programmes, books, and articles on the subject.

The way in which public opinion can be judged to have changed is in the reaction to particular incidents captured by the media. The lenient sentencing of the vicarage rapists, cited earlier, provoked widespread coverage of the anger the general public felt and prompted editorial comments in national newspapers (*Guardian*, 4 February 1987, p. 12; *Times*, 4 February 1987, p. 10).

Judge John Turner was recently reported to the Lord Chancellor for his lenient sentencing of a rapist. According to *The Independent* (18 May 1988), the 19-year-old assailant was convicted by a jury of raping a 16-year-old girl. It was reported that '[i]n passing sentence the Judge said: "Many people might criticise this sentence as light. But there is a difference in the varying circumstances in which this offence was committed. Rape can be serious and not so serious and this falls very much at the lower end of the scale, and I can pass the least possible sentence" '. Although not indicative of a judge who is aware of the implications of rape, the outcry and subsequent reporting indicates that many members of the community were angry with the judge's comments and sentence.

Recently, too, in another case already cited (*Daily Telegraph*, 6 July 1988, p. 3), there is evidence that the general public are no longer willing to accept that a woman is responsible for a rape offence even if she has behaved apparently 'provocatively'. A 22-year-old lorry driver was reported to have met a 42-year-old nurse at a New Year's Eve party. Apparently the woman had lifted her skirt to show her underwear. The man had 'insisted' on walking her home, they had kissed, and the woman had said 'no' to any further intimacy. The man left, but returned later that same night, broke into her flat and attempted rape. He was given a sentence of one month. The judge said that he hoped the man's employers would regard the sentence as 'holidays' and that the man would be allowed to keep his well-paid job. Vociferous outrage from women's groups who called the sentence 'a mockery' and an outcry from telephone callers to the *Jimmy Young Programme*, BBC Radio, on Wednesday 6 July 1988, declaring their anger at such a sentence, shows how public opinion is changing, despite the actions of some judges and journalists.

Although there is room for further improvement, it is clear that there has been change on a public level. Police forces are adopting a different approach to women who have been raped. The Metropolitan Police Commissioner, Sir Peter Imbert, fiercely criticized an insensitive rape interview scene in the BBC TV programme *Eastenders* (*Guardian*, 14 July 1988), in which the officer suggested that the victim had encouraged the sex attack. The chairman of the Police Federation, Mr Leslie Curtis, also condemned the portrayal and said 'for several years great emphasis has been laid on a sympathetic approach to sexual offences. This crude portrayal could undo public confidence and make victims of real attacks hesitate about going to the police.' Rape suites are available in some of the larger police stations, and it is now possible for a victim to ask that a woman police officer deal with her case. Some raped women have reported the 'very helpful and sensitive' treatment they have received from the police (Hall, 1985, p. 107), and requests for an examination by a woman police surgeon or one's own doctor can be made. Rape Crisis Centres, which began as a small enterprise in the early 1970s, are now national, and although still run and organized by volunteers are funded to some extent by the government. The Sexual Offences (Amendment) Act 1976 brought changes to the laws and women who make a charge of rape are provided protection through anonymity as well as protection from having to answer questions about their previous sexual experiences.

Conclusion

The research that was undertaken into the sexual harassment of schoolgirls by their male teachers did not reveal any incidents of this phenomenon at all. In this way the project failed. However, even though the project may not have met its stated objectives it is undeniable that valuable and interesting data were found. Therefore the first question which must be addressed is: does sexual harassment exist in this location and in this form or not?

In the face of the data I found it seems clear that there was none in the school in which I worked. Or was there? It is certainly true that ILEA has rigorous strategies for raising the awareness of teachers and students on such issues as sexual stereotyping and equal opportunities. INSET, ILEA policy documents and local school initiatives are testament to this fact. Given the scenario that the teachers knew the focus of my research and because of the high profile of gender issues in this authority, it is not surprising that if sexual harassment had been present, then for the duration of my research and in particular the sessions which I spent in the classroom, the male teachers would have been scrupulously vigilant about their behaviour, language, body language and teaching methods.

However on the other hand it must be recognized that I was invited by Dr Martin to conduct research in his school. I believe that had he been concerned that there was evidence of this phenomenon I would not have been so warmly welcomed. Headteachers of schools in which sexual harassment is a problem would not, one suspects, be eager to have a researcher on the premises. The invitation to conduct research in this school indicates Dr Martin's and the teachers' confidence that this issue was not a problem at that time.

However even though sexual harassment was not identified as a problem by the girls in this school I am neither implying that sexual harassment is not present in schools today nor that girls are not shown unwanted sexual attention from male teachers. For it is clear that sexual harassment is a problem and does occur in schools. I have already given examples of other research projects where it was identified (Mahony, 1984; Jones, 1985; Herbert, 1984).

Also there has been recent evidence of concern about this problem at a national level. In *The Guardian* (16 February 1988), an article was printed which exposed the seriousness of sexual harassment in schools and announced the setting up of the 'first campaign network for women who are, or have been, involved with their teachers'. This organization is called TAG (Teachers and Girls). Also in 1988 Celia Kitzinger presented a paper at the British Psychological Society Annual Conference at Leeds University which dealt in part with this issue.

Interestingly, in September 1988 I came across an example of sexual harassment of schoolgirls by a male teacher which fitted the sexual practices that I wished to document in my own research.

The details came to light whilst I was working as a supply teacher for Bedfordshire. It serves as an excellent example of behaviour which is elusive to define, normal in its manifestation, trivialized by others, internalized by the victims and an example also of how people who have knowledge of such practices remain silent and deliberately suppress the details. It came to my attention when I was with a class of fourth years in a girls' grammar school.

At the beginning of a maths lesson and after I had set the work suggested by the absent teacher, a girl in the front row asked me what I was reading. It was a draft copy of this book. The title was clearly printed on the front. She asked me what sexual harassment meant. I defined it for her and gave her a few examples. She asked me if she could look at the draft and I gave it to her explaining that the examples I had in it were not of the kind I was originally seeking for they had all occurred outside the school, and my intention had been to document examples inside schools. Within a few minutes the maths class which I had been supervising was abandoned as all the girls wanted to tell me of the continual unwanted attention they or their friends had received from one of the teachers in the school. Was this, they asked, sexual harassment? The list of offensive behaviour they described included: birthday kisses to second year girls in his class including putting his tongue in their mouths; putting girls over his knee and spanking them; running his hand down their backs to see if they were wearing bras; commenting on the size of a girl's breasts; pinning them to the wall with his hands; rubbing his crotch against the desk corner whilst he was teaching; rubbing his cheek against theirs; making comments about wanting to have sex with particular girls; leaning over them when they were working and breathing down their necks, suddenly picking up one of the smaller girls, turning her upside down so that her underwear was exposed; and taking PE lessons, which, according to the girls, gave him further opportunity to touch them as he showed them how to stand or hold a racquet in a particular way. I was told that one parent had demanded that her daughter was never to be taught by this man.

The behaviour they knew about had become part of the fabric and culture of the school. Apparently some of the girls' mothers had been taught by him and had had similar experiences. Throughout the two decades Mr Hardcastle had been at the school the unwanted attention had remained nameless. The girls in this maths class claimed that all the girls 'knew' he was a 'pervert' but that this was, perforce, accepted. They didn't like what he did but they felt they could do nothing about it. In order to minimize any potential incident the girls tried never to be alone with him and if he gave them a detention after school they would not stay for fear of what he might do. They all disliked his classes, declaring that they could not concentrate on their work for again they were afraid of what he might do, especially if he stood behind them.

The interesting facts about this case are that they so clearly show how male behaviour is excused and rationalized as 'normal', whilst at the same time controlling those it affects in a variety of ways. Further it shows how for twenty years this behaviour has been accepted by many cohorts of girls and staff members and how this man has continually escaped punishment in the form of dismissal, or even a reprimand. Clearly many people know and knew of these incidents. Clearly many people in the school still know today that the sexual harassment of girls is continuing. Clearly there are many people, adults and students, who remain silent. Why does silence and suppression still protect him?

From the girls' perspective the controls they are having forced on them are educational, social and emotional. Their autonomy is being controlled, as is their integrity. These issues will be taken separately. Educationally they do not work well in his class for they are frightened that they might be the next victim to be picked on. He disturbs their concentration by coming up behind them, touching them and making sexual comments about their bodies or what he might like to do to them.

Socially they are being controlled for they are being conditioned into believing that this is an acceptable way for men to behave and that women have to accept this behaviour as 'normal'. When they tried to complain their voices were silenced. They are learning that men have power to do these things, whilst women are powerless. Ideologies of masculinity and femininity are being constructed. Emotionally they are learning that whatever feelings they have cannot be trusted. Their perception of what has transpired have been ignored or redefined.

This case shows how societal-controlling-mechanisms work. The girls told me that Mr Hardcastle was a 'pervert'. They accept this label of 'pervertedness' and his behaviour as being acceptable and in fact 'normal' for a number of reasons. When some of them informed a teacher of his unwanted attention they were told they were imagining it. Another member of staff to whom they had complained who was in a senior position had not wanted to know any details and had sent them away. Another teacher had just not believed them. Two girls said that they knew of some girls who had been punished for 'making up stories' about Mr Hardcastle. When asked why they did not complain the girls said they were frightened of being disciplined themselves. Some had told their parents and the parents had suggested they 'keep away' from him. Was the list of sexually harassing behaviour listed above not considered, by the adults who had been told, to be serious enough to be detrimental, abnormal, atypical, unlawful, or obnoxious? For the only message the girls could deduce from the reaction they received was that this was 'normal' male behaviour and acceptable, even if distasteful. They told me on a number of occasions that I was the only person who had listened to them and who had believed them.

One of the ways behaviour of this nature remains silent is that those it affects and society in general do not have the language to describe it. This was the case with these girls. Initially they wanted me to define for them the behaviour which constituted sexual harassment. Once this happened they fitted practice to the name.

Interestingly, I tried to help the girls have their voices heard. I went to the headteacher and told him what the girls had described. Initially he was sympathetic and told me that he would make inquiries. When I returned to the school a few days later to do another day's teaching I was taken aside by the head and told that he had looked into the problem and sought advice from other senior teachers. However he was afraid that he could not discuss the case further with me because I was a supply teacher. Then he told me that as a supply teacher I had certain duties and one of these was to teach the lesson that had been set by the absent staff member. It was not my responsibility to talk about such issues as sexual harassment which was a sensitive and difficult area and one reserved for the pastoral care teachers.

Subsequently I was asked to see the deputy head teacher. She gave me the 'advice' that girls in an all-girls school often 'imagine' or fabricate such incidents, or perhaps exaggerate what has happened. I was told that it was extremely difficult for male teachers to teach in such an 'abnormal' environment and that they found it very hard to be friendly and caring without having their actions misconstrued. Interestingly it was nearly six weeks later that I was offered another teaching day at the school and this only after I had hinted that I hoped the lack of supply days had nothing to do with my 'reprimand'. I was assured that it hadn't.

Thus it can be concluded that sexual harassment does exist in some schools, that male teachers are perpetrators, girls are victims and that little notice is taken of the problem even if the girls try to speak out.

This raises an interesting point. The girls who were mentioned in this case study as having been victim to Mr Hardcastle's attacks, and the girls in my study, are two different groups. However there is also a third group which I wish to include in the discussion in order to argue that the girls in the research occupy a unique position amongst children who are abused.

The first group of girls (those in the school where sexual harassment is the 'normal' behaviour pattern for Mr Hardcastle) are in the position of being frequently sexually harassed during the school day. No one may have listened to them even though they have tried to talk. This type of sexual harassment is chronic. It happens frequently, always by the same man, often in full view of the whole class, is an 'expected' part of this man's teaching style, has happened for years and is a 'known', 'accepted' and talked about feature of this school's hidden curriculum, at least by the girls.

For the group of children who have been identified as those who are being sexually abused at home there are similarities. The sexual abuse is often chronic, the attacks frequent and regular, the man a known person, often the father or stepfather in the family, and the location of the attack is also known. The major difference beween these two groups is that the abused children are silent about their attacks, although of course there may be communication between the assailant and the victim.

However the girls with whom I worked did not have many features in common with these two other groups. Their experience was a 'one-off'. It happened totally unexpectedly, when they were alone, often on their way home, sometimes with a man they knew of, or about, unfortunately often when they were involved in doing something 'wrong', such as taking a forbidden short cut or being out of school, and as such the attack was seen by some of the girls as a form of retribution. The incident had never happened again, they had told no one, not even their friends, and they had subsequently become isolated by their experiences and thus silent.

The group of girls I have identified in this study have been ignored in most of the other literature because their experiences have never come to light before. What can be done for those students who have suffered sexual abuse and who have no one with whom to share their experiences? It is necessary for education authorities and schools to begin to understand that there may be a number of children in every classroom, over and above those who are sexually harassed by male teachers, and those who are being abused at home, who have experienced a traumatic sexual attack.

This raises a further problem. If the sexual abuse of girls is so common, yet so hidden, what is the incidence of boys' sexual abuse? Are the boys also silenced by societal-controlling-mechanisms of guilt, embarrassment, fear, blame, isolation, disbelief, trivialization and charges of fabrication or threats of repercussions? If not, are there other mechanisms which control men and boys? Further research must be conducted in this area if a picture of the extent to which young people are affected by sexual interference is to become clear.

What is important however for both girls and boys is that teachers become aware of this fact when teaching particular subjects such as health education, religious studies, aspects of literature, history, biology, and social and personal studies. New programmes can be introduced at a number of levels in schools. Young people must be taught that abuse is not their fault, that it should not be silenced and suppressed, and that if the controlling mechanisms are broken, help and counselling can be forthcoming. Teachers need to understand that the problem of sexual interference with children may be more prevalent than is currently accepted, and they need to have training in dealing with cases of sexual abuse. Education programmes too must be devised and written to challenge and change the power relationship between girls and boys and to provide an environment that is not predicated on gender conditioning and stereotyped assumptions.

This book has been primarily about the control of silence and the ways in which this operated. Nevertheless it is interesting that many of the girls during or immediately after attacks put up some resistance. It must be recognized that by resisting the girls were challenging some societal-controlling-mechanisms, for they were aware at the time that they were entitled to fight back, for it was not their fault that they had been attacked. The full force of the embedded societal-controlling-mechanisms only came later. When Alex encountered the men on the buses she either got off or told another person, whilst Zaheda shifted her bag or stepped on their toes. Collette informed her mother about the unwanted sexual experience she had with a schoolboy and action was taken. Carmel, Linda, Fitti and Annmarie when propositioned in the street either ran away, shouted abuse or said 'no'. Rukeya, Zaheda's sister, refused to be part of the sexual 'games' her brother wanted her to play. Alex ran away after her sexual attack by the man on open ground. The most defiant account of resistance however was from Jenny. She was attacked by two men and held first by one, then the other, in an underpass near the school whilst they assaulted her.

> 'Jenny: "I was struggling."
> Carrie: "And then how did you finally get away?"
> Jenny: "Well one of the men was holding me . . . and I bit his hand."
> Carrie: "Well done, well done, I'm very proud of you."
> Jenny: "It was round here," (indicating the thumb joint) "it was a big mark, do you see? And then I kicked him in his balls and the only way I could run was sideways . . . I bit the one man and kicked the other, and I had to move to the side you see to run".' (Int., 30 September 1986, p. 7).

The interesting, poignant and consistent factor was, despite the fight, verbal abuse or avoidance strategy which challenged the societal-controlling-practices of acceptance and 'normality' in their own unsupported way, the girls still remained silent about the episodes to other people, even though they had known at some point that the men had been in the wrong, had been abusive, had taken liberties or were perverted. Yet still they had been unable or unwilling to crack the silence they had learned to keep. In a recent edition of *Newstatesman and Society* (July 1988, p. 24) a mother, Susannah Cochrane, writes of the reluctance on the part of the authorities to take seriously her 3-year-old daughter's sexual abuse. Recalling her daughter's refusal to tell anyone else about the sexual interference by her grandfather, the mother wrote: 'How well she had been taught . . . that these things are private, and children who tell can be punished.'

I now wish to turn to a discussion of the methodology, and to describe how this was a fundamental aspect of the data which was collected. The research methodology was a synthesis of a number of relevant research strategies, some orthodox, others more experimental. The design which was planned to incorporate classroom observation, interviewing, diary writing and group meetings was abandoned in exactly this format at the end of the summer term of 1986. The refusal of the girls to write diaries and the problems associated with the participant observation method had forced me into directing more energy and effort into the remaining two strategies.

Informal interviewing and the group discussions became the prime methods for collecting data and they developed and grew in ways which were unprecedented in other ethnographic research models. It was the belief that these girls had something to say, but were unable to articulate their experiences, which encouraged me to persist with the interviewing sessions and the group meetings. Undeniably too there was the excitement of becoming closer and closer to a group of girls with whom the barriers of age, education and culture were gradually broken down. What emerged as a result was a new research design, containing an emphasis on two particular strategies, the interview technique and the group meetings. The way in which these two processes developed enabled the societal-controlling-mechanisms, which up until then had thwarted all attempts to gather data, to be displaced. In retrospect, the evolution of the research seems clear. But at the time, in common with ethnographic researchers, I acted as the situation demanded, and instead of 'catching what I could', I developed a research methodology 'as best I could' within the constraints and focus of the project.

In order to release the girls from the grip of what I was later to call societal-controlling-mechanisms, it became apparent that effective strategies had to be used. The girls carried with them a variety of feelings: an inability to disclose brought about by fear of not being believed, or anger from parents;

guilt in thinking they had been complicit in the abuse; disrespect for themselves in that they thought they were 'used', 'dirty', 'worthless' or 'defiled'; the contradiction that these behaviours were 'normal' and therefore unremarkable, yet unique in that they did not affect others; ignorance in that they could not name or describe them adequately; conformity in that they did not want to be singled out as being unusual; and anxiety brought about by the consequences for the assailant or others the disclosure might have had. All these feelings, not articulated but tacitly held, were significant and powerful enough to condemn the girls to silence.

The strategies which were used to combat the controls had to be strong and powerful too. Collecting data without their help would have been ineffective and it was to these ends that a variety of features emerged: intervention as a means of asking questions which researchers are not usually expected to ask; confrontation with the normal ways of perceiving the world; reciprocity in sharing my personal experiences; support for those that disclosed; time for the girls to express their own views in a way that suited them best; information which gave them more awareness of the way in which society is male-dominated; names with which to match experience with practice; and a safe and convenient place where discussions of an intimate nature could evolve. A methodology had been created which was different in design, technique and implementation and which produced a different order of data from other educational research projects in schools.

One of the most successful components of the methodology was that the girls became more and more confident about including their own ideas in the research. These have not been described because the data they revealed, although interesting, were not central to this dissertation. However the strategy that the girls could suggest ideas and that they were included whenever possible, as in the case of the trip to Stansted, drew them closer into the research, giving them an active and purposeful role, helping them identify with the research, its problems, its structure and its implementation, resulting in the feeling that the research belonged to them.

The methodology which I adapted from CARE and the research conducted by feminists had a great emphasis on feedback and follow-up. Even after I had left London I visited the girls on six occasions during 1987 and three times in 1988. In the summer of 1987, I wrote the first draft of the data analysis chapters. Once written I duplicated a copy for each girl in the research, marking each paper, so that each girl would know which part referred to her. They were sent off to the girls' private addresses with a note asking them not to show anyone else, and saying that I would be at the school a week later to discuss any changes, problems or deletions they might want to make. Some girls had been reluctant to have any correspondence directed to their house, in particular Zaheda and Annmarie, so these I sent to friends who passed them on. A week later I went to the school, met the girls and briefly discussed the work. On the whole the girls were disappointed with what I had written because so far as they were concerned there were few quotations but many pages of analysis and this had not been what they were apparently expecting. In particular, Collette was upset that she had not featured as centrally as had, say, Maria, Annmarie and Zaheda. Of course this was to do with the substance of her disclosures, not with the time or effort she had willingly contributed to the project. Although the girls had had the opportunity for deletions as the transcripts were handed back to them in the nine months of the research project, and during this time a few did ask for particular pieces to be omitted, at this meeting no changes were requested. The meeting dwelt briefly on the writing, but mainly on the way in which their lives had been spent since the project ended and on bringing me up to date with the school 'gossip'. On each of my visits I deliberately took Zaheda and Zohra inside and discussed with them specifically how they were feeling. But as the months went by, and the time grew longer between visits and the end of the project, the intimacies we had shared during those nine months became yet again silenced through embarrassment, estrangement and distance, and we talked no more about them.

All the girls have now left the school and gone either to a sixth form college, to a college of further education or to employment. Perhaps silence and suppression has yet again triumphed to all intents and purposes for these girls, for it must be recognized that keeping silent is easier than disclosure in an environment hostile to such claims. However each girl who disclosed has the satisfaction of knowing that however quiet she is now, her disclosure has contributed in a large way to the beginning of the fight against the sexual abuse of young girls and women.

The final issue to be dealt with here relates to the number of disclosures made and to the crucial point of 'validity'. I do not wish to discuss in detail again how I know that the girls were being 'truthful' but to link the issue of validity with societal-controlling-mechanisms. The disclosures all the girls made could not, by circumstance, be 'validated' in the usual sense of the word. All had happened when the girls were alone, or with others who were prepared to keep the silence, and the assailants who had perpetrated the abuse were either now unknown or somehow protected. Many had happened many years ago and in countries other than England. Claiming that research of this nature has to be 'validated' through particular avenues, such as 'triangulation', before it can be accepted at 'fact', is to employ societal-controlling-mechanisms. The 'normal' ways which have been used to 'validate' data in the past are clearly unhelpful in research of this kind. But there are other ways of 'knowing' if the experiences are credible. Many women and girls who read this book will find resonance with these accounts, because similar things happened to them or people whom they know. However, men may not be able to identify with the disclosures, for statistically it is less likely that they have been subjected to experiences of the type described here, and for this reason they may find the lack of 'normal' forms of 'validation' difficult to accept.

But this 'normal' way of creating 'truths' must not be allowed to persist and dominate research where corroborative evidence is impossible. If society does not want to know about the extent of sexual abuse, one powerful way to remain ignorant is to invalidate, and thus silence and suppress, research findings of this nature. This has been the problem for too long. Accounts of women and girls being sexually abused have until recently often been disregarded. To insist on verification, to question a woman's integrity, to refute her evidence and to suppress and silence this issue, is to submit to the forces of societal-controlling-mechanisms. Perhaps, instead of questioning the woman's account of her experience, a more appropriate question might be, why does society insist on corroborative evidence to ascertain the facts when we know how difficult it is to 'validate' incidents of this kind?

Appendix 1

Memorandum to all staff

Anti-sexist Monitoring

Colleagues will remember that Sue Ascot and I suggested at the final staff meeting of last term that we should invite Carrie Herbert, currently researching for a PhD in Cambridge to carry out part of her research here provided that Sue and Kate Wilson (now Equal Opportunities Advisory Teacher) studied the scheme and met and approved the researcher. This they did, and Sue, on behalf of the staff following last term's vote, recommended we went ahead.

I have asked Mike Taylor . . . to be Carrie's mentor, facilitating her work.

I am attaching the research scheme, which is to examine the girls' perception of male teachers' controlling techniques. Sue and I consider that the report will be of great interest and help in implementing an anti-sexist policy and, indeed, in simply knowing ourselves better.

Douglas Martin
May 86

Appendix 2

Research Project:
Redefining Classroom Interaction: a political critique of the impact of male-controlling-practice on schoolgirls.

Between the ages of 13 and 16, it seems that there is a common phenomenon in that some girls in schools begin to lose confidence, become more passive, publicly contribute less in class and generally lose their eagerness to participate in the way in which they did as pre-teenagers (Spender and Sarah, 1980; Spender, 1982; Whyld, 1983; Stanworth, 1981). For example although girls may be achieving at an above average level in maths at their primary schools, they drop to a level at the secondary stage whereby A-level maths is neither contemplated nor expected by either teacher or pupil. The figures of A-level mathematics entries in Summer 1980 were 73 per cent males and 27 per cent females (Whyld, 1983, p. 16).

There are of course many pressures contributing to this change in ability and attitude on the part of the female student. One of the 'normally' accepted reasons within a male defined paradigm is that the shift from childhood to adolescence is in itself traumatic, socially, emotionally and physically. It is thought that perhaps because biologically girls' bodies are maturing, this results in an exaggerated concern with sexuality and personal identification. It is also argued that on the whole girls are more emotional than their male counterparts as they try to cope with their changing position in society. And finally some argue that it is in fact 'natural femaleness' which accounts for the developing passive behaviour.

All these justifications are valid if one accepts the male-as-norm paradigm. However I believe that this way of looking at the world does not give a fair and just interpretation from a feminist perspective. I believe that more credence must be given to the social pressures and sexist influences on girls which make them see themselves in a less than positive light. And it is from a feminist perspective that I want to conduct this research.

I believe that there is a phenomenon which I have labelled male-controlling-practices [this label was only used temporarily, for I soon became aware that the practices were female based and perpetuated by both sexes, not just males] which may have some bearing on the change in the female students' attitudes to their academic abilities and their personal self esteem. I am hypothesizing that this male-controlling-practice is present in the normal everyday interactions between male teachers and female students. I believe it is present in speech, choice of words and intonation, in glance and gesture, in innuendo, facial expression, deliberate touches and other physical contact. I believe it affects many students, irrespective of their different racial and class backgrounds. Because it is so deeply embedded in the daily exchanges between pupil and teacher it has become invisible and 'normalized'. Its pervasiveness is so institutionalized that it has the effect of slowly but systematically reducing the girls' confidence which in turn has an effect on their learning ability.

This is the phenomenon I want to research. By closely working with a small number of the girls who perceive male-controlling-practices as problematic, I want to find out how they construct this behaviour for themselves. I want to find out the language they use to describe it, the methods they use to cope with it and the strategies they employ to avoid/thwart it. In short I want to re-construct with the girls what it is like to be a 15-year-old in a comprehensive school, as a receiver of male-controlling-practices.

Confidentiality

The research project is to be submitted as a PhD degree. It will be therefore written up in such a way that will explore the construction of male-controlling-practices. It is anticipated that the thesis will contain direct quotations and descriptions of incidents which have been collected and documented during the data collection period. All names will be changed to protect the individuals involved in the research. All care will be taken to assure confidentiality, although the constraints of working within a small community, such as one school, makes this impossible to guarantee. However my intentions are to investigate the way in which 15-year-old girls construct male-controlling-practices, not to damage or discredit in any way.

All the data is owned by those individuals from whom it is collected. They have the right of access and control over its publication. However if the data is used in such a form that conceals and obscures the identity of the individual then this will be considered fair. All those involved in the research will have the opportunity to read and comment on the fairness, accuracy and relevance of the parts which concern them. The researchee will also be asked for verification of contextual accuracy.

In all cases it is assured that as far as possible the data will be used with accuracy, validity and reasonableness. Because of the nature of the research it is expected that nothing is 'off the record'. (By 'off the record', I take CARE's interpretation that although particular pieces of information can be removed from the data, incidents which have been witnessed, or disclosures which have been made in private, and then deleted, cannot be removed from the researcher's mind, and in this way may ultimately affect the analysis and writing up). All communications and observations made by the researcher will be considered as valid data.

Appendix 3

17.5.86: Letter to Tutors

I have now completed the initial interviews for the research on 15-year-old girls and male-controlling-practices, and have selected fifteen girls to assist me in the project. I have chosen the girls primarily on their awareness of issues regarding sexism and their interest in this area generally, and secondly on the number of male teachers they have for their lessons.

In your tutor group the students I would like to include in the project are: . . . . .

I hope you will be supportive of their involvement in this research, and also that you will be willing to release them at various times to assist me. I anticipate at this stage a weekly interview with me on an individual basis, plus a group meeting at regular intervals, as well as my spending time with them in their respective classes.

If you have any concerns or queries regarding any aspect of the research, I will be more than happy to discuss them with you at a time convenient to you. I hope to make an appointment to meet you sometime this term if you have the time. Please do not hesitate to contact me at anytime.

Yours sincerely,

Carrie Herbert.

Appendix 4

Letter to Parents 27.5.86

Dear Mr and Mrs ......

Re: "Girls involved in the Research".

I think you will be pleased by the small scheme I am about to describe, but I certainly thought you would like to know about it in advance.

As you probably know, we are very keen indeed at this school to take special care of the girls, and to encourage them in the highest aspirations for their studies and their future careers. In so much of British education girls find that the structure of the school discourages some parts of their work.

We are also anxious here to have the work of the school studied by independent researchers, so that we can listen to their findings and consistently improve our practice.

Research in the United States and in this country has shown that if schools are not very careful girls are criticized, responded to by us teachers in ways that appear not to encourage their highest ambitions. We do not want this at this school!

We have been lucky enough to have the services of a Cambridge University researcher, Carrie Herbert, who has been studying the way in which male teachers control the behaviour of girls, and who has been studying whether teachers do this in a way that has the effect of reducing the confidence of girls.

The teachers of the school, with the agreement of your Parents' Association Committee have asked Carrie Herbert to look at work in Upper School, and to report back to us on what she finds.

She has found fifteen girls who have agreed to talk with her and to be observed through a series of lessons. By studying the perceptions and reactions of these girls, our Researcher hopes to build up a picture of the ways in which male teachers in this school are in the habit of speaking to and reacting to girl students. The Researcher would like not only to observe these girls through a series of lessons, but also to have confidential talks with them.

Your daughter happens to be one of those whom Carrie Herbert has found. Would you be willing for her to observe your daughter in a series of lessons and have a number of confidential conversations with her about how she finds the work in the lessons and the teacher's approach to her? All this would be in the strictest confidence, and I can absolutely assure you that the final report back from the Researcher to the school would not mention your daughter by name or allow her to be identified.

I do not think this is a major matter from the point of view of the individual girl student, but I do think that the report to us from the observation of a sample of fifteen girl students would be helpful in our strenuous attempts to make sure that girls are given the greatest encouragement.

I should be grateful if you could let me have your views by returning the slip at the foot of this letter. I do hope that you feel able to approve of this helpful scheme.

Best wishes
Yours sincerely
Douglas Martin, Headteacher.

Appendix 5

Letter to Class Teachers 27.5.86

Dear Subject Teacher,

I have now completed the initial interviews for my research, plus the final selection of the girls who will be involved in the project. I am writing to advise you that some of the girls are in your classes and to invite your support and involvement in this project.

The students are: . . . .

As part of the research involves documenting the interaction between the girls . . . and their subject teachers, it is important that I have access to their classes when possible.

At this stage I cannot give you any definite days or lessons when I should like to come to your classroom, but I felt it was necessary to keep you informed of the research's progress. I can tell you however, that this section of the research will only last until the end of this term, and I will be re-negotiating with teachers again when the new timetable is drawn up for the autumn term.

I hope you will be supportive of the project and that you will be willing for me to attend some of your classes. If you have any concerns or queries regarding any aspect of the research, I will be more than happy to discuss them with you. Please do not hesitate to contact me at any time.

Yours sincerely,

Carrie Herbert.

Appendix 6

Two examples of ideas the girls had for contributing to the research will be mentioned briefly. Firstly, because of the success of 'The Raving Beauties' poetry workshop the girls asked me to get another group to come to the school. However due to lack of resources it was only possible to arrange a group to perform to a larger audience than the thirteen in the project. 'Sensible Footwear', a drama-in-education team, came to the school one evening and many of the girls attended this performance.

Secondly, the girls wanted to ask some of the boys in the school to come to a meeting in order that they could monitor their own and the boys' reaction to the project. It is important to note that throughout the research some boys had been on the periphery in a number of ways. Some had continually asked if they could be interviewed; on one occasion a group meeting had been disrupted and invaded by three angry boys; the girls had found that the transcripts were highly priced on the school's black market, and if not protected could be easily stolen, and I had heard many stories and anecdotes about various boys in the fourth and fifth years whom the girls wanted me to meet. Thus, although the boys were in no way part of the research project, and for that reason I have deliberately omitted them from the account of the research, they did occasionally become an issue. The girls organized two mixed meetings in the last week of the Christmas term of 1986 in order to present to the boys some of the issues they felt strongly about and in particular the way the boys in class dominated the space, the time, the teacher and the resources. The reaction was perhaps predictable. In the meetings the boys expressed hostility and criticism for a number of reasons. They felt rejected because they had not been involved in a similar project, jealous that these girls had been singled out for special treatment, and finally they suggested that women's issues were boring and 'silly' and questioned the point of a research project on women.

In itself the reaction of the boys was a classic example of the female-controlling-practices with which this whole dissertation is concerned. Women and girls are controlled physically, verbally and psychologically. These controls can only be effectively challenged when girls or women recognize the behaviour for what it is. This is the crucial issue. As with my presentation of the new laws on sexual harassment in South Australia, men and women were continually trying to 'control' me because what I was saying lay outside the realms of their interpretation of the world, as defined as 'normality'. Thus I was met with resistance in the form of sexual harassment and sexual discrimination as they tried to silence and suppress the debate. Here too, in this forum with the girls, control was attempted by a handful of boys, and the normally effective societal-controlling-mechanisms were applied. Interestingly some girls were affected by them, despite the discussion we had had beforehand about how we were going to handle this meeting, and the prediction that I had made that the boys could become 'difficult'. Others, especially Collette, refused to be silenced and suppressed, and argued coherently and effectively throughout. However, change, as I mentioned earlier, is a slow process, and societal-controlling-mechanisms are invidious, powerful and divisive.

Bibliography

Abel, E., and Abel, E.K. (eds) (1983) *The Signs Reader: Women, Gender and Scholarship*, Chicago, University of Chicago Press.

Allen, C.V. (1980) (rpt 1986) *Daddy's Girl*, New York, Berkeley Books.

Alliance Against Sexual Coercion (1981) *Fighting Sexual Harassment*, Boston, Mass., Alyson Publications Inc., and The Alliance Against Sexual Coercion.

Amir, M. (1967) 'Victim Precipitated Forcible Rape', in *Journal of Criminal Law, Criminology and Police Science*, Vol. 58, no. 4.

Amir, M. (1971) *Patterns in Forcible Rape*, Chicago, University of Chicago Press.

Angelou, M. (1984) *I Know Why the Caged Bird Sings*, London, Virago Press.

Archer, J., and Lloyd, B. (1982) *Sex and Gender*, Harmondsworth, Penguin.

Ardener, E. (1975) 'Belief and the Problem of Women', in Ardener, S. (ed.).

Ardener, S. (ed.) (1975) *Perceiving Women*, London, J.M. Dent and Sons Ltd.

Ardener, S. (1978) *Defining Females*, London, Croom Helm in association with Oxford University Women's Studies Committee.

Armstrong, L. (1978) (rpt 1979) *Kiss Daddy Goodnight: A Speak-out on Incest*, New York, Pocket Books/Simon and Schuster Inc.

Ball, S.J. (1981) *Beachside Comprehensive: A Case-study of Secondary Schooling*, Cambridge, Cambridge University Press.

Barry, K. (1979) (rpt 1984) *Female Sexual Slavery*, New York, New York Union Press.

Bashar, N. (1983) 'Rape in England between 1550 and 1700', in London Feminist History Group (1983).

de Beauvoir, S. (1949) (rpt 1984) (Trans. and ed. H.M. Parshley) *The Second Sex*, Harmondsworth, Penguin Books.

Beechy, V., and Whitelegg, E. (eds) (1986) *Women in Britain Today*, Milton Keynes, Open University Press.

Bell, Q. (1976) *Virginia Woolf*, Triad/Granada Chatto, Bodley Head and Jonathan Cape Ltd and Granada Publishing Ltd.

Bem, S. (1974) 'The Measurement of Psychological Androgyny', in *Journal of Consulting and Clinical Psychology*, 42, pp. 155–62.

Benjamin, H., and Masters, R.E.L. (1964) *Prostitution and Morality*, New York, The Julian Press Inc.

Benn, M., Coote, A., and Gill, T. (1986) *The Rape Controversy*. National Council for Civil Liberties, London, Yale Press.

Bird, C. (1972) 'Demasculinizing the Professions', in Gross and Osterman (1972).

Bowles, G., and Duelli Klein, R. (1983) *Theories of Women's Studies*, London, Routledge and Kegan Paul.

Branca, P. (1975) *Silent Sisterhood: Middle Class Women in the Victorian Home*, London, Croom Helm.

Brownmiller, S. (1975) (rpt 1986) *Against Our Will: Men, Women and Rape*, Harmondsworth, Penguin Books.

Bryan, B., Dadzie, S., and Scafe, S. (1985) *The Heart of the Race*, London, Virago Press.

Burgess, R. (1983) *Experiencing Comprehensive Education: A Study of Bishop McGregor School*, London, Methuen.

Burgess, R. (1984) *In the Field: An Introduction to Field Research*, London, George Allen and Unwin.

Cameron, D. (1985) *Feminism and Linguistic Theory*, London, The Macmillan Press.

Cameron, D., and Frazer, E. (1987) *The Lust to Kill*, Cambridge, Polity Press.

Campbell, A. (1984) *The Girls in the Gang*, Oxford, Basil Blackwell Ltd.

Chapman, J.R., and Gates, M. (eds) (1978) *The Victimisation of Women*, Beverley Hills, California, Sage.

Clark, A. (1987) *Women's Silence, Men's Violence: Sexual Assault in England 1770–1845*, London, Pandora.

Clark, L., and Lewis, D. (1977) *Rape: The Price of Coercive Sexuality*, Toronto, The Women's Press.

Cline, S., and Spender, D. (1987) *Reflecting Men at Twice their Natural Size*, London, Andre Deutsch.

Cochrane, S. (1988) 'Torn Apart at Home', in *Newstatesman and Society*, 1 July.

Cohen, L., and Manion, L. (1981) *Perspectives on Classrooms and Schools*, London, Holt Educational.

Cole, S.G. (1985) 'Child Battery', in Guberman and Wolfe.

Connell, R.W. (1987) *Gender and Power: Society, the Person and Sexual Politics*, Cambridge, Polity Press.

Coote, A., and Campbell, B. (1982) (rpt 1987) *Sweet Freedom*, Worcester, Billing and Sons Ltd.

Coveney, L., Jackson, M., Jeffreys, S., Kaye, L., and Mahony, P. (1984) *The Sexuality Papers*, London, Hutchinson in association with the Exploration in Feminism Collective.

Dahl, T.S., and Snare, A. (1978) 'The Coercion of Privacy', in Smart and Smart.

Dahlberg, F. (ed.) (1981) *Woman the Gatherer*, New Haven, Yale University Press.

Dally, A. (1982) *Inventing Motherhood. The Consequences of an Ideal*, Burnett Books, Tiptree, The Anchor Press.

Daly, M. (1973) (rpt 1986) *Beyond God the Father*, London, The Women's Press.

Daly, M. (1978) (rpt 1984) *Gyn/Ecology*, London, The Women's Press.

Davidson, C. (1987) *Women's Work is Never Done*, London, The Women's Press.

Davis, C. (1983) *Action Research for School Development: A Focus on Classroom Learning*, published at Wattle Park Teachers Centre, Wattle Park, South Australia, 5066, for 'Bridging The Gap: A Project of National Importance'.

Deakin University (1981) *The Action Research Reader*, Deakin University Press, Victoria, Australia, 3217.

Dinny (1978) (rpt 1981) 'Feeling Sick With Doctors', in Feminist Anthology Collective (1981).

Dobash, R., and Dobash R. (1977) 'Love, Honour and Obey: Institutional Ideologies and the Struggle For Battered Women', in *Contemporary Crises: Crime, Law and Social Policy*, No, 1.

Dworkin, A. (1974) *Woman Hating*, New York, E.P. Dutton.

Dworkin, A. (1976) (rpt 1982) *Our Blood*, London, The Women's Press.

Dworkin, A. (1981) (rpt 1984) *Pornography*, London, The Women's Press.

Dziech, B.W., and Weiner, L. (1984) *The Lecherous Professor. Sexual Harassment on Campus*, Boston, Beacon Press.

Ebbutt, D. (1983) 'Educational Action Research: Some General Concerns and Specific Squabbles', unpublished paper presented at Qualitative Methodology and the Study of Education Seminar, Whitelands College, London, July 1983.

Edwards, A. (1987) 'Male Violence in Feminist Theory: An Analysis of the Changing Conceptions of Sex/Gender Violence and Male Domination', in Hanmer and Maynard.

Edwards, A.D., and Furlong, V.J. (1978) *The Language of Teaching and Meaning in Classroom Interaction*, London, Heinemann.

Eisenstein, H. (1971) *Contemporary Feminist Thought*, London, Unwin Paperbacks.

Elliott, J. (1980) 'Validating Case Studies', paper presented at British Educational Research Conference, Cardiff, Wales, Sept. 1980.

Elliott, J. (1983) 'Paradigms of Educational Research and Theories of Schooling', paper presented at Westhill Sociology of Education Conference, January 1983.

Elliott, J., and Adelman, C., (1976) *Innovation at the Classroom Level: a Case Study of the Ford Teaching Project*, Unit 28, Curriculum Design and Development Course E 203, Open University Course, Milton Keynes, The Open University Press.

El Saadawi, N. (1980) *The Hidden Face of Eve: Women in the Arab World*, London, Zed Books Ltd.

Eskapa, R. (1987) *Bizarre Sex*, London, Quartet Books.

Evans, M. (ed.) (1982) *The Woman Question: Readings on the Subordination of Women*, Fontana Paperbacks/Oxford, Oxford University Press.

Farley, L. (1978) (rpt 1980) *Sexual Shakedown. The Sexual Harassment of Women on the Job*, New York, Warner Books.

Feminist Anthology Collective (1981) *No Turning Back: Writings From the Women's Liberation Movement 1975–1980*, London, The Women's Press.

Firestone, S. (1971) (rpt 1979) *The Dialectic of Sex: The Case for Feminist Revolution*, London, The Woman's Press.

French, M. (1986) *Beyond Power: On Women, Men and Morals*, London, Abacus, Sphere Books.

Friday, N. (1973) (rpt 1976) *My Secret Garden: Women's Sexual Fantasies*, London, Quartet Books.

Friedan, B. (1963) (rpt 1983) *The Feminine Mystique*, Harmondsworth, Penguin Books.

Friedman, S., and Sarah, E. (eds) (1982) *On the Problem of Men: Two Feminist Conferences*, London, The Women's Press.

Furlong, V.J., and Edwards, A.D. (1977) 'Language in Classroom Interaction: Theory and Data', in *Educational Research*, Vol. 19, No. 2.

Garthwaite, A. (1984) 'All You Never Wanted to Know about Sex . . . But Were Forced to Learn', in Kanter *et al.*

Geis, R., Wright, R., and Geis, G. (1984) 'Police Officer or Doctor? Police Surgeons' Attitudes and Opinions about Rape', in Hopkins, J. (ed.).

Genovese, E. (1985) p. 380, cited in Kramarae and Treichler.

Goode, W.J. (1971) 'Force and Violence in the Family', in *Journal of Marriage and the Family*, Vol. 33, No. 4, pp. 624–635.

Gorman, D. (1982) *The Victorian Girl and the Feminine Ideal*, London, Croom Helm.

Grahame, K.M. (1985) 'Sexual Harassment', in Guberman and Wolfe.

Greer, G. (1970) (rpt 1981) *The Female Eunuch*, London, Panther Books.

Griffin, S. (1971) 'Rape: The All American Crime', in *Ramparts*, Sept., pp. 26–35.

Griffin, S. (1981) *Pornography and Silence*, London, The Women's Press.

Gross, R., and Osterman, P. (eds) (1972) *The New Professionals*, New York, Simon and Schuster.

Guberman, C., and Wolfe, M. (eds) (1985) *No Safe Place: Violence Against Women and Children*, Toronto, The Women's Press.

Hadjifotou, N. (1983) *Women and Harassment at Work*, London, Pluto Press.

Hall, R. (1985) *Ask Any Woman. A London Inquiry into Rape and Sexual Assault*, Bristol, Falling Wall Press.

Hamilton, D. (1976) *Curriculum Evaluation*, London, Open Books.

Hamilton, D., Jenkins, J., King, C., MacDonald, B., and Parlett, M. (1977) *Beyond the Numbers Game*, Basingstoke, MacMillan Educational.

Hammersley, M. (1983) *The Ethnography of Schooling*, Humberside, Nafferton Books.

Hammersley, M., and Atkinson, P. (1983) *Ethnography: Principles in Practice*, London, Tavistock Publications.

Hanmer, J. (1978) 'Male Violence and the Social Control of Women', in Feminist Anthology Collective (1981).

Hanmer, J., and Maynard, M. (eds) (1987) *Women, Violence and Social Control*, Basingstoke, Macmillan Press.

Hanmer, J., and Saunders, S. (1984) *Well Founded Fear. A Community Study of Violence to Women*, London, Hutchinson in association with The Explorations in Feminism Collective.

Hardy, T. (1891) (rpt 1984) *Tess of the D'Urbervilles*, London, Dent and Sons Ltd.

Hearn, J., and Parkin, W. (1987) *Sex at Work. The Power and Paradox of Organisation Sexuality*, Brighton, Wheatsheaf.

Hellerstein, E.O., Hume, L.P., and Offen, K.M. (eds) (1981) *Victorian Women. A Documentary Account of Women's Lives in Nineteenth-Century England, France, and the United States*, Stanford, Calif., Stanford University Press.

Hemmings, S. (ed.) (1982) *Girls are Powerful: Young Women's Writings from Spare Rib*, London, Sheba Feminist Publishers.

Herbert, C.M.H. (1984) 'The Power of the Personal: A Study of Sexism in Education', unpublished M.A. thesis, Centre for Applied Research in Education, University of East Anglia, Norwich.

Herbert, C.M.H. (1985) *TVEI; Equal Opportunities. A Report by the Local, Independent Evaluation of the Technical and Vocational Education Initiative on Equal Opportunities for Pupils in Suffolk Schools*, Norwich, Centre for Applied Research in Education, University of East Anglia.

Hey, V. (1986) *Patriarchy and Pub Culture*, London, Tavistock Publications.

Hopkins, D. (1984) 'Towards a Methodology for Teacher-Based Classroom Research', in *School Organisation*, Vol. 4, No. 3, pp. 197–204.

Hopkins, J. (ed.) (1984) *Perspectives on Rape and Sexual Assault*, London, Harper and Row.

Hosken, F. (1982) *Genital and Sexual Mutilation. Third Revised Edition*, Lexington, Mass., USA, Women's International Network News.

I.S.I.S. (1979) *Organising Against Rape*, International Bulletin 12.

Jacobs, H.A. (1987) *Incidents in the Life of a Slave Girl*, Cambridge, Mass., Harvard University Press.

Jeffries, S. (1984) 'The Sexual Abuse of Children in the Home', in Friedman and Sarah.

Jones, C. (1985) 'Male Violence in a Mixed Secondary School', in Weiner.

Kanter, H., Lefanu, S., Shah, S., and Spedding, C. (eds) (1984) *Sweeping Statements: Writings from the Women's Liberation Movement 1981–83*, London, The Women's Press.

Kelly, A. (1983) 'Action Research: Some Definitions and Descriptions', unpublished paper presented at Qualitative Methodology and the Study of Education Seminar, Whitelands College, London, July 1983.

Kelly, J. (1984) *Women, History and Theory*, Chicago, University of Chicago Press.

Kelly, L. (1987) 'The Continuum of Sexual Violence', in Hanmer and Maynard.

Kelly, L. (1988) *Surviving Sexual Violence*, Cambridge, Polity Press.

Kemmis, S., and McTaggart, R. (1982) *The Action Research Planner*, Deakin University Press, Victoria, 3217 Australia.

Kenyatta, J. (1938) (rpt 1987) *Facing Mount Kenya*, Nairobi, Martin Secker and Warburg Ltd.

King, R. (1978) *All Things Bright and Beautiful: A Sociological Study of Infants' Classrooms*, Chichester, Wiley and Sons.

Kitzinger, C. (1988) '"It's Not Fair on Girls": Young Women's Accounts of Unfairness in School', paper presented at the British Psychological Society Annual Conference, University of Leeds, 15–18 April 1988.

Koso-Thomas, O. (1987) *The Circumcision of Women. A Strategy for Eradication*, London, Zed Books Ltd.

Kramarae, C., and Treichler, P.A. (1985) *Feminist Dictionary*, London, Pandora Press.

Kushner, S., and Norris, N. (1980) 'Interpretation, Negotiation, and Validity in Naturalistic Research', reproduced from *Interchange*, Vol. 11, No. 4, 1980–81, published by Ontario Institute for Studies in Education.

Lacey, C. (1970) *Hightown Grammar*, Manchester, Manchester University Press.

Leavitt, R., Sykes, B., and Weatherford, E. (1975) 'Aboriginal Women: Male and Female Perspectives', in Reiter.

Lees, S. (1986) *Losing Out: Sexuality and Adolescent Girls*, London, Hutchinson.

Lewis, J. (1984) *Women in England 1870–1950*, Sussex, Wheatsheaf Books Ltd.

London Feminist History Group (1983) *The Sexual Dynamics of History*, London, Pluto Press.

London Rape Crisis Centre (1984) *Sexual Violence. The Reality for Women*, London, The Women's Press.

Lowe, M. (1984) 'The Role of the Judiciary in the Failure of the Sexual Offences (Amendment) Act to Improve the Treatment of the Rape Victim', in Hopkins, J.

MacDonald, B., and Walker, R. (1974) *Safari: Innovation, Evaluation, Research and the Problem of Control. Some Interim Papers*, published jointly by Safari Project, CARE, University of East Anglia, Norwich, and Workshop Curriculum No. 1, Arbeitspapiere zu Problemen der Curriculumreform, Arbeitskreis Curriculum, Yerlag Lothar Rotsch, 7401 Bebenhausen 45.

MacDonald, B., and Walker, R. (1977) *Safari One, Innovation, Evaluation, Research and the Problem of Control*, CARE Research Monographs.

MacKinnon, C.A. (1979) *Sexual Harassment of Working Women*, New Haven, Yale University Press.

MacKinnon, C.A. (1983a) 'Feminism, Marxism, Method and the State: An Agenda for Theory', in Abel and Abel.

MacKinnon, C.A. (1983b) 'Feminism, Marxism, Method and the State: Toward Feminist Jurisprudence', in *Signs Journal Of Women in Culture and Society*, Vol. 8, No. 4, pp. 635–658.

McRobbie, A., and Nava, M. (eds) (1984) *Gender and Generation*, Basingstoke, Macmillan Press.

Mahony, P. (1984) *Schools for the Boys. Coeducation Reassessed*, London, Hutchinson in association with The Explorations in Feminism Collective.

Malcolm, J. (1984) (rpt 1986) *In The Freud Archives*, London, Fontana Paperbacks.

Marland, M. (ed.) (1983) *Sex Differentiation and Schooling*, London, Heinemann Educational.

Masson, J. (1984) (rpt 1985) *The Assault on Truth*, Harmondsworth, Penguin Books.

Mayhew, H. (1851) (rpt) *Mayhew Characters*, Spring Books, London, The Hamlyn Publishing Group.

Mead, M. (1949) (rpt 1981) *Male and Female*, Harmondsworth, Penguin.

Measor, L., and Woods, P. (1984) *Changing Schools, Pupil Perspectives on Transfer to a Comprehensive*, Milton Keynes, Open University Press.

Medea, A., and Thompson, K. (1974) *Against Rape*, New York, Farrar, Straus and Giroux.

Mies, M. (1983) 'Towards a Methodology for Feminist Research', in Bowles and Duelli Klein.

Miller, J.B. (1976) *Towards a New Psychology of Women*, Boston, Beacon Press.

Millett, K. (1970) (rpt 1983) *Sexual Politics*, London, Virago Press.

Millman, M., and Moss Kanter, R. (eds) (1975) *Another Voice*, New York, Anchor Press/Doubleday.

Minority Rights Group (1982) (revised 1983) *Report No. 47. Female Circumcision, Excision and Infibulation: the facts and proposals for change*, Minority Rights Group, 29 Craven Street, London.

Mitchell, J. (1971) (rpt 1981) *Woman's Estate*, Harmondsworth, Penguin.

Mitchell, J., and Oakley, A. (eds) (1986) *What is Feminism?*, Oxford, Basil Blackwell.

NALGO (n.d.) *Sexual Harassment is a Trade Union Issue*, Research Section, NALGO Headquarters, 1 Mabledon Place, London WC1H 9AJ.

Nash, C.L., and West, D.J. (1985) 'Sexual Molestation of Young Girls: A Retrospective Survey', in West.

National Council for Civil Liberties (NCCL) *see* Sedley and Benn (1982), and Benn *et al.* (1984).

Nicholson, J. (1984) *Men and Women. How different are they?*, Oxford, Oxford University Press.

Nightingale, C. (1988) *The Nightingale Roars: An Incest Survivor's Journey to Freedom*, leaflet prepared by Thames Television and Constance Nightingale to accompany the television programme of the same name, first shown on ITV in June 1988.

Norris, N. (ed.) (1977) *Safari: Theory in Practice. Papers Two*, CARE, University of East Anglia, Norwich.

Oakley, A. (1972) (rpt 1985) *Sex, Gender and Society*, Aldershot, Gower/Maurice Temple Smith.

Oakley, A. (1974a) (rpt 1985) *Housewife*, Harmondsworth, Penguin.

Oakley, A. (1974b) (rpt 1985) *The Sociology of Housework*, Oxford, Basil Blackwell.

Oakley, A. (1981) 'Interviewing Women: a Contradiction in Terms', in Roberts.

Ohse, U. (1984) *Forced Prostitution and Traffic in Women in West Germany*, Human

Rights Group, 8 Scotland Street, Edinburgh.

Okely, J. (1978) 'Privileged, Schooled and Finished: Boarding Education for Girls', in S. Ardener (1978).

Open University (1982) *The Changing Experience of Women*, Milton Keynes, Open University Press.

Partnow, E. (1977) (rpt 1982) *The Quotable Woman 1800–1981*, New York, Facts on File, Inc.

Partnow, E. (1985) *The Quotable Woman From Eve to 1799*, New York, Facts on File, Inc.

Perkins, R., and Bennett, G. (1985) *Being a Prostitute*, London, George Allen and Unwin.

Prager, E. (1983) *A Visit from the Footbinder*, London, Chatto and Windus.

Radford, L. (1987) 'Legalising Woman Abuse', in Hanmer and Maynard.

Raving Beauties The (ed.) (1985) *No Holds Barred; The Raving Beauties Choose New Poems By Women*, London, The Women's Press.

Read, S. (1982) *Sexual Harassment at Work*, London, Hamlyn.

Reason, P., and Rowan, J. (eds) (1981) *Human Inquiry. A Sourcebook of New Paradigm Research*, Chichester, John Wiley and Sons.

Reinharz, S. (1979) *On Becoming a Social Scientist*, San Francisco, Jossey-Bass Publishers.

Reiter, R.R. (ed.) (1975) *Towards an Anthropology of Women*, New York, Monthly Review Press.

Rhodes, D., and McNeil, S. (eds) (1985) *Women Against Violence Against Women*, London, Onlywomen Press.

Rich, A. (1980) (rpt 1984) *On Lies, Secrets and Silence*, London, Virago Press.

Roberts, H. (ed.) (1981) *Doing Feminist Research*, London, Routledge and Kegan Paul.

Rohrlich-Leavitt, R., Sykes, B., and Weatherford, E. (1975) 'Aboriginal Women: Male and Female Anthropological Perspectives', in Reiter.

Rosenkrantz, P.S., Vogel, S.R., Bee, H., Broverman, I.K., and Broverman, D.M. (1968) 'Sex role stereotypes and self-concepts in college students', in *Journal of Consulting and Clinical Psychology*, 32, pp. 287–295.

Rowbotham, S. (1972) *Women, Resistance and Revolution*, New York, Pantheon Books.

Rowbotham, S. (1973) *Woman's Consciousness, Man's World*, Harmondsworth, Penguin.

Rubin, G. (1975) 'The Traffic in Women: Notes on the "Political Economy" of Sex', in Reiter.

Rush, F. (1980) *The Best Kept Secret: Sexual Abuse of Children*, New York, McGraw-Hill Book Company.

Russell, D.E.H. (1975) *Rape: the Victim's Perspective*, New York, Stein and Day.

Russell, D.E.H. (1982) *Rape in Marriage*, New York, Collier Books/Macmillan Publishing Company.

Russell, D.E.H. (1984) *Sexual Exploitation. Rape, Child Sexual Abuse and Workplace Harassment*, London, Sage Publications.

Russell, D.E.H. (1986) *The Secret Trauma. Incest in the Lives of Girls and Women*, New York, Basic Books.

Sarachild, K. (1975) 'Consciousness Raising: A Radical Weapon', in *Redstockings*, P.O. Box 413, New Paltz, New York, 12561.

Savage, W. (1986) *A Savage Enquiry: Who Controls Childbirth*, London, Virago Press.

Schram, D. (1978) 'Rape', in Chapman and Gates.

Seager, J., and Olson, A. (1986) *Women in the World: an International Atlas*, London, Pluto Press.

Seddon, V. (1983) 'Keeping Women in their Place', in *Marxism Today*, Vol. 27, No. 4, July, p. 20.

Sedley, A., and Benn, M. (1982) (rpt 1984) *Sexual Harassment at Work*, NCCL, 21 Tabbard St., London SE1 4LA.

Sheffield Men Against Sexual Harassment (1984) *S.M.A.S.H. An Information Pack for Men: Sexual Harassment, Rape and Sexual Abuse of Children*, S.M.A.S.H., P.O. Box 281, Sheffield S1 2HN.

Shipman, M. (ed.) (1985) *Educational Research: Principles, Policies and Practices*, London, Falmer Press.

Simons, H. (1977) 'Building a Social Contract: Negotiation, Participation and Portrayal in Condensed Field Research', in Norris.

Smart, C. (1984) *The Ties that Bind. Law, Marriage and the Reproduction of Patriarchal Relations*, London, Routledge and Kegan Paul.

Smart, C., and Smart, B. (1978) *Women, Sexuality and Social Control*, London, Routledge and Kegan Paul.

South Australian Department of Education (1984) *Sexual Harassment*, S.A. Ed. Dept., Flinders Street, Adelaide, S.A. 5000.

Spence, J.T., Helmreich, R., and Strapp, J. (1975) 'Ratings of self and peers on sex role attributes and their relation to self-esteem and conceptions of masculinity and femininity', in *Journal of Personality and Social Psychology*, 32, pp. 29–39.

Spender, D. (1980) (2nd ed. 1985) *Man Made Language*, London, Routledge and Kegan Paul.

Spender, D. (ed.) (1981) *Men's Studies Modified: The Impact of Feminism on the Academic Disciplines*, Oxford, Pergamon Press Ltd.

Spender, D. (1982) *Invisible Women: The Schooling Scandal*, London, Writers and Readers Cooperative.

Spender, D. (1983) *Feminist Theorists. Three Centuries of Women's Intellectual Traditions*, London, The Women's Press.

Spender, D. (1986) 'What is Feminism? A Personal Answer', in Mitchell and Oakley.

Spender, D., and Sarah, E. (eds) (1980) *Learning To Lose*, London, The Women's Press.

Spring, J. (1987) *Cry Hard and Swim*, London, Virago Press.

Stanko, B. (1985) *Intimate Intrusions: Women's Experience of Male Violence*, London, Routledge and Kegan Paul.

Stanworth, M. (1981) *Gender and Schooling: a Study of Sexual Divisions in the Classroom*, London, Hutchinson in association with Explorations in Feminism Collective.

Staus, M.A. (1978) 'Sexuality Inequality, Cultural Norms and Wife Beating', in Chapman and Gates.

Steedman, C. (1986) *Landscape for a Good Woman. A Story of Two Lives*, London, Virago Press.

Steinem, G. (1983) *Outrageous Acts and Everyday Rebellion*, New York, Holt, Reinhart and Winston.

Strachey, R. (1928) (rpt 1978) *The Cause: A Short History of the Women's Movement in Great Britain*, London, Virago.

Taylor, D. (1985) *Women: A World Report. Part 1*, London, Methuen.

Trades Union Congress (1983) *Sexual Harassment of Women at Work: A Study from West Yorkshire/Leeds Trade Union and Community Research and Information Centre*, Aug. 1983: ISBN 0946891028.

Turnbull, C.M. (1981) 'Mbuti Womanhood', in Dahlberg.

Walker, B.G. (1983) *The Woman's Encyclopedia of Myths and Secrets*, New York, Harper Row.

Walker, R. (1974) 'Classroom Research: A View from Safari', in MacDonald and Walker (1974).

Walker, R. (1977) 'Descriptive Methodologies and Utilitarian Objectives: Is a Happy Marriage Possible?', in Norris.

Walker, R. (1985) *Doing Research: a Handbook for Teachers*, London, Methuen.

Ward Jouve, N. (1986) *The Streetcleaner: The Yorkshire Ripper Case on Trial*, London, Marion Boyars.

Warren, M.A. (1980) *The Nature of Women: An Encyclopedia and Guide to the Literature*, Inverness, California, Edgepress.

Weeks, J. (1981) *Sex, Politics and Sexuality. The Regulation of Sex since 1800*, London, Longman.

Weiner, G. (ed.) (1985) *Just a Bunch of Girls*, Milton Keynes, Open University Press.

West, D.J. (ed.) (1985) *Sexual Victimisation. Two Recent Researches into Sex Problems and Their Social Effects*, Aldershot, Gower.

Whitbread, A. (1980) 'Female Teachers are Women First: Sexual Harassment at Work', in Spender and Sarah.

Whyld, J. (ed.) (1983) *Sexism in the Secondary Curriculum*, London, Harper and Row.

Willey, R. (1984) *Race, Equality and Schools*, London, Methuen.

Williams, J.E., and Bennett, S.M. (1975) 'The definition of sex stereotypes via the adjective check list', in *Sex Roles*, 1, pp. 327–337.

Willis, P. (1978) *Learning to Labour*, Farnborough, Saxon House.

Wilson, E. (1980) *Halfway to Paradise, Women in Postwar Britain: 1945–1968*, London, Tavistock.

Wise, S., and Stanley, L. (1987) *Georgie Porgie: Sexual Harassment in Everyday Life*, London, Pandora Press.

Wollstonecraft, M. (1792) (rpt 1982) *A Vindication of the Rights of Woman*, Harmondsworth, Penguin.

Wood, J. (1984) 'Groping Towards Sexism: boys' sex talk', in McRobbie and Nava.

Woods, P. (1979) *The Divided School*, London, Routledge and Kegan Paul.

Woods, P. (1986) *Inside Schools*, London, Routledge and Kegan Paul.

Wright Mills, C. (1959) (rpt 1983) *The Sociological Imagination*, Harmondsworth, Penguin.

Index